The Selected Essays
of Cyril Connolly

The Selected Essays of Cyril Connolly

edited and with an introduction by

Peter Quennell

A Stanley Moss Book • Persea Books, Inc.
New York

A Stanley Moss Book/Persea Books, Inc.
225 Lafayette Street
New York, N.Y. 10012

Library of Congress Cataloging in Publication Data

Connolly, Cyril, 1903-1974.
    The selected essays of Cyril Connolly.

    "A Stanley Moss book."
    I. Quennell, Peter, 1905- . II. Title.
PR6005.0393A6 1983   824'.912   83-22147
ISBN 0-89255-072-4

Manufactured in the United States of America

ACKNOWLEDGMENTS

The essays in this volume appeared in the following books:

The Condemned Playground (1945): "Spring Revolution," "England Not My England," "Distress of Plenty," "The Ant-Lion," "Writers and Society, 1940-3," "Imitations of Horace," "Ninety Years of Novel Reviewing," "More about the Modern Novel," "Felicity," "Felicity Entertains," "Told in Gath," "Where Engels Fears to Tread."

Ideas and Places (1953): "Bordeaux-Dordogne," "Hommage to Switzerland," "The Elegiac Temperament," "Farewell to Surrealism."

Previous Convictions (1963): "The Grand Tour," "Revisiting Greece," "Impressions of Egypt (1955)," "One of My Londons," "On Re-reading Petronius," "In Quest of Rococo," "James Joyce: 1," "James Joyce: 2," "James Joyce: 3," "Oscar Wilde: 1," "Oscar Wilde: 2," "Living with Lemurs," "Beyond Believing," "Bond Strikes Camp."

Cyril Connolly as Critic

Ten or fifteen years ago, a middle-aged Englishman, a small package clasped beneath his arm, could, now and then, be observed, looking rather anxiously around him in the crowd outside a Spanish airport—Cyril Connolly, who was staying with a friend nearby, and, having just dashed off his weekly book review, hoped to persuade a homebound British tourist to carry the manuscript back to London, and stamp and mail it on arrival. Often his plan succeeded, and the article duly appeared; but his efforts to put off a piece of hackwork until the eleventh hour frequently caused him—and, indeed, his editor—a good deal of temporary vexation. Cyril was a reluctant journalist, yet simultaneously a born critic. To everything that confronted him—a new book, an old book reissued, a monument, a canvas, a landscape, a dish, a precious bottle of wine—he had an extraordinarily quick and keen response. There could be no doubt exactly what he thought, and he announced his opinion with the utmost firmness. Even though one might wish to disagree, one respected his wit and learning and imaginative choice of words.

All his life, Cyril had aimed at perfection; in the opening paragraph of *The Unquiet Grave* he had gone so far as to assert that "the more books we read the clearer it becomes that the true function of a writer is to produce a masterpiece and that no other task is of any consequence," and he deeply resented the economic problems that had thrust him into newspaper criticism and equally time-wasting jobs. He had submitted, however. After publishing his only novel, *The Rock Pool*, in 1936, *Enemies of Promise* in 1938 and *The Unquiet Grave* in 1944, and after editing a monthly magazine *Horizon* from 1939 to 1950—an occupation he found comparatively agreeable, in 1951 he joined the staff of the London *Sunday Times* as its leading book critic, a post he continued to hold for the remainder of his literary career. Yet he still regretted the creative freedom he had given up, and both the first and the last of his three volumes of collected essays—*The Condemned Playground*, which appeared in 1945, and *Ideas and Places* and *Previous Convictions*, which came out in 1953 and 1963—include poignant prefatory allusions to the reviewer's sorry fate:

> . . . I wish I had been a better critic [he lamented, prefacing *The Condemned Playground*] and that I had not written brightly, because I was asked to, about so many bad books. What merits I have are somewhat practical and earthy. I stay very close to the text—no soaring eagle but a low-swung basset who hunts by scent and keeps his nose to the ground. . . . Experience develops in the critic an instinct, which, like the water diviner's, agitates him when near to treasure.

Similarly, while introducing *Previous Convictions*, he admits that "writing for a Sunday paper has tempered my improvidence and widened my knowledge," yet complains that he might have written "longer and better," had he escaped "the weekly stint."

The contents of the present book are drawn from all three volumes and exemplify the full range of his critical activities. It was a wide range. The earliest essay reprinted here is a study of Laurence Sterne, which he wrote in 1927, at the age of twenty-three. Horace Walpole, he recollects, had shied at Yorick's dead donkey, and perceived Sterne's "terrible flaw," his "habit of luxuriating in emotion he thinks creditable, which turns his sympathy to self-congratulation and sets a smirk on all his tenderness. . . . It is this latent insincerity . . . by which Coleridge was offended, that has made so many enemies for Sterne and turned nearly every biographer into an apologist." Yet, given these shortcomings, and the fact that the tempo of his masterpiece, *Tristram Shandy*, "must be the slowest of any book on record," so that it often reminds one of the "youthful occupation of seeing how slowly one can ride a bicycle without falling off . . . such is Sterne's ease and mastery that . . . he will always keep his balance and soon there will follow a perfect flow of words that may end with a phrase that rings like a pebble on a frozen pond."

Cyril's comparison of Sterne's bravura passages to the sound of a pebble ringing across a sheet of ice strikes me as particularly expressive, and, meanwhile, he has neatly and accurately balanced the novelist's defects against his virtues. The whole essay is an admirable specimen of what, eleven years later, when he discussed contemporary writing in *Enemies of Promise*, he would dismiss as "Mandarin" prose, and it is interesting to watch his gradual acquisition of a more relaxed and somewhat less "literary" style. Not that he ever lowered his standards; he remained a staunch champion of new books he considered good, and of the old masters, Congreve, Rochester, Dryden, Pope, he had admired since boyhood. Their genius he was always glad to celebrate. True, in common with every critic, he would sometimes make mistakes, and over-applaud or undervalue, but then, the great Sainte-Beuve himself had committed some astounding errors, for example, when he likened the son of a family friend, young Charles Baudelaire, author incidentally of *Les Fleurs du Mal*, to a capricious opium-smoking hermit, seated in a fantastic kiosk on the island of Kamskatchka.

The excellent classical education Cyril Connolly had received at an old-fashioned English school was among his many assets. It gave him a wider view of life and deeper sense of the past than the average newspaper critic today possesses, and to this grounding of scholarship he added an acute if disillusioned interest in the modern world and an exceedingly vigorous imagination. Once his imaginative talents had been aroused, his subject quickly came alive, whether he were criticizing a book, describing his own travels or devising a Rabelaisian caricature of some preposterous twentieth century scene. The essays chosen for publication here have been divided into three main groups, critical, topographical, satirical; and in each we are aware of the same qualities—insight, wit, and erudition—which may suddenly and enjoyably illumine an otherwise more or less prosaic page.

As a specimen of Cyril's method at its more effective I would cite *The Ant-Lion*—a complex pattern of memories and ideas, in which, after evoking a favorite Southern landscape, he provides a vivid description of a predatory insect, a fiendish embodiment of evil, engulfing and devouring its prey, and next sweeps us on to Bishop's Palace at Albi, where, surprisingly and perhaps inappropriately, hang Toulouse-Lautrec's wonderful nightmarish pictures of the Parisian underworld, "nocturnal, gaslit, depraved and vicious," and draws an ingenious comparison between the fiendish ant-lion and the wickedly accomplished artist. Cyril was a lifelong traveler and sightseer, and wrote with special appreciation of the Augustan Grand Tour. He had not only a naturally inquisitive spirit, but, an invaluable gift, "the seeing eye," accompanied by a feeling for the proper use of language that enabled him to pin down his impressions in a few revelatory words. Despatched by the *Sunday Times* on a journalistic tour of Egypt, he managed to depict the country, its splendors and its squalors, from a refreshingly unfamiliar point of view. Cairo depressed him: "We are in one of those numerous cities whose commonest vista is of a big block of flats in bilious concrete, a patch of blue sky, some very poor people and a hoarding." Nor did the Cairo Museum please him—"the marvellous statues are ill-lit and overcrowded"—until he confronted the image of Tutankhamen and soon developed "an affection for the sleepy Valentino who died at eighteen in an atmosphere of religious conflict which recalls our own Edward VI. . . ."

I remember reading Cyril's article when it was first printed, and being momentarily startled, yet delighted and amused, by his suggestion that the ancient pharaoh bore an odd resemblance to the twentieth century film actor. Cyril alone, I thought, would have so sympathetically observed and so tellingly recorded it. He had always the knack, both as a learned writer and a lively conversationalist, of producing the kind of detail that throws brilliantly unexpected light upon a situation or a personality. Hence the charm of his essays, which, although we may sometimes disagree with the opinion he voices—he cherished certain prejudices and prepossessions, which he seldom troubled to conceal—illustrate the workings, in almost everything he wrote, of a restlessly intelligent and active mind. In this collection we follow him around the New and Old Worlds, and through the magic universe of literature and art. None of his observations is second-hand; he and Edmund Wilson, I think, were the most individual critics to appear during the last half of the twentieth century; and Cyril, we must not forget, was also the finest satirist and parodist we have had since Max Beerbohm. Bound up with his knowledge, his appreciation of ideas, and his feeling for the right word was an inextinguishable sense of fun.

PETER QUENNELL
LONDON 1983

Contents

I
TRAVEL

The Grand Tour

I have always been fascinated by the Grand Tour. In how many biographies over the last three centuries does it not form the pleasantest chapter? The hero's first encounter with the wonder of Europe, the sense of the past, the attraction of foreign minds, the acquaintance with love, and then the belated return from the little foreign courts with their polished manners to the crudities of the pocket borough, the club, and the gaming table. . . .

It redeems adolescence and breathes some fresh air into the political fiery furnace. But is there an age limit? And what survives in the present day from that enchanted circuit? I have just been given the chance to find out.

What are the essentials of the Grand Tour? A visit to Italy, in particular to Florence, Rome, and Naples (which in those days was a capital with a glittering court). These could be approached by Paris, Lyon, and Turin (another court) or by the South of France (Montpellier was a favored resort) or by the republic of Geneva, Lausanne, and the Simplon. Voltaire at Ferney was a "must," and Milan and Venice were capitals of pleasure.

I broke all the rules and took my wife, who had never been to Italy, thus falling into the old Grand Tour role of bearleader. We concentrated on the essentials, which were Florence and Rome, and substituted Palermo for Naples, now shorn of so much of its glory.

The Grand Tour is a mood and a state of mind. There must be no worries about money; one must be able to buy a book or a tie or give somebody dinner; one must feel like an heir coming into his inheritance who has nothing to do every day but live it from morning to midnight, without anxiety or remorse. One must be consumed with curiosity and permit no misgivings about the leaky receptacle where all the new information (much of it forgotten from previous visits) will be stored. Our duty is to learn and feel, not to reason why.

On the Grand Tour we owe something to ourselves, a little relaxation of an evening. The Englishman of the eighteenth century was not guilt-ridden; he brought a mask and a domino, he did not crawl through museums as if preparing for an examination.

I suppose in our time the Grand Tour should be undertaken by car or by making use of the new special car-and-sleeper services, but there seemed no point in motoring to Sicily. Flying, on the other hand, would deny the benefit of the slow plunge southward and set us down in Rome before Florence, which is inartistic. We chose the Simplon Express, and so sleepers were booked and one cloudy morning we set off with reserved Pullman seats and meal tickets on the Golden Arrow.

I am partial to trains; I belong to a generation which grew up to worship flight for flight's sake; I was an original member of the Oxford Railway Club. I also have a weakness for good hotels and experience a satisfaction at going to ground in one of them with the pack at my heels.

The Golden Arrow, especially with a cabin on the boat, is still the most luxurious and therefore the most exhilarating way of getting out of the country. It provides a good breakfast on the English side and an excellent luncheon on the other. On both train and boat there still survives that perfect attentive service from an assortment of mellow Jeeveses that one is accorded nowhere else.

At the Gare du Nord one must take the first decision. "How gaily I used to jump into a taxi and visit the bars while the train crawled round the *Ceinture*. Nowadays . . . I sit glumly in my compartment." When I read this sentence of Evelyn Waugh two years ago I felt rather sorry for him. Now I, too, sat on in the *Ceinture*, thinking of the money saved on tips and taxis, and sipping champagne.

How Parisian is the *Ceinture!* And how Parisian one would be if one could recognize its landmarks. Even following it with a map we got lost. A glimpse of the Sacré Coeur, of razor-sharp corner houses, of leafy boulevards which we trundled over, then some splendid inland waterway with locks and harbors, some woods and precipices—could they be the Buttes Chaumont? A cemetery—was it Père la Chaise? A forest—the Bois de Vincennes? And then we seemed to be returning again to the heart of the city in the slanting sunset—somewhere very near the Seine.

Here at the Gare de Lyon the magic ended; we ceased to be Grand Tourists; crowds of sinister little people milled about; something seemed vaguely wrong. Our sleeping car attendant wore no uniform and was having a row with a porter-like creature, the kind who so pointedly explains that he does not go any farther. "Je connais mes droits," he screamed. "Je vous *emmerde!*" Our attendant (an Italian) bellowed back and seemed rather tipsy. We left them and went to get our tickets for the *wagon-restaurant*.

Should we choose the first or the second service—dine as we left, at half-past eight, or let appetite simmer till nine forty-five? A nice problem. But all the tickets for the first service were already booked by Vampire's Tours. The second then, but all the tickets for that had been reserved by the Locust Agency. Monsieur would have to wait and see if there were any cancellations.

Well, there are always cancellations. The Simplon Express slid off into the dusk with packed carriages to Venice and Trieste, Florence and Rome. As we moved out, the fifty members of the first party filed by us. There were no vacancies, only some rather good smells.

When it was time for the second service we tried again. The corridors were now jammed with waiting couples and impatient business men. Once more a party of fifty Nordic harpies pushed past. There were indignant murmurs.

Then the word went round. There would be a third service, the wagon-restaurant would not be disconnected at Dôle. Till then it remained locked, and by Dôle the whole corridor was

packed with hungry people. The diners left; the train stopped
—and the wagon was disconnected with a dreadful clink. We
had been betrayed.

A woman screamed, "At least give us some bread," and was
handed a biscuit. A business man thundered, "If there were a
journalist here he would write that in France there was not
enough to eat"—"I am a journalist," I rumbled, "and I shall
write precisely that."

Few sights are more beautiful than the Lombard plain in the
thick morning mist from the lower berth of a wagon-lit, with
the leather curtain slightly raised and the blue *veilleuse* still
gleaming. With a net full of guidebooks and the little reading
light, the enclosed wash basin and one's clothes swinging on
the hanger, one is snug as a Pharaoh. Now we leave the poplar
alleys and quiet waterways and take to the mountains with a
tunnel nearly as long as the Simplon, until the acacia scrub on
the hills gives way to olives, a stream tumbles southward and
we descend by Prato to the sunlit valley.

> Amid those cypress-wooded hills that mount
> Beyond Vinciliata and quarried Ceceri
> To where by San Clemente we so often have seen
> Tuscany spread its grave and gracious landscape out
> From Vallombrosa to the far Carraran peaks;
> A vision of enchantment, a delight more deep
> Than ever elsewhere spirit or sense may hope to know.

I used to dislike Florence, its inadequate river, its medieval
bankers' machicolated fortresses miscalled palaces, its inade-
quately Mediterranean climate and rainy *rentier* reminders of
Bath and Cheltenham, its pale priggish culture-stricken *pen-
sionnaires*—and now it is Ferney without Voltaire, for this is
the first time I have been here without visiting Berenson.
When first taken to stay with him I was young and rebellious,
I kicked against the prigs, read Joyce, and stole out looking for
night life. I never imagined I would one day quote from his
old friend Bob Trevelyan's poem to him. It took the last war
to make me see he was right, that culture, as he used to say,
was precarious, like a match lit in the surrounding darkness
that everyone is trying to blow out.

To some extent my attitude had been due to B. B. himself. He felt an ambivalence to the city of his election which seemed provincial to him now that the Russians had gone, and he didn't much like his guests going into the town. Sightseeing in the Val d'Arno was something they were supposed to have got over long ago; one could do it better in his library. Up the hill came the world of fashion and the American professors and art students, while down below lurked people whose talent he admired but whose "bohemianism" he deplored—Norman Douglas inseparable from Orioli, Reggie Turner, the friend of Wilde, and the Lawrences, then at work on "Lady Chatterley"; the *trattoria* set whom "one couldn't possibly know if one lived in the place." I wish I had tried harder to meet them.

Afterward I came to love B. B., the sage who enjoyed every happiness except that of artistic creation, the only kind he truly wanted, and now I found myself returning to Florence haunted by his silken voice yet also deeply curious about that more gifted and yet forbidden society which too had passed away.

There was also the Florence of Uncle Eustace in Huxley's *Time Must Have a Stop*, Florence considered above all as a pleasure city. With this in mind we made for the Grand Hotel (the modern equivalent of staying with Walpole's friend, Sir Horace Mann) and were never for a moment disappointed.

About ten days' extravagance is enough before the *cafard de grand luxe* sets in and there emerges the point of tension which will become intolerable; the pianist in the bar who projects his personality, the electric clock that suppresses a click before not striking, the staring lift-boy, the concierge who seems to know too much about us. But on this first morning, with the sun shining on a breakfast of hot chocolate and saffron scrambled eggs, nothing could be more friendly.

There is a message from Harold Acton and an invitation from Osbert Sitwell, both of whom hold through the present the keys to the past. Later in the afternoon Harold calls, a grave Florentine patrician who is also an English aesthete, and takes us out to dinner at Pratolino, where we question him about the *Côté de chez Norman*.

Alas, even the *trattorie* which he haunted, "half king and half cabbie," have disappeared, the lighthearted world so minutely described by him in *Looking Back* and *D. H. Lawrence and Maurice Magnus* and in Osbert Sitwell's *On the Continent* is gone for ever.

And now the Florentine week begins in earnest, a round of rain and sun, of churches and villas, work and play. For sightseeing is work and one clocks into a museum like an office, arriving fresh and leaving with jangled nerves and a furious hunger, still several rooms behind schedule, yet with a satisfaction comparable only to that felt in wartime by those "engaged in work of national importance." In a city like Florence, all along our route in fact, one is conscious of a host of predecessors all busy passing judgment until it seems quite impossible to find anything new to say.

"One grows to feel the collections of pictures at the Pitti Palace splendid rather than interesting." (Henry James was here.) "None of the works of the uncompromising period, nothing from the half-groping geniuses of the early time . . . a princely creed I should roughly call it—the creed of people who believed in things presenting a fine face to society." I gave one star to Raphael's *Fornarina*, another to the little Flemish pictures in the corridor with Breughel's magical *Orphée aux enfers*. The Pitti remains one of the few examples of what a royal collection was actually like in its original surroundings, but we have grown used to the more simplified presentation of works of art.

For this we must go to the Uffizi, after pausing to give these royal palaces credit for one feature so pleasing to Medicis and Hapsburgs—the jewel room. I have always loved the chill of rock crystal, the blue of Lapis, the combination of gold with ivory, small sea monsters in the shape of baroque pearls or bearing elaborate saltcellars, agate loving cups, sapphire and emerald mermaids, satyrs in sardonyx—all the devices by which the princes of the high Renaissance and their goldsmiths sought to carve a chain of hand holds back to antiquity.

The only "three stars" for Florence we awarded to the Botticelli room in the Uffizi, as far as contents are concerned perhaps the most beautiful room in the world. We can have reservations about him, we can read volumes explaining the symbolism, the techniques, the doctrinaire significance of these two paintings, the *Birth of Venus* and the *Primavera*, but nothing can prepare us for the shock when we are confronted by this flowering of the human spirit, the conjunction of an artist whose powers are at their highest, whose erotic sensibility is at full flood, with the moment historically ripe for him, when, after mortifying the flesh for a thousand years, the mind of man is avid for a religion of beauty.

Even without Savonarola to maim Botticelli, even without the sack of Rome to end the "middle summer's spring" of humanism, the room is instinct with sadness; one weeps first and analyzes after; there is something in the breaking water, the whorl of pale wavelets under Venus's whorled shell, or in the pose of the youth examining a fruit with outstretched arm, which confers a benediction on man's search for knowledge and eases the weariness of living. A goddess is present and by believing in her the painter has revealed to us for ever the divinity within himself.

There is another small roomful of Botticellis with the mysterious *Calumny*, there are Flemish rooms (always my favorite), Leonardos, Guardis, and Longhis; the Uffizi is perhaps the most perfect picture gallery in the world and the least tiring. In Florence the Renaissance began a hundred years before anywhere else. This accounts for its fortress-like civic architecture but also gave rise to Giotto and the major breakthrough of Masaccio's frescoes in the Carmine. The Tombs of the Medici close the cycle. Michelangelo is independent of place, the Duke seated in meditation, the figures of Day and Night belong to a timeless world of the imagination, frighteningly adult. Like the Laocoön or *Paradise Lost* they exist outside the cage of history.

There is nothing like the contemplation of works of art above one's head to provide an appetite; we rush out to find our level. . . .

Florentine cooking is delicious, digestible without being monotonous; besides the tender steaks, the enormous asparagus, the wild strawberries and the fish stew from Leghorn, there are one or two agreeable dishes one can find everywhere, the artichoke omelette (yet it is not really an omelette), *tortino di carciofi* and *fagioli all' uccelletto*, white beans simmered with oil, garlic, sage, and tomato in a big earthenware pot until they are impregnated with the aroma and deliciously tender.

Villa-visiting took us out into the country, first to Mrs. Trefusis, who at the Ombrellino owns one of the most civilized views in the world and a terrace which might be the setting for the big scene in one of James's novels. Then farther afield to La Pietra with its renaissance garden, an arrangement of grass and gravel, bay and myrtle, light and shade created by Arthur Acton to absorb the unique collection of statues which he went on making through the first half of the century, salvaging them from abandoned gardens and dilapidated palaces of the North, a work of art in its own right.

Still farther away in the cheerful chianti country Sir Osbert Sitwell directs from his hilltop castle the production of his excellent vermouth, flinty-fragrant as his wit. We saw these houses with roses and wistaria in bloom, when the lemon trees in their huge tubs were emerging from their winter quarters.

The sun shone for us at Montegufoni but when we revisited I Tatti, Berenson's humanist sanctuary, it was pouring with rain. The great buff house with its magnificent library is now the property of the University of Harvard, to which he bequeathed it as a center for the study of Italian art. The villa remains exactly as he left it, and I wandered through the empty rooms with their familiar objects, the Sienese paintings, the Chinese porphyry lion "that had listened," he once said, "to so much good conversation," even the array of thin gilded glasses that were used at his dinner parties, while I puzzled over the nature of existence.

A man who lives to a great age and who acquires both fame and wisdom in the process, remaining for upward of sixty years in the house which he has built, comes to seem more permanent and indestructible than many a landmark beside which we grew up. And suddenly he is there no longer; the order and ceremony with which he was surrounded prove an illusion and all the affectionate encouragement which he gave to others, that too has vanished. However lovingly the home may be preserved, the personality evaporates with its discrimination and mischief; the perfect house becomes like a dead tooth; unswept, the cypress avenue grows older than its planter.

How many ghosts gallop round with us on our journey like riderless horses! It is time to move on.

There is no pope in Florence, no pagan monuments, scarcely any baroque, no *dolce vita*. Rome has them all; we deal stars thick and fast. Two for the Piazza di Spagna at azalea time, the steps all the way up a forest of blossom, two more for the Piazza Navona where one can dine quietly in the open while tracing the lines of Domitian's stadium for Greek footraces in this loveliest of Roman squares.

Round the stadium were grouped the brothels where Saint Agnes won her martyrdom under Diocletian, and her church by Borromini combines with the Bernini fountain of the four rivers to complete the sumptuous baroque ensemble. There are two good restaurants and a café on the square, and the youthful coproprietor of one of them was during our visit involved in a killing. He had pursued and unfortunately contrived to shoot a teenage gangster who was stealing a transistor set from a client's parked car.

The hotel we had chosen was an old favorite. A hundred years ago the King of Portugal had stayed there and its furnishings and pictures have remained in keeping with his visit. Some of the rooms are palatial, and ours was a converted salon with four long windows and three beds. There is a rumor that furring of the pipes has long prevented hot water ever rising above the first floor, but this I consider unfounded.

The hotel is really very comfortable, it leaves us to our own devices, and it converges on one of the most attractive quarters of Rome, the Via Condotti with its beautiful shops, and such resorts of ancient elegance as the Caffè Greco and Ranieri's,

the Spanish Steps, and all the narrow streets leading toward
the Piazza del Popolo or the Piazza Colonna.

Another road slants uphill to the Pincio Gardens and Val-
adier's, still the best place from which to view at sunset the
whole tawny prospect of old Rome with its bridges and cupo-
las. The hotel is a favorite with people like ourselves and so
old friends keep popping up which saves us the uncertainties
of waiting on letters of introduction and frees the whole day
for sightseeing. This life within the hotel becomes part of the
Roman day, like the *Rome Daily American* which inaugurates it
and which soon seems to contain all one ever wants to know of
the world.

The walk from the hotel to the foot of the Spanish Steps,
where husbands cross over for the American Express and
wives turn right for the hairdresser, to meet again on the red
plush seats of the Caffè Greco for chocolate or Negronis, is a
daily ritual, when all the hotel habitués are encountered.

One hears of other hotels in Rome: the Edwardian magnifi-
cence of the Grand, the papal charm of the Nazionale and the
Minerva, the view from the top rooms of the Hôtel de la Ville,
the chic of the Hassler, the gaiety of the Flora, the august
obscurity of the Croix de Malte; but none of us ever dream of
moving to them. The Inghilterra is in our bones.

There are three sights which I always revisit on the first
day: the Pantheon, the Piazza Campidoglio, and the National
Museum (delle Terme). The Pantheon is one of the seven
wonders of my world; it is certainly the oldest roof in Europe
whose bronze dome delighted Rutilius Namatianus when he
sailed away to France in 416, the last poet of the Roman Empire. All the credit for it is now given to the Emperor Hadrian, who incidentally borrowed the idea of a circular opening
to admit the light from Nero's Golden House.

The bronze doors are original, so is the pavement; the vast
octagonal temple is as broad as it is high. The Barberini Pope
removed the bronze from the roof for the Baldacchino of St.
Peter's, but the gilt-bronze of the interior dome was taken to
Byzantium in the seventh century. Both should be restored.

One can climb to the top of the Pantheon and look down

through the hole (thirty feet across), but I have never dared. It is enough to stand by the tomb of Raphael and look up. "The game is to describe a sphere in a cylinder: if the curve of the dome were projected beyond the point where it meets the vertical walls of the drum, the bottom of the curve would be just tangent with the floor."

If the Pantheon is a building which did away with the monotony of the rectangular Greek temple, the Piazza Campidoglio is a space—but what a space! It was designed by Michelangelo, flanked on three sides by palaces, two of which are museums, while in the center is the equestrian statue of Marcus Aurelius, surely the most perfect evocation of power tempered by wisdom, even by compassion. "Extending its arm with a command which is in itself a benediction," as Hawthorne put it. "I doubt if any statue of King or captain in the public places of the world has more to commend it to the general heart," wrote Henry James. "Irrecoverable simplicity—residing so in irrecoverable style . . . in the capital of Christendom the portrait most suggestive of a Christian conscience is that of a pagan emperor."

It is a certain wistfulness of expression that captivates us and which is found also in the portraits of the philosopher emperor on the reliefs in the adjoining museum. For both the flanking palaces, Renaissance masterpieces in their own right, house magnificent collections more or less as they were seen by the Grand Tourists of old.

In the Capitoline museum are Hawthorne's *Marble Faun* and the *Dying Gladiator* [or Gaul], and the extraordinary room of Roman portrait busts: soldiers, emperors, and sages— cagey Augustus, beatnik Heliogabalus, bull-necked Nero, Socrates looking like Verlaine, and a lady who is the image of Virginia Woolf. What a wealth of information about personality, a typologist's casebook.

The museum of the Conservators, opposite, is even richer. I think of a friend of mine who arrived in Rome in the small hours after a long day's journey and drove his car round and round Aurelius's statue (a perfect turning circle) for half an hour in a state of ecstasy. The fourth side of Michelangelo's square (where once the Sibylline books were kept) is open to the Capitoline steps by the statues of Castor and Pollux and here Horace, in the poem which was also his farewell, pictured priest and silent vestal for ever ascending

> dum Capitolium
> Scandet cum tacita virgine pontifex.

The National Museum is opposite the station, inside the Baths of Diocletian where it is always cool. It contains some beautifully laid out modern rooms and I make my way first to the top where the garden frescoes from the Empress Livia's villa occupy four walls of an otherwise empty room. An apparently monotonous design of fruit trees and flowering shrubs meanders round the wall across a low painted trellis which invites one to step over. But the effect is magical for we are seeing nature through the eyes of the first Roman empress.

This was how the world looked, this was what a garden meant to her . . . or rather, it had only just begun to look like that, owing to the painter Ludius, "noted for having been the first to introduce in this kind of pictorial composition views of buildings and ports, and famous for the freshness, the vivacity and the sense of reality that he knew how to bring out in his landscapes . . . in the rendering of the continuous garden the artist obtains, by means of light and shade, atonal gradations of colour, the desired spatial effects" (Rizzo).

One can almost touch them in this misty orchard, bursting pomegranates, golden quinces and the illusory fruit of the strawberry tree. Roses bloom underneath, oleanders are in flower and cypresses with birds perching wherever they can while quail or a tame pigeon waddle by the low railing. Irrecoverable simplicity! "The distance remains magically impenetrable," wrote the ninety-year-old Berenson, "veiled as it was in the gardens of Lithuania where I lived when I first came to awareness."

Quite as remarkable are the finds from the Roman villa of the Farnesina, where in 1879 were discovered "the most beautiful mural paintings that had ever been admired in Rome." These frescoes (another triumph of preservation) are among the most vivid and haunting to be seen outside Naples, and yet they are inferior to the exquisite stuccoes which adorned the ceilings of three of the rooms. These are light and airy *chinoiserie:* delicate bridges span ravines or link gossamer temples where poets meditate and goatherds sacrifice, a boy is led up to an old Silenus, a satyr raises a leather bottle, a sentry Priapus salutes from the hip.

A museum of such perfectionism is a powder magazine where the imagination can suddenly be blown sky-high. Perhaps the mosaics will set off the train—for whereas a few years ago I found Pompeian painting the supreme art, now I give mosaic the palm—its colors are fresher, it is less blurred and also less conventional. What we all need is another Berenson to give us a great work on Greek and Roman painting and mosaics which will make correct attributions and identify certain painters as Sir John Beazley has done for Greek vases. Then Ludius (or Studius) and lofty Fabullus and Dioscorides of Samos, or Seleucus (whose signature is found in the Farnesina), will come into their own.

Somehow every Roman evening is different while the days, clotted with sightseeing, are all the same. Except when one gets out in the country—where more museums, more neck-stretching await us. One day it is an open car to Tivoli and Palestrina and a morning at Hadrian's villa with its broad canal lined with statues and its marine theatre where the manic-depressive emperor could haul up the drawbridge and dine on his tiny island.

On the way we stopped at the tomb of the Plautii, with its superb lettering, and then went on to the permanent aquatic striptease of the Villa d'Este where water spurts and foams and billows to take the shape of every known fountain. Compared to Hadrian's villa or the Temple of the Sibyl it is insubstantial, superficial almost, yet nothing is more satisfying than its impressive water organ or the looping cascades that run along the Alley of the Hundred Fountains. Only the Nile mosaic in the museum at Palestrina, a floating paradise islanded with temples and enlivened by crocodile and ibis, religious processions, soldiers, duck hunts, hippopotamus chases, houseboats peddling lotus seeds, can compete with the Cardinal d'Este's caprice in homage to wetness.

Alas for Palestrina and Hadrian's villa, I never understood them till yesterday, when I read Mr. Mackendrick's excellent *The Mute Stones Speak*. Then I learnt how much the bombing of Palestrina had revealed of Sulla's Temple of Fortune: "a turning point in the history of architecture, perhaps the most seminal architectural complex in the whole Roman World." We saw nothing of this, and climbed up and down in vain—any more than we saw (with informed eye) Hadrian's palace-block in the Piazza d'Oro: "Here the vastness, sweep and richness comes to a climax in a design which has been called lyrical, feminine and even Mozartian." So much curiosity; and so little discovered!

We were a little better prepared—by Georgina Masson's *Italian Gardens*—for Caprarola and the Villa Lante, another formal water paradise where a stream is made to evolve through the phases of a river, an Anna Livia in miniature, from a basin down a series of terraces to a square "sea" with stone boats and a sculptured island.

The Villa Lante, like the Villa d'Este, was the design of a Cardinal (Gambara). The gardens were begun by Vignola— his masterpiece—in 1566. Montaigne admired them in 1581 and Sacheverell Sitwell has written, "Were I to choose the most lovely place of the physical beauty of nature in all Italy or in all the world that I have seen with my own eyes, I would name the gardens of the Villa Lante."

Only eight miles away in the same Viterban foothills is the Villa Orsini at Bomarzo with its abandoned valley of monsters. Giants held an appeal for Vicino Orsini, who (around 1564 perhaps) made use of extraordinary outcrops of stone which could be carved into threatening shapes, a dragon or a giantess or an elephant—there is even a giant tortoise. They have been ignored for centuries, and we still know nothing of owner or sculptor. The whole suggests the workings of a bizarre but highly erudite and congenial imagination.

All this appreciation and Christian Rome still untouched! Where can one start? With the vine mosaic of Santa Costanza?

Or with a sophisticated baroque gem like the oval Sant' Andrea del Quirinale? The Grand Tourist would begin with St. Peter's and brush the rest aside. Fortunate hidalgos—they didn't have to write about it.

Here in Rome one would wish Christianity to be radiant with happiness and promise as befits the seat of the head of the Church and on a Sunday afternoon we found the Basilica hung with banners and crowded with pilgrims for a saint had just been canonized.

Here in St. Peter's, as in the earliest and most primitive of churches, we are reminded that Christianity is a religion of joy. One certainly does not feel it in the Sistine Chapel where the personality of Michelangelo (five stars, I am afraid) seems obsessed with crime and punishment. The beardless almost florid Christ of the Last Judgment is a truly terrifying arbiter whose patience with our wickedness is (in one furious gesture) exhausted. Yet this same artist could depict the heart-rending figure of Remorse or the impersonal lonely wisdom of the Sibyls or the sublime creation of Adam and then insert himself only as a grimacing mask on a flayed skin. Whenever we encounter Michelangelo we are baffled and humiliated in our littleness even while we marvel.

Nothing is more reassuring than Bramante's Tempietto prototype of so many enchanting pavilions, which we visited next, or more poignant than the tombs in San Pietro in Montoro of the two Irish exiles, Tyrone and Tyrconnel who ended their days here after the "flight of the Earls" in 1607. From the Janiculum, with its tranquil panorama, we went on to the Aventine, nearer to the Rome of the last century than any other part I know, with the lovely early church of Santa Sabina and then came back by the little temples of Vesta and Fortune.

And now the pace quickens. Aqueducts of the Appian Way flash past us between the tunnels, the hills seem brighter and greener; a glimpse of sea-girt Gaeta and then the fertile gardens of the *Terra di Lavoro* whose tall poplars are garlanded with vines.

Three stars for the Naples museum pulsating with life from the Campanian cities. Once again that tremor before the small still lives, the peaches with a jug of water, the glow of Pompeian red in architectural *trompe-l'oeil*, the "genre" scenes of Dioscorides, the exquisite mosaic of marine life with squid and octopus, crawfish and John Dory (art forms that were to disappear for the next 1,500 years).

Shall we give up everything to the study of these flickering foreshortened landscapes and harbors? Not just yet, for we are taking the night boat to Sicily. It is most comfortable and we dine well and watch Italian television as the silhouette of Capri slides by, hung with lights like a cruise boat and we enter the freshening Tyrrhenian.

It is many years since I was in Palermo, and I was distressed to see so much bomb damage still unrepaired along the waterfront, and behind it all such slums and overcrowding. Several travelers returned from Sicily had told us of the sinister atmosphere they found there; we may have been suggestible but it did seem as if the gaiety and welcome of the mainland was clouded with apprehension and as if there was much truth in the stories of the "honourable society," the Mafia, which was now being modernized on American lines and spreading its rackets everywhere. One had the impression of well-organized exploitation in every petty detail increasingly threatening toward the west and center of the island.

Hitherto the tour had confined us to cities but here our hotel stood somewhat outside in a large garden by the sea and we breakfasted under the palms. The Villa Igiea is a very good hotel indeed and noise free, and possesses a beautiful *art nouveau* salon of 1908, left as a memorial to its architect, Basile. As most of the company filming *The Leopard*, including Visconti and Burt Lancaster, were installed there, it proved an almost too absorbing spectacle and caused us to miss several chapels by Serpotta, the late baroque sculptor whose plaster compositions of saints are so moving.

Huge crowds and building programmes make sighteeing in Palermo a torment, a new "West End" is draining the elegance away from the old center of the *Quattro Canti*; the baroque palaces along the Via Alloro are coming down, the Arab *Khalsa*, once the most picturesque quarter of fisherfolk and fine buildings will soon be a thing of the past. The Arabs are represented by one or two small palaces, the Hohenstaufen Emperors by their superb tombs in the cathedral where that unhappy family seems to brood in Byzantine aloofness.

Nearly everything that wins a star is the work of the Normans; especially the happy little botanically-minded cloister of San Giovanni degli Eremiti whose domes rise out of a former mosque, the Capella Palatina which merits two stars and Monreale which deserves three. The general effect is overpowering and enhanced by the grandeur, dignity and brightness of the interior with not an inch left bare. I found the mosaics here warmer and bolder, better conceived and more original than those in the much smaller Capella Palatina which seemed a rehearsal for them, though others prefer its more miniature scale and subtler lighting.

Monreale alone makes a visit to Sicily essential, even if it were without its view and Norman-Arab cloister. I have seen these Norman wonders of Palermo four times now and I find that memory has completely obliterated my other visits. Just precisely what is the point of sightseeing if everything goes in at one eye and out the other so that after ten years the whole of Europe has to be mugged up again? But hush! This is the Grand Tour.

And now we come on something seen for the first time— Sicilian Rococo. I remember vividly the glass furniture—colored glass with brocade covers—that Mr. John Richardson had installed in Mr. Douglas Cooper's château near the Pont du Gard, and which had come via the auction room from the Villa Rosebery at Naples where it had been acquired from the Villa Palagonia outside Palermo; the prettiest furniture I had ever seen.

And I remembered Goethe's description of meeting in the street a distinguished elderly gentleman in Court dress followed by liveried servants holding out dishes for alms. It was the Prince of Palagonia, creator and owner of the villa, collecting money to free Christian slaves. This does not tally with

other reports of him as a lecherous hunchback, "a poor miserable lean figure shivering at every breeze." This was the Prince
Ferdinando who was responsible for the fantastic decoration;
the villa itself was begun by an earlier Ferdinando in 1715.

A curved open staircase leads up from the outside and the
main façade is also curved which lends it an enchantment not
marred by the circular garden with its ubiquitous evidences of
decay. It is otherwise with the interior. What was a highly
original, even surrealist décor has almost entirely disappeared
including, besides the glass furniture, ornaments composed of
fragments of broken mirror, old picture frames, barometer
tubes, brocaded sofas with iron spikes concealed in them,
rusty iron mobiles and chandeliers, columns and pyramids of
broken china encrusted with tea-pots. . . . Now all is derelict
and though help is supposedly on its way, it may arrive too
late.

There is a large domed room with a looking glass ceiling and
rococo decoration, with polychrome portrait busts of the family, and a long dining room in bad repair. These rooms are
faced both with marble and with glass to look like marble. A
sculptured frieze of musical dwarfs survives on the coach-
house. "It is eccentric surely; it is amusing; it may even be
pretty," writes Mr. Lees-Milne. It would do very nicely for
me.

Bagheria, except for its eighteenth century villas, is like a
straggling town in Andalusia but a little way up the hill the
Villa Valguarana boasts a superb façade and an enchanted
view.

The next day, after bidding farewell to our resourceful and
patient mentor, Mr. Archibald Colquhoun, we left at crack of
dawn by bus, the most practical way to see the island. There
is much to be said for the touring bus, especially in a not
wholly developed region. A polyglot hostess describes what
we are about to visit in three languages so that we will never
forget it. Although each spot can be reached by train or car,
only a maniac could get to all of them and when hotels are so
indifferent the bus enforces a certain standard. We all become
coach-proud. And sometimes our hostess tells us in three lan-

guages there is nothing to see and we can go to sleep and then we drop off obediently. What I liked best was calling at the different hotels to set down passengers so that we could make our choice for the next time.

We leave Palermo past the Favorita palace (said to equal the Brighton Pavilion) and then along the lovely north coast to Segesta—three stars, and for the last time. It is in a romantic position on an isolated hilltop, a large unfinished Doric temple (the columns are unfluted) perhaps abandoned because of fire or invasion but of the perfect period. For temples must not be judged by how complete they are but by the moment when they were built, and after the fifth century (Segesta is safe by forty or fifty years) some virtue goes out of them.

We went on to lunch at Erice, a high mountain plateau covered with grass and pine woods where a medieval village and castle perch on the site of the great temple of Venus (attributed to Aeneas), a landmark to sailors of the ancient world. Late in the afternoon we came by Trapani and Marsala to Selinunte, still unspoilt, its colossal columns and chaos of ruins abutting on to rushy sand dunes by the loneliest of seas and then to coffee in cheerful Sciacca (the poor man's Nerja) before being squirted out for the night in Agrigento, a booming and most *mafioso* town.

The next day was begun with the temples which are in wonderfully preserved condition, but later in date than Segesta and somewhat lacking in inspiration, except for the scanty remains of the colossal temple of Zeus and the early temple of Hercules. A broad new asphalt road with petrol station winds round the temples that I once approached on foot over the fields and adds bitumen to their numen. We are now in the far south; it is already very hot by breakfast; we drive round Licata through a pale empty heat-haze with scattered new settlements in cube shaped houses and a landscape of strange crops—early tomatoes and groundnuts.

Gela with its oil-derricks, like a boom town on the Texan gulf, and Caltanisetta (inland) mark the easternmost limits of the Mafia. It is a relief to take to the hills and ascend the lovely green valley with its hazel orchards to Piazza Armerina. This was what we had come to Sicily to see for the greater part of the excavations are only ten years old.

The Palace of the Emperor Maximian (A.D. 286 to 305), the colleague of Diocletian, is as ambitious as any from Nero's Golden House to Diocletian's Spalato. It is an enormous agglomeration which has been enclosed in perspex to preserve the mosaics until it looks like some *avant-garde* prizewinner at an international exhibition. The site, 2,000 feet up a wooded green valley with a high mountain protecting it to the north, is one of the pleasantest on the island. The Emperor was identified by Gentili through the portraits of a small boy who is twice represented with a squint. (The Byzantine chronicler John Malalas described Maximian's son Maxentius as crosseyed.)

The huge area of mosaics was the work of hundreds of craftsmen imported in a hurry from North Africa. Most scenes have to do with the chase or the bringing back alive of large animals for the circus. There are also some gruesome studies of agonizing giants and the famous Bikini girls of later and more delicate workmanship. The Imperial latrines must be the envy of tourists from all over the island.

Although the father-in-law of Constantine, Maximian seems to have been aggressively pagan; a ruddy well-pomaded Hemingwayesque tycoon mad on big game and bloodsports, deplorably square, with a bevy of daughters all taking after him. Or are they more probably a Windmill cabaret of water girls?

Syracuse, in spite of the new approach past chemical factories, is still a sacred island. It is the only place in Sicily where one could settle; the air, the light, the sea breeze, the baroque squares, the promenades round the seawall contribute, but above all it is a city where the isolated outposts of the world of antiquity of which we have seen so many are concentrated and constitute the place where we live. "What one feels here," wrote Gregorovius beside the fountain Arethusa, "is love for Hellas, the fatherland of every thinking soul."

Our hotel is about to be taken over but the view across the Great Harbor redeems it and there is a good sea food restaurant round the corner. The cathedral combines some great columns of a temple to Athena with a dazzling rococo façade.

In the museum is an archaic *ephebus* of the early sixth century and the Venus of Syracuse. According to Maupassant *"C'est la femme telle qu'elle est, telle qu'on l'aime telle qu'on la désire."* I thought the guardian seemed unduly watchful. Bathing had already begun by the Anapus. There was an American yacht in the harbor with special equipment for locating statues under water and hauling them up. Summer was as tempting as Venus.

On our last day we reached Noto, one of the most southerly towns in Europe with its baroque palaces and blue-green araucarias, the lightly swaying Norfolk island pines which guarantee a mild winter. And now begins the long, lovely, exciting, exhausting journey home, at first under the lee of Etna by Catania, Acireale and other cities, past the little tempting islets below Taormina and many unspoilt beaches and then by the train ferry to the mainland with the Sicilian coastal range bidding us an oblique farewell. If I were a rich man looking for a property, I would be tempted by the Calabrian coast between Palmi and Tropea with its groves of huge olives and the many lovely strands and coves far from the main road which cluster round Cape Vaticano.

We had allowed for a day and a half in Rome, just enough, as it happened, to see the end of the fine weather. One morning we spent at the Etruscan museum in the Villa Giulia, finding the Apollo of Veii slightly repellent by comparison with the archaic Apollo of Tiber in the Terme, but enraptured by the jovial couple on the Caere sarcophagus carved in what looks like orange-pink blancmange, by the thin Giacometti figurines and by the bronze cauldron over the edge of which alternate figures of men and dogs peer to see what's cooking.

On our last morning, a Sunday, we stopped on the way to the station to hear some Gregorian singing at Sant' Anselmo. The modern church, which belongs to the international Benedictine College, is spacious and austerely elegant. The monks file in and sing unaccompanied, a balm to the soul and the ceremony proceeded with a clear-cut distinction and suavity, with visiting priests and nuns and even a cardinal in the congregation.

No railway addict could have contrived a brighter homeward journey. Our tickets permitted a choice of Alpine routes. We decided to go by Zurich. Leaving Rome at 10.20, the streamlined Settebello (one of the beautiful trains of the world) with unhurrying anapaests (and only three stops) set us down from our armchair seats at Milan in time to catch the Gottardo, of the network of Trans-Europe expresses, which stops only twice before Zurich.

The Settebello is American style with not very good food but enormous washrooms. The Gottardo is beautifully Swiss like the lakes and waterfalls and spruce-woods past which it thunders. A young *maître d'hôtel* in morning coat announces dinner which is served by uniformed waitresses from a vast *à la carte* menu. And in Zurich later that night we sipped our Fendant underneath the photograph of Joyce in what is my favorite old-fashioned restaurant.

Gray houses, green hills, a lake and two blue rivers, arcaded quays where one can still recapture the charm and exhilaration of pre-1914 Central Europe—Zurich was the perfect place to return to the North while we cashed the last of those colored slips which had brought us all that sunshine and San Pellegrino, which had unlocked so many doors and rolled back so many centuries. After this we were able by means of another brilliant Trans-Europe (the Arbalète) to breakfast in Zurich and dine in London thirteen hours later, muttering with Maecenas "Lubricos quate dentes" (shake out our last tooth) "vita dum superest bene est" (while one's alive all is well).

Revisiting Greece

After examining a clutch of well-made travel books, I have sometimes wondered for how many pages one could keep it up by setting out to tell the truth, not only about places but about the inadequacy of our feelings. (I have known the Acropolis to resemble a set of false teeth in a broken palate.) When at last we take our long-wished-for holiday what really happens?

There is, first, the period of preparation (in a sense the only time we are abroad); guidebooks are compared; experts are consulted; a mirage of a brown, lean summer self descending on an obese island dances before our eyes and we are convincingly importuned by the wrong clothes, the wrong books, the wrong introductions. "Of course you will need a white dinner jacket and a cummerbund"; "you must take the *whole* of Pausanias"; "an ultra-violet filter"; "stout walking shoes"; "the rubber flippers should be made to measure."

At twenty we travel to discover ourselves, at thirty for love, at forty out of greed and curiosity, at fifty for a revelation. Irresponsible, illiterate, shedding all ties and cares, we await the visitation, the rebirth. Gradually the present dissolves, England becomes totally unreal; we have in fact already left, not yet airborne but anxiety-cradled; "if the flippers are not ready, they cannot possibly be sent on"; "you quite understand that these traveler's checks are not negotiable on Mount Athos"; "don't go to the new hotel but the other one"; "don't go to the old hotel"; "there are three new hotels"; "Corfu is the place for you: it has everything"; "yes, if you like a green island. I prefer Mikonos"; "it's never too hot on Corfu"; "you would hate Corfu."

D-Day. Running in the new dark glasses in the car to the airport. Livid clouds, infra-red buses, a lurid day-of-judgment air about the hoardings along the clotted avenue. Signs of panic, cleverly concealed, as I board the plane, where I suffer from a private phobia, dispelled only by champagne, that the signal "Fasten your safety-belts" is staying on for the whole voyage.

Paris: the heat advances across the tarmac, our gaoler for the next six weeks. "Thick brown overcoat, stout walking shoes, whole of Pausanias," it mumbles; "Mr. Connolly? I think we can take care of all that." Inevitable contrast between London and Paris, the one muffled under its summer cloud-cap, all Wimbledon and roses, the other with a migraine of politics, bleached and persilled in the heat. The bookstall at London Airport for a nation of magazine readers—if that; at Le Bourget full of expensive works on art and philosophy. The paralysis of suburbia contrasted with the animation of the *banlieue* where a fair is in progress and a horse-drawn dray of children jingles under the catalpas.

How much of a holiday is spent lying gasping on one's back, in planes, trains, cabins, beaches, and hotel bedrooms, the guidebook held aloft like an awning? We really travel twice—as a physical object resembling a mummy or small wardrobe-trunk which is shuttled about at considerable expense; and as a mind married to a "Guide Bleu," always reading about the last place or the next one.

It is suddenly apparent that the heat permits no reading of any kind; whole areas of consciousness must be evacuated, the perimeter of sensation shortened; no past, no future. Only the guidebook survives and the other books we have brought sneak to the bottom of the suitcase. And now the Seven Indispensables perform their ghostly jig from pocket to pocket. The passport, the traveler's checks, the tickets, the dark glasses, the reading glasses, the pen, the comb. Where are they? I could have sworn I had them a moment ago.

A flying visit to Versailles to see the *petits appartements* rendered famous by the Pompadour, the Dubarry and Madame de Mitford. Intense disappointment; so much redecoration, and everywhere the milling multitudes, locusts of the post-war summer. Illumination: *The human eye deteriorates all it looks at.* Why is the decoration of the House of the Vettii at Pompeii so much less exciting than the new excavations? Because the human eye has faded the colors, vulgarized the painting. The camera also enfeebles its subject, and being photographed too often I believe to cause cancer of the soul.

And now, Venice, city of sore throats, frayed tempers, and leaking wallets; alas, never the same for me since I reviewed Hemingway's last novel but one. Much as I disliked the book I remain obsessed by his terrible colonel. I drink Valpolicella and take the fatal stroll to Harry's Bar, stopping on the little bridge where the colonel had a heart attack on his way from his wine to his martinis. How he would have hated the Biennale! So much painting that should never have come South of the Alps, North of the Po, West of Suez, or East of Saint Louis, all maltreated by the heat, the humidity, and the merciless light—except the paintings which have some secret poster quality, Delvaux's clustering cowlike nudes or Bacon's agonizing tycoons. Art is bottled sunshine and should never be exposed to it.

And everywhere art critics, never a painter; symbol of the age of culture-diffusion when publishers and village-explainers travel while authors have to stay at home, when painters in Maida Vale hear from their dealers in Mozambique or Mogador, when Byron would have received a postcard: "Dear B. London must be very hot. Just off to Ravenna to join the Galignanis and then to meet some Greek publishers at Missolonghi. Hope to be able to do something for you. How goes the Canto?—Yrs., John Murray."

Revisit the equestrian statue of Colleone in its dingy square. The base is too high. Better in a photograph. Failure to experience any emotion over Tintoretto. Horror of Surrealist masters in Biennale. Moved by nothing later than Pompeii. Great paintings should be kept under lock and key and shown as seldom as wonder working images. The real connoisseurs of art were the Pharaohs; they took it with them. Intoxication with Venetian gardens, the oleander drooping over the canal at some scabrous corner, the ubiquitous freshwater sea smell and the best drink in Europe, a tumbler of ice-cold peach juice in the colonel's bar. More hordes of milling tourists, squeaking *lederhosen;* Clapham Junction of the mechanized masses in the Piazza. Everybody is somebody. Nobody is anybody. Everyone is everywhere.

At last the boat: survival of an earlier form of travel, obeying the strange psychology of "on board ship." Whom we hate on the first day we shall love on the last, whom we greet on the first we shall not bid farewell; boredom will become its own reward and change suddenly to ecstasy. The *Achilleus* is a charmed vessel, trim, white, gay, its inmates friendly and delightful. The islands of the lagoon bob at their moorings as we churn through the warm night and the next blue day past Monte Gargano and Brindisi, with its lemon ices and Roman column, and across to Corfu where we stay for three hours instead of a week, just time to see the famous view at Canoni, so called because the tourist is fired at it like a cannonball.

That evening we are streaking through the Corinth Canal like mercury rising in a thermometer. The *Achilleus* has now gone completely Greek. The food is interesting and local, the crew sings, the married couples no longer flash their signals of distress, "save me, rescue me." The passengers crane over the rail to where the distant corona of Athens glows above the dark bulk of Salamis. We enter the sooty bustle of Piraeus as the last evening steamers beetle forth to fertilize the expectant islands and are extracted from our carefree cabin like ticks from a dog's ear. Nothing on shore will quite come up to it, even as Nice is never worthy of the Blue Train or New York of the *Queen Mary. Arriver, c'est déjà partir un peu.*

Great heat, like a smart doctor, begins every sentence "You'll have to cut out. . . ." With the temperature always around ninety, generalities alone can be appreciated, details and detours must be ignored; we are but fit for the simplest forms of sightseeing.

Air throbs, marble hisses, the sea glistens with malice, the exhausted landscape closes at lunchtime and does not reopen

before six o'clock when the sun ceases its daily interrogation.
We stagger across the grilled slabs of the Propylaea with only
one idea—which is both idea and sensation—the juice of a
lemon and an orange in equal proportions poured again and
again over cubes of ice. After this postwar duty visit we flee
the Parthenon and rush to take the first boat at the Piraeus. It
is crowded and unbelievably noisy but there is a cool breeze as
we round Sunium.

Bathed in lemon-yellow light like Rabat or Casablanca,
Rhodes has some claim to be the perfect island. Neither too
large nor too small, too hot nor too cold, fertile, hilly, legendary and exotic, it lives in the present as well as the past. The
medieval city of the knights has been so perfectly restored by
the Italians as to outdo Carcassonne; it is a golden flypaper for
tourists who are led to it like bombers to a dummy target,
leaving the real town uninjured. Between the austerity of the
medieval fortress and the flamboyant Fascist concrete outside
the walls the old Turkish quarter sprawls in exquisite decay.

The few simple elements required by the Moslem conception of beauty, the dome and minaret, fountain, plane tree,
and arcaded courtyard are here combined into a dozen similar
but never monotonous patterns . . . we are in a tiny Stamboul,
a sixteenth and seventeenth century quarter of dignified exiles
with their Persian tiles and Arabic inscriptions, their memories of fallen grandeur. No farther from the comfortable but
hideous Hôtel des Roses than you can spit a pomegranate seed
stands the little mosque of Murad-Reïz, its cemetery planted
with mulberry and oleander. Few places are more soothing
than a Turkish graveyard, where the turbaned tombs are
jumbled like spillikins around the boles of cypresses and the
cicadas zizz above the silent koubbas.

Here sleeps the commander who captured Tripoli, and
probably the administrators who lost it, heroes and footlers
together, the generals and admirals, the Beys and Pashas of
that cruel, clean, pious, frugal horticultural community. The
great admiral's grave is well kept-up and hung with Mecca-
green cloth; otherwise the nodding conversation pieces are
abandoned to shade and sun, each stone turban proudly pro-

claiming its owner's status or bearing a verse from the Koran by which we linger in bewilderment—even as one day in some far-flung graveyard a passing Chinese may halt, baffled by the enumeration of our meager virtues.

Mikonos by contrast is a rude stone altar erected to the stern god of summer. The town is a white African sneer arching brightly round the bay where a row of little restaurants vie with each other in disappointments. The heat swaggers through the spotless alleys where bearded Danish painters seal every exit with their easels.

To swim one must bump across the bay to some blinding cove or trudge the iron-hot mountain path, paved with mule-dung and brown thistle. The sun needles the brain cavity, desiccates the lung and obtains a garnishee upon the liver. Doors bang, nerves jangle, little waves bristle and buffet through the afternoon and in our sleep fashionable voices cry "Mikonos for me," "*il y a toujours du vent à Mikonos.*"

After this stony sanatorium its humble neighbor seems to flower with statues, tremendous in its exuberant and irretrievable collapse. Whereas Delphi's mountain womb remains one of the holy places of the human spirit, Delos is complex and baffling, irreverent even in its piety. With its swans and geese and cafeteria, the sacred lake where Apollo was born must have been not unlike the Round Pond in Kensington Gardens; the commercial Roman town survives in better shape than the Greek; the shrines of Isis and the phalloi of Dionysus have stood up better than Apollo's altars. In this center of the ancient slave trade, this eclectic battener on the world's religions whose moneylending priesthood were the Rothschilds of antiquity, the god of man's fulfilment in this world, the wielder of the lyre and the bow, is noticeably absent.

Yet Delos is magical. According to the admirable Greek usage, no fence surrounds the ruins nor is there an entrance fee; black with tourists and lizards, prostrate in the sunshine, the ancient stones are part of the world's daily life. Among the Roman pavements is the mysteriously haunting mosaic of anchor and dolphin which was found on the seals of the wine jars on the Greek ship salvaged outside Marseilles by M. Cou-

steau, and which aided him to identify his Sextius, owner of
the vessel, with the proprietor of this sumptuous villa. By
such means are we enabled to creep backward into time, liberated by significant detail such as the hand, in the museum,
from that colossal archaic Apollo which was broken off by the
fall of the sculptor Nikias's fabulous bronze palm tree.

Delphi remains sacred to Apollo while Delos had permis-
sion to exploit him; both became enormously rich, both tot-
tered to destruction after Julian's reign in A.D. 363 with full
treasuries, gold ceilings and colonnades of marble statues
(Delos had 3,000 intact under the opprobrium of the Chris-
tians). Abandoned to pirates through the Dark Ages, Delos
must still have been one of the wonders of the world, a desert
island carpeted with temples and matchless private buildings,
a thousand years of sanctity still clinging to the shrines and
avenues while Delphi, pillaged by Byzantium, issued its de-
spairing last oracle and the bronze horses of St. Mark's, as I
like to think, were reft from the impassive Charioteer.

We may walk across the sacred lake or stand on Apollo's
temple at Delphi where the earth-dragon fumed and fretted
and the priestess gave out incoherent moans for the priest to
polish into the double meanings which answered our desire.
But it is difficult to feel aware of the terrible god of youthful
strength and intellectual beauty. He exists only in museums.
For though Greek architecture has barely survived, and Greek
music and painting not at all, we have at last learned how to
display sculpture at its best.

In the new museum at Athens we no longer need to pretend
to ourselves; here the chain of masterpieces signal to each
other down the ages. This is how Greece was; this is what
man can do. Apollo is manifest at last with his smile which
seems instantly to annihilate all time and all suffering. Joy is
under everything and if we feel pain it is our fault because we
are not divine enough. Death has an appropriateness which
transcends sorrow; the world belongs to the beautiful charm;
is welded to courage, thought to action—even the serpent is a
friend.

But humanity could not grow up without a religion of the

mother; the world could not always belong to the graceful tactless hearties with red curls, bulging eyeballs, stocky behinds, a try-anything-once look below their waving helmets. Can one think of any archaic sculpture which takes even Zeus beyond early middle age? In this art "Hippocleides doesn't care" triumphs over the maxims of the seven sages. Irresponsible perfection went out about 475 B.C.; yet is it my imagination or are not the contemporary Greeks one of the happiest as well as the most friendly nations in the world?

Bordeaux-Dordogne

BORDEAUX

Bordeaux, the fourth city of France, and once, after London, York and Winchester, of England, is no place for the sightseer; it is a climate, a rest cure, a state of mind whose principal charm is that there is nothing to see. The Palais Gallien is the dimmest of Roman ruins, the cathedral just gets by, the churches, gates and towers, except for a collection of mummified human remains, are quite without interest, while the architecture of the eighteenth century, for which it is famous, is so discreet or so damaged that one is hardly conscious of the golden age except as an atmosphere.

A great yellow river crossed by a long and lovely red-brick bridge (1810) sweeps in a semi-circle past lines of dignified *quais*. The focal point of these *quais* is the Place de la Bourse, which resembled a corner of the Place Vendôme, until a British bomb fell on it. Then comes the Quinconces, an enormous open square which is either very dull and empty or enclosed for a noisy industrial fair, and the picturesque docks. A little way into the town from the river is the true heart of the city, the holy place which is in the form of an equilateral triangle from whose apex a circle is suspended.

Contemplate this circle within the triangle for a few moments. For a stay of inside a week it should not be necessary to leave this area; it contains all that one could wish for, and those who demand more and break the magic bounds will, it is rumored, nearly all meet with misfortune.

The sides of the triangle are three streets laid out by the

33

Marquis de Tourny, *intendant* or governor of Bordeaux in the reign of Louis XV. At point B is the Place Gambetta, a charming and unspoilt two-storied square of the period, with a magnolia garden in the center. From B to C is the Cours de l'Intendance, the principal shopping street. At point C is the Place de la Comédie, with its theatre, the most beautiful building of the city (1773-80) and one of the loveliest theatres in the world in the purest classic of Louis Seize. Opposite is the Café de Bordeaux, the pleasantest in the town (restaurant ruined by fluorescent lighting), where one should sit in the evening to enjoy the green sunset.

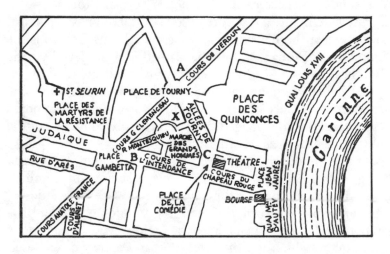

From C to A runs a wide esplanade or narrow piazza, the pleasure promenade of the Allées de Tourny (1744), delicious in the evenings when the theatre is floodlit. At point A is the circular Place de Tourny, somewhat spoilt but including a charming bar and nightclub (when not too crowded), the Palm Beach, whose salons, with their "Empire" *boiseries*, overlook the Allées de Tourny, and round off the evening. (As it is forbidden to serve food after midnight, a wild night-out in Bordeaux will usually end with a visit to a speakeasy where *soupe à l'oignon* is consumed in the strictest secrecy.) From A to B is the Cours Georges Clemenceau which completes the design of the Marquis de Tourny for a shopping street, a promenade, and a boulevard.

Now for X, the magic circle, the holy of holies. This is the Marché des Grands Hommes, a covered market approached by four little streets, the Rues Montesquieu, Voltaire, Montaigne, Buffon, which are a perpetual feast for the eye. Here in the market, surrounded by great names, is the evidence of the delicious soil, sea, and climate of Bordeaux, often sultry in summer, sometimes raw and humid in winter, but as near perfection as a temperate maritime climate can be: *ver longum, brumaeque breves*. It is southern England removed to the furthest point south at which it would remain both green and industrious. (Mean monthly temperatures of over seventy in summer or below forty in winter bespeak a different climate. Bordeaux—a drier, harsher version of Biarritz—is our own south coast but riper.)

Pyramids of Dublin Bay prawns, lobsters, *langoustes*, cod, sole and skate vie in the market with more unusual fish: lamprey, sturgeon, huge red *chapons*, and enormous shad. Salt-marsh mutton, butter, cheese, ortolans, and *palombes* from the Landes lead us on to the fruit and vegetable section, as fine as anywhere in the world; nectarines and muscat grapes in autumn, melons of all kinds in summer; asparagus, wild strawberries, cherries, peaches, gourds—and, in savory stacks, the color of Havana cigars, the *cêpes bordelaises*, glorious fungi like giant Bath buns which, when fried in oil with garlic, form the perfect link between Pauillac lamb and Gruyère cheese while a dynasty of clarets is being accommodated.

The line joining point B to the circle is the Rue Montesquieu, and here is the Hôtel Montré, which still preserves the atmosphere and Empire furniture of the great days of the European coaching inn. Henry James might well be in room 19, with its red and gold salon, writing a story about the uneasy American family next door. Opposite is the Chapon Fin. *Reverentia!*

This restaurant has the best wine list in existence for those who consider claret superior to Burgundy and brandy preferable to *alcools blancs*. It has a light, dry Château Olivier which is a perfect white wine for the fish; afterward we can matriculate at will among the older bottles, half-bottles, and magnums before we finish up with a tawny but flawless Yquem and an historic *fine maison*. The food is delectable in its simplicity; a plate of *haricots verts* is a meal in itself; eggs, fish, meat, and fruit are all impeccable.

The restaurant is built in the grotto style which was fashionable in Bordeaux around 1900, and which is found in fish stalls along the *quais* and in the amazing *art nouveau* gardens on the road to Macau. It is large, cool, quiet, and comfortable and seats the full French cabinet in times of crisis. M. Sicart has managed it for fifty years, and the old wine waiter, as expert as anyone in these matters can hope to be, has presided for nearly as long. The hotel is very pleasant, the rooms somewhat noisy. At the other end of the triangle, on the Allées de Tourny, is Dubern's, the rival establishment, a luxury grocery and wine merchant whose window display is a combination of the best from the market with caviare and *foie gras* as seen at Fortnum's before the last war. Upstairs are two or three small paneled rooms in which excellent meals are served. The fashion is now to prefer this restaurant to the Chapon Fin; it is indeed a serious rival, but the one is unique, sole survivor from the age of Foyot and Voisin's, the other an engaging upstart.

Within the triangle in a somber little square there is also the church of Notre Dame, in the Jesuit style of the end of the seventeenth century, and a feeble museum of antiquities. There is a good bookshop in the Place Gambetta and an *antiquaire* in the Place de Tourny.

After two days in Bordeaux one becomes conscious of a liver: at best we are sluggish and irritable, at worst bilious and racked with headache. This silent critic of our pleasures will have to be placated. Exercise must be taken, luncheons cut down. We were able to begin by a visit to this year's admirable Goya exhibition, testimony to the vision of Bordeaux's vigorous young Mayor and member of Parliament, M. Chaban-Delmas, ex-general of the Resistance and international Rugby player, then on to the public garden, another creation of M. de Tourny, full of lovely southern trees and romantic charm. A longer walk may be taken to the town hall, cathedral and picture gallery, and back via the *quais* and bridge. The river is always soothing, and little boats take one over to Lormont, where the country begins, and there is usually a breeze. Just off the Place de Tourny is the terminal bus station, and here buses radiate in all directions: an ideal regime, we found, is to take a bus every morning and return to dine at the Chapon Fin, Dubern's, or the Château Trompette every night. Here are some of the most pleasant excursions:

1. Southeast down the Garonne to Labrède, where the Château of Montesquieu can be visited, a moated castle in which the noble author's mid-eighteenth century study and bedroom are preserved intact. From Langon one can go south to the Sauternes country, to Bazas with its unrestored cathedral and then seek out the chain of churches and castles associated with the *bordelais* Pope, Clement VII (fl. 1300). Cadillac, St. Macaire, and La Réole are interesting places along the river, before vines give place to tobacco as we approach Agen.

2. Due east, along the Dordogne, stands Libourne, with its reminders of the English occupation, and St. Emilion, a sparkling southern hill village full of Romanesque churches and crypts, the best antiquarian value of the whole neighborhood, and Vélines whence Montaigne's château can be visited, with the painted tower where this most modern of all ancient writers had his library. An evening autorail goes right up the Dordogne to Bergerac, Souillac, and eventually the mountains of Aurillac. The Dordogne is a far more beautiful river than the Garonne, despite the latter's villages and vineyards, but becomes spectacular only above Lalinde, at a considerable distance from our base.

3. North up the estuary of the Gironde, here a noble stream like the Mississippi at New Orleans, lie Bourg and Blaye, both charming places, and Jonzac, Pons, and Saintes which are remarkable indeed: silver Romanesque cities, far more southern than anywhere between Bordeaux and Biarritz, and unpolluted by the general stream of tourist traffic. It is a country,

towards Angoulême, of bright limestone hills and precious twelfth century churches. Royan, on the coast, was almost blown to pieces in the last war, but Talmont, a white village islanded on the estuary, repays a visit.

4. Northwest to the claret country. The journey to the vineyards of the Médoc is indispensable, but if several vineyards are to be visited it must be undertaken by car, and introductions provided by a wine merchant will be necessary.

We shall take as an example a visit to Mouton, one of the best managed and most welcoming of vineyards, whose wines, relatively heavy for the Médoc, have a certain bulllike grace and solidity. "*Ça fait très Mouton,*" as they say of some particularly noble specimen.

As a region, the Médoc illustrates all the subtlety of the Bordeaux climate. Until the seventeenth century it was unreclaimed marsh, and compared to the great names of Saint Emilion, whose wines were prized by Ausonius, its châteaux seem absurdly *nouveau riche.* The vine-ripening belt is a narrow strip running north-northwest; on one side lie the salt marshes and the brown estuary, on the other the sandy Landes with their commons and pine forest. Between the sand and the mud runs the magic vein of stony soil. The flints, the light earth, the rainy spring, the hot blue summer, and the lingering autumn have all contributed to this perfection of the grape: fruit of sunny sea-wind radiance, of Dutch polders silver-gilt by the warmth of the Midi. To understand the Médoc is to begin to love Bordeaux, to which it forms a companion piece.

Flat, bright, dusty—subject to sudden storms and lowering clouds which as suddenly clear—the plain, between the tidal water and the dark belt of forest, is peppered with sacred names: Latour, Lafite, Margaux, Cantenac; each vineyard marked out by an army of knotted green bushes whose powdery clusters dangle among the pebbles, whose wine gives out the most delicate of civilized aromas; fragrant, light, and cavernous as myrtle-berries from an Etruscan tomb, the incomparable *bouquet du vieux Médoc,* offspring of sunshine and hard work, parent of warmth, wit, and understanding.

The châteaux are strung out irregularly along the strip. Two at all costs must be seen, Beychevelle and Margaux. They are the loveliest of the region, the one Louis Quinze (1753), the other Louis Seize. As befits the age of Adam, Margaux is the statelier pile, while Beychevelle is lower and more rambling, with a garden pavilion to each wing and fine wrought iron gates. Classical perfection or rococo charm? We must examine both from as near at hand as impertinence will take us and then forever take our stand. Other enchanting neighbors are Issan, with its moat, the British owned Léoville-Barton, with its cypress, and the eighteenth century tower of Château Latour, stoniest of all vineyards, most perfect of all wines.

Mouton seems more like a pleasant English villa—until we enter the group of low buildings across the courtyard. The first room, which one might call an ante-chapel, contains old prints, decanters, documents, and statues likely to induce a mood of reverence: vestry would be a better term for it, the robing room of Bacchus. Great doors silently open and we look across an enormous low nave with the heraldic sheep of Mouton emblazoned on the far wall over the pewlike rows of silent barrels in which the new wine rests for three years, before being bottled, numbered, labeled, and sent out to the world on its goodwill mission.

We walk down the nave to its far end, rinse our mouths with the sharp new wine and, lighting our pious candles, descend to the crypt. Here stand the enormous vats in which the newly pressed wine ferments before being stored in barrels, each vat as big as a Nissen hut, with the temperature chart and case history of its tumultuous inmate pinned up outside. Here also is an electric wind machine which will dry grapes gathered in wet weather; and at the end of the crypt, in greater darkness, heavy iron doors which lead to the catacombs, the long dry cellars where the bottles themselves mature in their cobwebby cages.

A vista of shiny black disks recedes before us, the bottled vintages of the last few years, then come the years we covet most, the *reserve de Monsieur le Baron* and lastly the "museum"

of rare and ancient wines from this and neighboring properties, where fabulous bottles, too precious to drink, may peace-
fully end their days like kings in the Escurial. *"Ça fait très
Mouton."*

At last we must climb back from catacombs to crypt, crypt
to cathedral, cathedral to vestry to visit the winepresses themselves, where the grapes are poured in by the pickers, then
sifted and trodden by laborers with wooden rakes and paddles
who shuffle round to the music of a fiddle. M. Marjory, the
enchanting manager, will imitate the motions for us as a special favor. This age-old sifting of the grape and pressing of the
wine (before it flows into the huge vats below) is performed by
human hands, or rather feet, and wooden implements. More
complicated modern machinery has been tried and found
wanting, and the process illustrates the archaic and dedicated
life of the great vineyards, where quantity is sacrificed to quality and where the munificent owners sometimes prefer to
carry on the business at a loss rather than lower the standard
or destroy the tradition to suit the declining taste and coarsen-
ing palate of our frantic epoch.

It is always hard to keep awake at Mouton; the sea air, the
sun, the wines (decanted and served again from their own bottles) and the simple but outrageous perfection of the cooking—*risotto aux truffes, gigot de pré salé*—deal one knock-out
blow after another—or I would recommend a prolonged stay
in the district to all painters and writers. But the region is anti-
art and the villages lack the Romanesque beauties and pastoral
surroundings of those across the estuary. Tennis, hospitality,
and big business occupy the claret-kings, with their American
cars and English nicknames, and there are few walks and
fewer books in the artificial landscape. Fleecy clouds drift
across the high blue sky, slow carts with spraying machines
pass between the squat regiments of vines, "ole man liver"
rumbles a warning against *galanteries vinicoles;* it is time to go.

Southwest of Bordeaux lies its principal pleasure ground,
the Basin of Arcachon, an inland sea like a glorified Poole Harbor, ideal for yachting, safe for children, famous for oysters,
cool in summer, mild in winter, surrounded by undulating

pine forests with a back cloth of arbutus. A mile or two down the coast, where the Basin joins the Atlantic, stretch the beaches of Le Moulleau and Le Pyla, each with an hotel, and beyond them the Dune de Pilat, the highest in Europe.

The view from this dune is one of the loveliest that I know. The white sand runs for several miles in a steep hog's back; on one side it descends to the Atlantic in a long deserted beach, on the other to the pine forest which extends without a break or a building to the limit of the horizon. To the north the violet waters of the Basin and its sea channel wind before us. The woods come right down to the argent shore and hardly a villa is to be seen, only the curving sand and the green pine trees. It might be some vast inlet of the Carolinas as viewed by the first explorers.

It will have taken us about ten days to visit Arcachon, the Médoc, the Sauternes, the lower Dordogne, and the Gironde, returning to Bordeaux, if we choose, every evening. After ten days the traveler may have seen enough and may even depart complaining that Guyenne is not nearly so interesting as Provence or the Pays Basque. But he will never be cured of it. Months later, generally at the beginning of March or by the middle of September, the bridges across the Dordogne at Libourne or Saint André de Cubzac will rise before his inner eye. If he is in Spain the image of the old wine waiter at the Chapon Fin, with his brown face and twinkling eye, will appear in a dream, he will just distinguish the words "*Prenez le Dix-huit, c'est plus léger*" before awaking to his sultry flagon of Rioja or Valdepeñas. If he be in the mountains, he will suddenly envisage the delicious flatness of *Entre deux mers*, the land of the two rivers, he will remember the rose-red arches of Napoleon's bridge stemming the yellow eddies, the sober *quais* with their *mascarons*—carved faces, all different—above each doorway. If we are in the South of France, it will be the waters of Arcachon we covet, cool and tidal, its unspoilt beaches and the nights without mosquitoes, the south-west wind— and if we are in London it will be something of them all, with the limestone grays of Saint Emilion, the tall magnolias of the public garden, the evening patina of the Place de la Comédie, and the pale clear sunshine of the Médoc.

For when we say there is nothing to see at Bordeaux we mean that there is everything to feel, if we would enjoy the sensuous atmosphere of this Bristol three hundred and fifty miles south, an atmosphere witty, inquiring, earthy, a little complacent and provincial, the climate of eighteenth century philosophers like Montesquieu, of its wise mayor who gave Shakespeare the idea for *The Tempest*, Michel de Montaigne, or of its last Roman Governor whose vineyard at Saint Emilion is still famous as Château Ausone and who celebrated in one of his most charming poems the air of his native city, that green and yellow harmony of the South West, the climate of humanism.

THE DORDOGNE

The Dordogne is exactly 300 miles long, which puts it into the second rank among French rivers; no town of any size, except Bergerac, lies on its banks; it does not even reach the sea. Yet year by year it grows in prestige and when people say they are going to the Dordogne (and they never say they are going to the Garonne or the Seine or the Loire) they mean something which the words do not express and which is intelligible only to those who have already taken the cure—for that is what the visit is.

What is the essential quality of this "Dordogne?" It means a certain climate, a certain relationship between man and nature, a special blend of landscape and architecture, which, taken together, form a complete and self-dependent little world somehow different in time from our own and exercising an extraordinarily soothing effect on all who stay there more than a week. The climate is peculiar to the southwestern slopes of the Massif Central which are influenced by the Atlantic. The winters are not very cold, the springs and autumns are dry and sunny, the summers wet and thundery. The plateaux are bleak but the long river valleys, Dordogne, Lot,

Vézère, Isle, are soft and balmy. Mediterranean evergreens bloom on the cliffs of Les Eyzies while the Basins of Brive, of Beaulieu and Souillac enjoy the same climate as Pau. Early vegetables and delicious fruit thrive round Brive. The plateaux are covered with oak copses, rich in truffles; in the valleys maize, walnuts, tobacco, vines spread out. The vegetation is northern; the air and light are of the south. Oxen are in general use and if we replace the cypress by the poplar we receive an impression of Tuscany which accounts for the epithet "Vergilian" which is sometimes applied.

Each river has certain characteristics: the Lot is wild and lonely, the Vézère seems consecrated to prehistory, the Isle, which passes through Périgueux, is quiet and placid. The Dordogne alone combines a noble grace and austerity with a civilized overtone of feudal castles and Romanesque churches. If one were to sum up its appeal, especially to English visitors, one would be tempted to ascribe it to a quality of remembered childhood. If we go for a walk anywhere along the Dordogne, we find everything is English—the flowers, the trees, the fields, the hedges—but multiplied to a vast size and enriched by the southern light with a kind of radiance. Things look as when we first saw them and recall by their luxuriance the indelible sensation of the turf round Corfe Castle or the heather at Oban when for the first time we apprehended them with wonder. Summer showers pelt down but never create a sensation of darkness: the vast landscape stretches out in its lowering greens broken by the white cliffs along the river, the brown of a castle—and suddenly the sun reappears. The turf is warm and springy, steam rises from the wild quinces along the hedges, the enormous blackberries glisten, the lemon-yellow walnut trees or dazzling chestnuts shake themselves, the geese go back into single file, the rainbow forms across the Cirque de Montvalent; the deluge is over.

The villages are among the most beautiful in the world: the pointed roofs are covered with round gray tiles, the walls are of unhewn stones, there is a profusion of small towers and dovecotes, of rough stone steps leading up to lofts, and tall vines cover every door. The castles of the Dordogne are on a gigantic scale but every village boasts a small manor or *gentil-hommière* (they are graded according to whether they have four towers or two towers or one) which fits perfectly into the landscape, like the little Romanesque church with its carved porch and ruined cloister. These small manors seem the ideal retreat for the present time and it is a pleasant daydream to search for one's favorite—Autoire, St. Sozy, Salignac, Terregaie, or the magnificent Latreyne.

The Dordogne rises high in the Puy de Sancy and for many miles remains a mountain river flowing through somber gorges and newly made lakes. From Argentat to Beaulieu there is a road along it for twenty-five kilometres; this stretch is very little known and most beautiful. At Beaulieu civilization begins, there is a good hotel and a wonderful Romanesque church and portico. Five miles further on, near Bretenoux, is the first of the enormous castles, a triangular block of red masonry with a stupendous view and a series of rooms "restored" by a retired tenor from the Paris opera. Two miles south is the most beautiful of all the Renaissance buildings of the Dordogne, the Château de Montal, which M. Fenaille almost put back into its original state, recovering its carved chimney-pieces and dormers from all over the world. Only the South Kensington museum has refused to disgorge its *lucarne*. The frieze in the courtyard with the old family motto for the son who never came back from the war in Italy, *"Plus d'espoir,"* is exquisite. From here a road runs up through the lovely village of Autoire to the Causse, the scrubby plateau which conceals the *bondieuseries* of Rocamadour and the preposterous Gouffre de Padirac with its chilly underground river. The Causse de Gramat with its snakes and pot holes forms a southern rampart to the ravishing valley of the Dordogne which now enters its most beautiful reaches. There is a road along the left bank to Carennac where the hotel is part of an old monastery in which Fénelon wrote some of his *Télémaque*, making golden apples of the quinces on "Calypso's Island" below in the river. Carennac is the sunniest and loveliest of all the Dordogne villages. The road continues through the walnut orchards over high ground and one can walk to the edge of the cliffs which overhang the river and look down on the landscape of Claude and Poussin. After Floirac we cross over and take a cobbled lane which runs from Gluges, with its underground church, to Creysse. We are now in the Cirque de Montvalent, an amphitheatre of rock through which the river meanders; the road goes under the cliff through woodland with endless glimpses of broken water and sandy beaches. Creysse, by its variegated stone colors and its church, is a water-bound rival to Carennac. From here one can go straight to Souillac or else follow the river by Meyronne and Lacave and the Louis XIII Château de Latreyne, rising out of the water, to Pinsac and Souillac.

Souillac is the capital of the upper Dordogne; it is on the main line from north to south, possesses a first-class hotel and two good cafés. The church has a statue of Isaiah which is one of the most graceful, even dandified triumphs of the Romanesque. Souillac is the only small town of the region to make an appeal to the mind. The *Syndicat d'Initiative* is in the charge of M. Pierre Betz who edits from Souillac his art magazine *Le Point*. M. Couderc's hotel used to be a favorite of writers and painters (though now swamped by charabancs in the high season) and many Paris intellectuals, who made the district their headquarters during the Resistance, return for holidays. Souillac is the best center from which to explore the region, not only of the Dordogne, but of the surrounding Causses. Martel with its towers is the most interesting of the neighboring towns and a few miles to the north, in the direction of Brive and Tulle, is an area of hill and forest, the Massif de Meyssac, which has an appeal of its own. The soil is red sandstone, the bracing uplands are covered with heather and enormous chestnuts, the villages unspoilt, the views superb. The rich earth has none of the gloomy aridity of the Causses, and Collonges, where the vines make arbors of every rose-red house, is full of those bargains in masonry which tempt one to settle. Brive is worth a visit, if only for its admirable train services; there are expresses to Bordeaux, Paris, Barcelona, Milan, and it has a good bookshop. In the last two years new hotels have been opened south of Souillac in two old country houses set in wild country and enormous parks, one near Gramat and one outside Cahors. Both these can be reached from Souillac by the main line and may help those travelers who wish to get away from the bustle of Souillac in summer where the hotels have never recovered from "*l'article*"—as they call an enthusiastic description of their beauties which appeared simultaneously in the French and American *Vogue*.

Below Souillac the Dordogne becomes more public and for the rest of its course is kept company by the railway. As the hills dwindle and the valley widens, the castles grow more and more magnificent until we reach a stretch between Domme and Beynac which can compare in beauty and interest with the Rhine and the Loire. Domme is one of those rectangular thirteenth century *bastides* which shows the English influence of the Hundred Years' War; it is built on a cliff some 500 feet above the river and enjoys one of the most beautiful prospects in the world. Below, on the river level, is the village of La Roque-Gageac which some consider to be the loveliest in France. At Beynac, a little lower down, is a good inn and two of the finest castles on the river. The Château de Beynac, of the thirteenth, fourteenth, and sixteenth centuries, is restored and sumptuously kept up. The view from its ramparts, if we can gain admission, embraces another château, Fayrac. Across the Dordogne is the ruined stronghold of Castelnaud whose construction was completed by the English, who added the dungeon. Many of the Dordogne castles are difficult of access, but the ruins of Castelnaud are like some English feudal beauty-spot; the wild thyme and valerian grow over the walls and the pomegranate flowers in the courtyard. Even without its view it is one of the most romantic corners on the whole river and its white battlements and crumbling arches are for ever safe from the rich owner in Paris and the careful restorer.

The center for this part is Sarlat, a pleasant sleepy little town renowned for its truffles and its medieval architecture. Here lives the bookseller made famous as a symbol of French culture by Henry Miller in his *Colossus of Maroussi*. The Vézère enters the Dordogne near Le Bugue and the combined rivers flow through the Périgord Noir with its sandy tracks and pinewoods to Bergerac and prosperity; but from Sarlat a road cuts across to the Vézère at Les Eyzies. The prehistoric cave drawings are disappointing after the new discoveries higher up at Montignac, but the situation is more beautiful and there is a particular charm about the nineteenth century civilization which grew up round the caves; the wistaria-hung hotels, with their comfortable sitting rooms, have something of the atmosphere of Olympia and Delphi. There is no space to go into the mysteries of prehistory, we can only say that the warm sheltered valley with its low bluffs and easily tunnelled rock must have had some special appeal for a vanished race of artists and hunters. The caves at Lascaux, near Montignac, are one of the wonders of the world. The recently discovered paintings have a scope and freshness that make one proud to belong to a species which so many thousand years ago was able to create this pictorial magic. Lascaux is the Parthenon of prehistory: the valley of the Vézère is the foundation of humanism, a landscape where the work of man is like a mineral flower on the tunnelled rock, as exciting and beautiful as the stalagmites and stalactites of Lacave and Padirac are monotonous and unfriendly. To all who have not quite given up hope for mankind this is holy ground. So accomplished are the paintings of this race which was suddenly to vanish, so peculiar are the sites chosen for them, that one wonders if the valley of the Vézère was not a site specially allotted to an élite, like the castles where Hitler perfected his future *gauleiters*. If the paintings, as many think, formed part of magical rites which conferred on the huntsmen particular powers over animals, their inaccessibility might itself have been a test of prowess.

The people of the Dordogne are nearly all peasants, they do not emigrate like the Auvergnats but remain on the land; they are sober, honest, and hard working nor have they yet been much affected by the spread of tourism or by contact with the foreigner. The whole region was one of the fairest provinces of the old feudalism of the Languedoc and contact with the north has not benefited it. The English or rather the Anglo-Normans brought the ravages of the Hundred Years' War whose vestiges remain in ruined castles and regular bastides; the Albigensian Crusade enabled the northern French to sack all the treasures of the castles where troubadours and courts of love had flourished. There is little architecture of the Renaissance, of the seventeenth and eighteenth centuries; great families like the Turennes and Noailles moved north and built elsewhere. The whole of this "other château country" would have fallen into decay were it not for a movement back to the great castles with their wonderful outlooks which arose among the rich world of nineteenth century Paris in search of summer enchantment. It is to Parisians that we owe the saving of so many fine buildings, like Bretenoux and Montal. If exchange restrictions are ever lifted, there remain any amount of delicious, if ramshackle, small houses to be acquired for a thousand pounds or two where writers, painters, retired people, or refugees from our climate can enjoy a warmer version of English rural life in fertile surroundings. The cost of living is much lower here than in the south of France, the Pays Basque or the coastal regions. Everything grows here and ripens but the cooking is apt to be monotonous. There are all the dishes with truffles as an ingredient, but one gets tired of goose and chicken, and the spectacular *lièvre à la royale* is hard to come by. Sea food is sadly lacking and one must remember that the higher Dordogne, under the patronage of Fénelon, whose château is midway between Sarlat and Souillac, is, apart from the valley, an austere and infertile region, very different from the lower river, with its *primeurs* and vineyards, its shad and salmon, whose presiding genius is Montaigne.

The most interesting city of the department is certainly Périgueux, which adds Byzantinism and Roman remains to the riches of the province. It has a château country of its own to the north, with Brantôme and Bourdeilles, in the delicious valley of the Dronne, as members by courtesy of the Dordogne fraternity. But somehow it is to Beynac, Souillac, or Les Eyzies that one is constantly returning, the evening autorail from Bordeaux or the *rapide* from Paris deposit one at the high station of Souillac and soon we are wandering under the planes in the main street, inspecting the two rival cafés and

M. Couderc's tables opposite, surrounded by geraniums and oleanders in tubs. One English novelist has left, we hear with relief. Some Americans have arrived *depuis l'article;* it is not too hot and not too cold, there is still some of the old *eau de vie de prunes,* not too sweet, tomorrow we shall walk along the river, not too far, there is a one-towered farm to let at Meyronne, not too dear. "How shall I find words to describe my pleasure in this countryside," wrote Delacroix a hundred years ago, from the Château de Croze. "It is a mixture of all the sensations that are lovely and pleasant to our hearts and imaginations."

Hommage to Switzerland

The journey from Paris, in the July heat wave, was a night-mare of discomfort. The train, leaving at nine in the evening, did not reach the Swiss frontier till noon the next day; food-less, waterless, seatless, the occupants stood in all the car-riages as well as the corridors while the train passed the long hours of tropical night panting and blowing beside some dried-up water hole. Old, wild-eyed, and orange with grime, those who persisted into the Jura, reached the Swiss escarp-ment, stretching their legs by the buffetless frontier station. Then suddenly Canaan, a land flowing with milk and honey, the Val de Travers! After trout and ham and two kinds of white wine at the first Swiss station, Les Verrières, we be-came tourists—no longer those mean suspect civilian figures, shady and shadowed, which anyone not in uniform on a Euro-pean train invariably appears—but tourists with guidebooks, hotel folders, packages of cigarettes, and the *Journal de Genève* under our arms, while the neat bright electric train rattles over the torrents, brushes the spruce trees, cascades from bright sun into black pine shadow and back again, coasting along the mountain shoulder of the Val de Travers, whose chalets and trout streams and widening pastures, unfurl far below.

Such was our intoxication, Alp-starved since 1939, that every sleeper on the track, every cable and pylon, every newly born aroma of mountain sunlight and fir forest and the name of every station appeared the last unbearable saturation point in the rebirth of feeling—and then when this saturation seemed reached came the spectacle, quivering in the noontide haze, blue as the Aegean, green as Cumberland, shot by the copper sulphate and the azure of the sky, of the blue-green iridescence of the vineyards tumbling down, between their limestone walls with the name of the grower painted on them in bright black letters, into the lake of Neuchâtel. This dazzling lake, first reminder that fresh water can be colored, we follow through the afternoon heat, until we can truly no longer feel anything. The names become German, the vines vanish and suddenly we are on the hotel balcony in Berne. I had almost forgotten that hotels had balconies. This one surely overlooks one of the most lovely views in the world; a near vista of pleasant hill suburbs gives way to mountain and forest, beyond these ranges are the perpetually white peaks of the Oberland with their creamy glaciers, while directly underneath the hotel, uniting all the landscape and seeming to rush straight at the spectator like a giant sword-blade, flows the green arrowy torrent of the Aar. On these summer evenings, or in the morning for breakfast, one would sit out on this balcony, under the awning, with coffee and fruit and some immensely provincial Swiss newspaper, watching the lights come out or the extraordinary procession of heads in the water (for the Bernese method of bathing is to throw yourself into the Aar at one point and let the current carry you down for half a mile). The bodies shoot by like brown matches, occasionally followed by some shavings which turn into a riotous canoe. I know of no city of Berne's size where the country and the pleasures of the country are carried like this right up to the hotel door. The town of Berne is, after five years of England, sheer hallucination. The streets are all arcaded and interrupted only by baroque churches and palaces. The houses are all window boxes, the squares all fountains, the lighting like a new ballet, the air dry oxygen. The shops are like our first Christmas tree; indeed the shops of Berne and of the Bahnhofstrasse in Zürich must rank at this time among the best in the world. Watchmakers have such dazzling exhibitions of gold and chronometry that one ends by annihilating desire through the multiplicities of choosing. Watches with old-fashioned Second Empire lettering whose case is a flat twenty-dollar gold piece neutralize the angular affairs of cubist pin-points;

white gold kills red; submersible, waterproof, anti-magnetic, altitude-proof creations cancel out the kind that wind themselves up by the motion of the wrist; fingernail size creations in platinum and diamonds vie with monsters which bear on dials large as a florin, the days of the week, month, year, signs of the Zodiac, and phases of the moon. Patek Philippe (*très chic*), Zenith, Longines, Omega (*très à la mode*), Universal end by reducing the purchaser, like a Pavlov dog, to a state of nervous breakdown and one turns gratefully to the clock department, where the mysterious Atmos clock by Jaeger Lecoultre (an experiment in perpetual motion working from the minute daily changes in the room's temperature), reigns in solitary splendor. And what is not a watchmaker's is a clothes shop, or a Bally shoe window or a tobacconist, where every known make of cigarette and cigar can be supplied in hundreds. One comes to hate the tobacconists in the end almost as much as the jewelers—or the chemists with their innumerable layers of vitaminized toothpastes and hair restorers, their nylon brushes, and electric razors, with all these gadgets which exert an increasing tension on our newly born free will. This fantastic luxury, this high bloom of materialism, carried out also in wine shops, pastry cooks, and hotels, where laundry comes back the next day and where waiters are never rude, is undoubtedly the supreme achievement of Switzerland today. There is no country in the Old World where the Craft of Living (I am not so sure about the Art) has reached such perfection, where, for those who have the money, the commonplace routine has been brought to such a peak of aesthetic efficiency and pleasure. Witness Swiss trains, paradises on wheels, clean, fast, silent, superbly windowed, wonderfully catered for; hotels like eighteenth century engravings; cities where the old and new architecture is indistinguishable; towns which are solidly compact of beauty and tradition as a Renaissance woodcut, yet to which plastics and new light-metal alloys or experiments in street illumination have given a strange abstractionist grace and lightness, floodlit town halls, dust-free offices, suburbs worthy of great Corbusier, to whom in fact they gave birth. . . .

To fly from London to Zürich, as one could in the past in one hop, is to leave a city three-quarters of which is dirty, unhealthy, moribund and obsolete, and be transported to the most progressive industrial town in Europe, with the best-built workers' dwellings, the healthiest factories, to a city which is fighting a constant battle to keep itself from expanding, where the proportions kept between man, mountain, and lake are regarded as the key to a general harmony and where the wonderful salubrity of the air, manifested in experimental thought, encourages in art a daring and rarefied curiosity—as witness Klee, Gideon, Dada, Joyce, and Jung.

What has Switzerland had to pay for this bracing and ever-present material progress? A certain price in guilt and smugness—for guilt and smugness are the hallmark of the Neutral; not to have been bombed, not to have been invaded, not to have been ruined in the cause of freedom, for a country whose love of freedom is hereditary, must occasion much subconscious uneasiness. And an internal price has been paid as well, for Switzerland is now a country surfeited with luxuries, choked by its own gold, yet where the necessities of life are still scarce and dear. The working-class cannot afford the tea shops and the hotel balconies, their housing conditions are often bad, they have suffered from the strict food rationing, for the luxuries to alleviate it have been outside their reach. The Swiss predicament is partly due to the country having no commodities to sell but jewelry and precision instruments on the one hand, and sun, air, snow, and lake water on the other. The selling of these elements it has, through its hotel industry, raised to a fine art, but they must be sold only for textiles and foodstuffs, and few today are the countries which can supply them.

The Swiss townsman is still but at one or two removes from the peasant. The peasants have had to contend for centuries with the intractable Alps and consequently the character of Swiss industrialism is greedy and thrifty. The typical German Swiss, with their close-set eyes, thin lips, and shrewdly stupid expressions, sometimes fanatically gangling and idiotic, are not among the most immediately appealing of men. Yet these philistine urban peasants of German Switzerland, through its great wealth, are now the rulers, potentially, of Central Europe, and this is another factor in the Swiss predicament. Formerly the German Swiss looked to Munich, or Vienna; the French Swiss to Paris; the Ticinese to Milan; they were consciously provincial. Now the roles are reversed. The provinces of Switzerland have unexpectedly gained the economic mastery over their moral and intellectual capitals.

But it's really too hot to listen to these arguments. Let's be tourists again. First a practice run; the early train to Interlaken, an open carriage to the lake; a swim in the cobalt water of the Thünersee. Lying on one's back in the water, until forced to submerge against a dive-bombing attack from horseflies, one looks up at the icy pinnacles of the Jungfrau. The glaciers tower above us, the water temperature is seventy degrees. After lunch and some hours of sunbathing we return on the lake steamer, sometimes hugging the cliffs and woodlands of the shore, sometimes dashing across to a lake village with its vineyards and bulbous yellow church, its ruined castle and its café under the chestnut trees, while we exchange one group of sunburnt summer visitors for another, and the swans glide round the landing stage. After this preparation the real circuit begins; we invite you, reader, to Lausanne and Geneva. It's too hot to get out at Fribourg, home of the catholic aristocracy, with its convents and palaces, its admirable university publishers (L.U.F.) and its Maritainist intellectuals; too hot to leave the train till the evening, when a new balcony looks over the smooth sliding Rhône at the Hôtel de l'Ecu. This little corner of old Geneva is almost Venetian: the river, intensely blue, looped and coiled in a swirling kaleidoscope of vanishing eddies, washes the very walls of the old down-at-heels hotel, where Stendhal, Dickens, Balzac, Ruskin, Byron, Chateaubriand and an intolerably distinguished clientele of nineteenth century beards haunt the corridors. Here let us evoke for a moment the vanished Geneva of Ruskin and Henry James a century ago, the small provincial city which Beckford considered had been corrupted by Voltaire from its Calvinist austerity. "A little canton, four miles square, and which did not wish to be six miles square! A little town, composed of a cluster of water mills, a street of penthouses, two wooden bridges, two dozen of stone houses on a little hill, and three or four perpendicular lanes up and down the hill . . . And this bird's nest of a place to be the center of religious and social thought, and of physical beauty, to all living Europe . . . this inconceivable point of patience"; Ruskin describes in *Praeterita* the old town, "the group of officially aristocratic houses round the cathedral and college presenting the same inaccessible sort of family dignity that they do today." There is the inevitable visit to the jewelers (which Henry James has so well narrated in the "Pension Beaurepas") and then Ruskin returns, fascinated, to the Rhône—"But the Rhône flows like one lambent jewel; its surface is nowhere, its ethereal self is everywhere, the iridescent rush and translucent strength of it, blue to the shore and radiant to the depth.

"Fifteen feet thick, of not flowing, but flying water; not water, neither—melted glacier, rather, one should call it; the force of the ice is with it, and the wreathing of the clouds, the gladness of the sky, and the continuance of Time.

"Waves of clear sea are, indeed, lovely to watch, but they are always coming or gone, never in any taken shape to be seen for a second. But here was one mighty wave that was always itself, and every fluted swirl of it, constant as the wreathing of a shell. No washing away of the fallen foam, no pause for gathering of power, no helpless ebb of discouraged recoil; but alive through bright day and lulling night, the never-pausing plunge, and never-fading flash, and never-hushing whisper, and, while the sun was up, the ever-answering glow of unearthly aquamarine, ultramarine, violet-blue, gentian-blue, peacock-blue, river-of-paradise blue, glass of a painted window melted in the sun, and the witch of the Alps flinging the spun tresses of it forever from her snow. . . . And in the midst of all the gay glittering and eddied lingering, the noble bearing by of the midmost depth, so mighty, yet so terrorless and harmless, with its swallows skimming instead of petrels, and the dear old decrepit town as safe in the embracing sweep of it as if it were set in a brooch of sapphire."

When I used to visit Geneva between the wars, it seemed a dull, respectable, expensive, and luxurious city, most conventionally Swiss. Then it was the capital of Savoy, and, through the League of Nations, of the world. Now, cut off from both, it has become a somewhat forgotten and undernourished corner, a "dear old decrepit town" again. The life has receded from the boulevards and from the huge hotels along the lake and withdrawn itself into the older quarters. The whole place has become more French; packed with French refugees, it has become a little bit shabby and *louche*—if *louche*ness were imaginable in Switzerland—and taken on something of the atmosphere of forbidden Provence. There are "cafés de la Marine," "brasseries de la Navigation," the Place du Molard with its pollarded plane trees, its flower market, its kiosk and large cafés full of unobtainable French *apéritifs*, is like the Boulevard of Aix. Here congregate the open-shirted "Montparnasse" of Geneva, the painters, sculptors, and art critics who gravitate about Albert Skira, former editor of *Minotaure* and now publisher of the only *avant-garde* art magazine in the country, the monthly *Labyrinthe*. A more academic literary group, less surrealist or preoccupied with the visual arts, centers round Pierre Courthion and his review *Lettres*. These editors, like Skira and Courthion, all come up against the essential uncreative smallness of Switzerland, which is a country meant to publish and to propagate the arts, to produce fine books, to distribute European editions and live by exporting them, rather than to nourish its own song birds by regularly drawing out its checkbook. So let us thank heaven for the Place du Molard and for any other still existing pockets of indigenous European culture, before we wander back to bed through the French-smelling streets and watch the moon over the water from the haunted hotel. "I am sitting in our old family *salon* in this place, and have sat here much of the time for the last fortnight in sociable converse with family ghosts. . . . I have treated myself, as I say, to the apartments, or a portion of them, in which we spent the winter of '59-60, and in which nothing is changed save that the hotel seems to have gone down in the world a little, before the multiplication of rivals."

So wrote Henry James to his brother, with "the shooting blue flood directly under his windows," and since October 1888, when he was at the Ecu, it has gone down, except for the food, a little bit more—bowed under, perhaps, by the ghostly impact of literary imaginations, all suffering from the terrible "wear and tear of discrimination." So come, reader, let's go to Lausanne—for you have guessed by now that this is to be a literary pilgrimage—where it lies on its high clean sunny ledge above the lake—embalmed in the prose of Gibbon.

"Of my situation here I have little new to say, except a very comfortable and singular truth, that my passion for my wife or mistress (Fanny Lausanne) is not palled by satiety and possession of two years. I have seen her in all seasons, and in all humors; and though she is not without faults, they are infinitely overbalanced by her good qualities. . . . In a word, my plan has most completely answered; and I solemnly protest, after two years' trial, that I have never in a single moment repented of my transmigration. The only disagreeable circumstance is the increase of a race of animals with which this country has been long infested, and who are said to come from an island in the Northern Ocean."

There are even times when Gibbon seems to sing with the same voice as Rousseau—can you distinguish between these two paeans?

"*Ce paysage unique, le plus beau dont l'oeil humain fût jamais frappé; ce séjour charmant auquel je n'avais rien trouvé d'égal dans le tour du monde.*

"*Je perdrois de vue cette position unique sur la terre, ce lac, ces montagnes, ces riants côteaux; ce tableau charmant, qui paroit toujours nouveau aux yeux mêmes accoutumés dès leur enfance à le voir—sur tous les pays de l'Europe j'avais choisi pour ma retraite le pays de Vaud, et jamais je ne me suis repenté un seul instant de ce choix.*" And yet Lausanne today is not what it was; it is with Lucerne the smuggest of Swiss cities, the most sport- and tourist-ridden; there is too much tennis and golf and exiled royalty, it's all too much of a *Musée Bourgeoise*; one wants, as in so many Swiss towns, to let loose some Senegalese, some French sailors or workmen, some drunken American women, some props and pillars of moral worthlessness, someone to walk on the grass or spit in the funicular. Now we leave Geneva and the Pays de Vaud, the stronghold of Gallic humanism, for the Catholic Valais, where nature is worshipped rather than man, and whose writers have an added mystical savagery in their attitude. St. Maurice, Martigny, Sion (the loveliest of all Swiss towns according to Cingria, and certainly the most romantic) and we enter the burnt-up white landscape of little African hills, like the homes of Spanish troglodytes, the rainless apricot country between Sion and Sierre. Here the cicada is found, and up each long lateral valley is some curiosity of wildness; women of Saracen descent, smugglers' headquarters, rare Arolla pines, or the archaic village-kingdom, with strange costumes and marriage laws, of Evolène. Above Sierre, pitiless in the sun, we struggle up through the vineyards and peach or walnut orchards, past the ragged tawny romanesque villages, with their untidy and sunny poverty which is so soul-refreshing, after the northern neatness, to our last literary pilgrimage, Rilke's tiny castle at Muzot.

"It lies some twenty minutes above Sierre, set steeply in a less arid, but happy countryside gushing with many springs— with views of the valley, of the mountain slopes and far into the most marvellous depths of sky. . . . For the Valais (why is it not included when one counts earth's loveliest places?) is an incomparable country. At first I did not understand the truth of this because I *compared* it—with the most significant things in my memory, with Spain, with Provence (with which it is, indeed, via the Rhône, related by blood), but only since I admired it for its own sake has it revealed itself in all its grandeur and at the same time, as I gradually came to see, its sweet gracefulness and its strong, passionate traditions. . . . Shrines, crucifixes at every crossroad, uplands ribbed with vineyards and in late season all curly with their foliage; fruit trees, each with its tender shade and (oh, so rightly!) single fully grown poplars dotted about, exclamation marks of space crying 'Here!'"

The Lötschberg is one of those tunnels which separate north and south; baroque Brigue and the Valais, the vines of the Rhône and the baked white earth with the Catholic villages, are left behind; ten minutes of darkness and we are back in the Oberland, among the heavy, broadeaved, opulent chalets, the cows and the ski lifts. At Spiez the lake of Thün reappears, and a branch line takes us to Gstaad, the last lap of the journey. Gstaad is an up and coming Kitzbühel, not too high, not too enclosed—a mountain village open to the sun, surrounded by fir woods and fat pastures. A Mozart festival is on, directed by M. Kuriel. The whole ambience has that exquisite stimulation of a mountain resort assured of a future. In the evening I would usually dine with charming and hospitable friends, who own an ancient chalet. To reach them I had to cross a small ravine and would often pause half-way down, surrounded by dark firs, with the gray torrent below me, while the grasshoppers subsided, their day's barracking over and the cold night air assumed and rarefied the scents of hay and clover. In those magic twilights I came to understand what Switzerland now was—no longer a place one rushed through on the way to somewhere else, nor even a general playground whose inhabitants one ignored, but a fascinating and unexplored vital organ of European civilization. I had not yet discovered the Tessin, nor revisited the Engadine, I had seen none of the famous baroque monuments, I had never been to Lucerne, Lugano, St. Gall, or Winterthur, but I knew this was a stronghold of civilization, a country which had new power thrust upon it, and whose federal system was an object lesson to the miserable rivalries of its battle-scarred neighbors. After the last war the Swiss refused to adopt the Vorarlberg province of Austria; it was an example which the four great powers have yet to follow. They may seem prudent, cautious and unromantic, invincibly bourgeois, but they are also admirably unambitious, unconsciously liberal, wholesomely sceptical of ideologies, and, although perhaps too attached to money, independent, wise; tolerant, humane, and free.

I returned to Berne, to one last desperate act of indecision in the shops, a last farewell to the Anglophil staff of the Bellevue, and then the new through carriage to Paris, a carriage which returned to the Jura in full Swiss cleanliness, only to become poorer and dirtier with each hamstrung league through crisis-ridden France. I had said good-bye to a radiant hospitable country, to which I hope now constantly to return, a bower of bourgeois bliss with its pre-war standards of health and courtesy, the complex land of Rousseau and Calvin where all Nature cries "Forgive yourself!" and Man, defiant, answers "Never!"

Spring Revolution

The boredom of travel! There is an acute condition which develops in enforced lulls before the wholesome drudgery of getting from place to place makes a brute of one again. If you knew how bored we were in Athens! Stagnation and self-disgust engender a low fever that lays waste the curiosity and resolution which might have cured them. The weather was too bad to go anywhere, and the nearest sun was in Egypt. Sleeping late to shorten the day, one went to the window and found the Acropolis and the Parthenon blocking the horizon. A thing of beauty, that is a joy once or twice, and afterward a standing reproach. Downstairs it would be nearly lunchtime. In the bar, which was an embottled corridor smelling of gin and Gold Flake, the Greek business men jollied each other up in cinema American and Trocadero English. The somber dining room was like the Dickensian coffee room of a Midland hotel. The French dishes all tasted the same, like food on a liner; the Greek joints seemed made of sweetened gelatine. Coffee was served in the lounge amid the engineering papers, and snatches of conversations.

"I hope you are never troubled by the green-eyed monster."

"Pliss, Mr. Insull?"

"Why, you know what the green-eyed monster is! Jealousy!"

"O yais, Mr. Insull, Pliss?"

A walk in the afternoon. Tramlines, blocks of yellow houses, demolition, everywhere the metamorphosis of a tenth-rate Turkish market town into a tenth-rate Californian suburb. A pause in the bookshop where one must choose between

61

expensive art books on the Acropolis and diseases of the stomach, or sixpenny editions of Edgar Wallace and Wilhelm Meister. There were also the newspapers, and glancing at them phrases would enter with a little stab and begin to fester. "Ruskin, one felt, would have disapproved," "wherein promise and achievement touch hands very agreeably," and "Bébé is painting a portrait of Baba." Before the gossip-writer's ingenious vulgarities I would gape like a mesmerized chicken.

In the hotel *thé dansant* will have begun. A hundred bearded ladies have brought their black little daughters. The ballroom reeks with stale flowers and cheap scent. All the tables are taken. The fathers in spats and clean collars try to eradicate from their faces the expression which forty years of Levantine practices have implanted. The mothers employ the vocabulary of the underworld of elegance. *"Très réussi . . . convenable . . . on aura dit . . . ça se remarque."* The daughters fidget. The young men attempt polish. All move in the psychologist's wonderland which is revealed to us when we watch charmless people trying to be charming.

At dinner a piano and a violin play evening music, with *Peer Gynt, Rosamund, Chansons sans Paroles, Toselli*, wistful and gallant compositions that empty over one all the slops of capitalist sentiment. Afterward, there are the cinemas with wooden seats and German films unknown to the Academy, and a few places for supper. In Greek cabarets one is not allowed to sit with a woman unless one has champagne. The sexes are therefore divided on opposite sides of the floor. If a young man dances with a "hostess," he scurries back at the finish like a male spider trying to escape from the nuptial embrace before he is eaten. The girls are sulky, the whiskey tastes of sawdust. Back in the hotel there are mosquitoes in February, and, four days old, the Continental *Daily Mail*. This day, repeated ten times, was typical of Athens. As boredom gathered momentum one felt all the ingredients of personality gurgling away like the last inch of bathwater. One became a carcase of nonentity and indecision, a reflection to be avoided in mirrors. Why go abroad? Why travel? Why exchange the regard of a clique for the stare of a concierge?

On the day of the elections the sun was shining. It was one of those Sundays in early spring when there is an air of displacement. A sensation of keels lifting from the mud, of new skin, and of new acquaintances. We motored to Kephissia for lunch. The butter was good. Refugees paraded about in their hideous best, and gramophones were playing in Tatoi. At Hagios Mercurios we looked down over the plain to the blue lake of the Aegean, Chalcis, Eretria, and the snows and forests of Euboea. In the wet weather we could not conceive a reason for being here, in this moment it became impossible to imagine being anywhere else.

When we got back to Athens everybody had voted. The bars and cinemas were closed, and in the restaurant wine was served from teapots and drunk in cups as in an old-fashioned speakeasy. Crowds cheered. Venizelos was sweeping the polls. "The best thing for the country." As in all companies where politics are discussed, to compensate the dullness of the subject one began to feel an illusion of far-sightedness and worldly wisdom.

Next morning the town was quiet. I was particularly annoyed to find an antique shop closed, and tried to get the concierge to rout up the missing proprietor. Down the empty street moved a kind of gray Noah's Ark on wheels. At the English tailor's we heard the news. Venizelos had lost the election. Tsaldaris, the head of the Royalist-Popular party, was in, but he and all his colleagues had been put in prison. There had been a revolution in Macedonia. The shops were closing and the proprietors of travel agencies stood in the doors with the keys in their hands. Lorries of mud-colored soldiers passed down the street distributing handbills. Martial law was proclaimed, newspapers suppressed, groups of people shot at sight, by order of the Chief of the revolution, Plastiras. By lunchtime it was accepted that we were under a dictatorship. All the *plats du jour* were "off," and we bawled out the head waiter. An aeroplane flew over, dropping pamphlets in which Plastiras described the collapse of parliamentary government. Rumors collected. "Plastiras was a Venizelist." "He was going to cancel the elections and keep Venizelos in office."

"He was not a Venizelist and was going to govern by himself."
I walked down the University boulevard. It was warm and
sunny. A straggling crowd that was moving about suddenly
thickened and made way for two archaic fire engines, whose
hoses were playing over it. The smell of wet earth followed
their path through the sunshine. Everybody laughed and
teased the soldiers on the engines, who laughed back at them.
The crowd began to cheer a motor car from which a very ugly
man waved his arms, and to follow it up the avenue clapping;
with them went the police and the fire engines. One could not
tell if they were shouting Tsaldaris or Plastiras. In the hotel
we received more explanations. "Plastiras was in prison. It
had all been done very quietly. Venizelos and Tsaldaris had
arranged it with the President of the Republic. The soldiers
had fraternized. The dictatorship was a wash-out. General
Condylis had flown last night to Athens from Salonica. Plastiras had taken him prisoner, but he had escaped and was
marching with his army from Thebes on Athens. Tonight
there would be a big battle as Condylis wished to avenge Plastiras' execution of the Cabinet in 1922."

We went out again. "Tsaldaris" was being shouted everywhere. There were still crowds in the boulevard, but suddenly down a side street we saw a ragged collection of men
marching with staves in their hands, on many of which the
olive leaves still remained. Some carried only small un-
trimmed branches. They looked like a woodcut of Jack Cade's
rebellion from a child's historybook. It was at this moment
that we heard the rattle of machine-guns. Everyone ran gig-
gling into doorways. "They're only blank, of course," was
said knowingly. Turning into Stadium Street some soldiers
rushed up to us pointing down and crying, "Katô, Katô." The
machine guns began again.

The street, in normal times so straight and dull, became an
enormous affair of shadows and relief, of embrasures and exposed spaces. The kiosk at the corner seemed as far away as it
would to a baby who could just walk, or to a very lame old
man. As we ran round the corner volleys seemed to come from
every direction. People threw themselves flat on the ground

and hid behind trees. The Noah's Ark passed down the end of the street with the snouts of machine guns thrusting from the wooden windows. We came to a little restaurant where we had dined the day before. The crowd surged on the steps and the doors were barricaded, but when they recognized us we were let in. In the falling night more men with staves could be seen from the balcony. A small cannon boomed at intervals and shook the windows. A man was helped along with a bleeding arm. While one-half of my brain dealt in realities—"revolution, street fighting, baptism of fire"—the other continued to function as if nothing had happened, and remembering that a friend was coming for a cocktail, I insisted on trying to telephone to the hotel that we should be a little late. The wires were cut, but if we went back directly we should still be in time for him. From the balcony we saw a crowd collecting at the foot of the University. A man ran up the steps waving something. A machine gun rattled, the crowd fell apart, and he was revealed lying in a growing pool of blood and brains. An ambulance bell sounded and a man with a woman in a mink coat walked down the middle of the street from the other side. Slipping out, we made our way round by narrow alleys and crossed the Place de la Constitution in the yellow dusk. We reached the side entrance to the Grande Bretagne. It was heavily barricaded. We knocked and rang, when another crowd of people surged round the corner and up the steps. There was a sudden feeling of complete hopelessness and panic. After the crowd, turning elaborately, glided the armored car. What had once seemed comic and antediluvian was now implacable and fatal. The machine guns pointed straight at us; a fat woman tried to turn us out from behind a pillar where we were, but we quickly shoved her away. The car passed without firing and we got round to the other entrance. Inside the hotel all was cheerfulness and commotion; everyone felt important and with a reason for living. We dined in a large party which included several people whom we had avoided for weeks, and retired upstairs with a gramophone and a bottle of whiskey. The inevitable business man explained everything. "Plastiras was master of the situation. He was a patriot. He would force a coalition between Venizelos and Tsaldaris. The latter's victory was illegal because he had promised the refugees bonuses which he hadn't got." "Plastiras does not play," he said with admiration. "He knows his head is at stake. If he fails he will shoot himself. He had eight officers shot who tried to arrest him. General Condylis was locked up. He sent him a telegram signed 'Tsaldaris' telling him to fly to Athens. When he landed he took him prisoner. There would be no battle. The army was with him. It was the best thing that could happen for Greece." Outside, the night was dark and cold; a few small tanks patrolled the streets. From the balcony of the palace machine guns looked down. In previous volleys the armored car had chipped bits off the masonry along the front of the hotel. All was quiet, and with the cessation of firing people began to experience the anti-climax and grow irritable. One wondered why one was cooped up with the tiresome businessman; with the young Frenchman and his crisp platitudes; with the "clergyman's daughter" chorus girl of dubious status, who was explaining why she would "never have a lady dog in the house." Everyone separated, secretly hoping for the roar of Condylis' artillery.

Next morning we were woken by the noise of trams. There were no guns trained from the palace. Newspapers arrived. The shops were open, and of the day before nothing remained but the pool of wet blood by the University, surrounded by gaping students. At a time when Plastiras was supposed to be master of the situation, he had surrendered to the eight generals who commanded the rest of the army for Venizelos under Zaimis and Tsaldaris.

The dictatorship was over, and had been over since eight o'clock the night before. Plastiras had seized the government with only one regiment; his party had repudiated him. Whether a patriot or a power-grabber, he was ridiculous. He had wounded thirty-three people, killed one, and cured two or three discontented pleasure-seekers of a curious stoppage of the sensibility to which they had fallen victim. They, while secretly admitting the futility of the eye-witness, the meaninglessness and stupidity of all that had happened, knew also that they had tasted the intoxication and the prestige of action, and were soon rearranging the events of the day on a scale, and in an order, more worthy of the emotions which had been generated by them.

Impressions
of Egypt (1955)

"Flight 159 for Rome, Cairo, Khartoum, and Nairobi"; from the early morning London drizzle we are shepherded into our plastic no-man's-land. Our emblem is the air hostess: she smiles and life is good; our pastor is the Captain who broadens in the doorway and tells us where we are, and where we are is right. Sunshine above the cloud carpet, "nothing but well and fair." The Alps scatter beneath us; surprised Elba blushes and we descend from euphoria to luncheon, sealed off from wintry Rome. A glimpse of Capri, of Cape Palinuro, a lingering sunset over Etna, "visibility about two hundred miles" and night is served with a good dinner. The hours slip by and suddenly we are circling concentric boulevards, neon-lighted avenues and a large sign "Welcome to Egypt." No greatcoats; much khaki; a mild luminous dusk and a loudspeaker blaring Arab music. I recognize that voice like broken toffee, it is indeed the celebrated Om Khalsoun and I learn that she appears on this first Thursday of every month in a Cairo music hall. Through Southern streets, past silent villas, I rush there in a taxi, but— my first disappointment—am offered only a black market seat at two pounds for the end of her performance.

The first view of Cairo is another. The streets resemble downtown Athens; we are in one of those numerous cities whose commonest vista is of a big block of flats in bilious concrete, a patch of blue sky, some very poor people and a hoarding. The Nile at first sight bewilders, in color not unlike the Thames in summer, yet its opposite shore is fringed with palm trees and the skyscrapers and warehouses down the river remind one of New Orleans. But lime replaces lemon in long drinks, first hint of the tropics.

The great museum is a further disappointment for the "new look" of modern showmanship has hardly reached it; there is a basement feeling and the marvellous statues are ill-lit and overcrowded. To spare him the contrast with the austerity of the Old Kingdom I go straight to Tutankhamen. Here the arrangement is more spacious and worthy of the greatest treasure trove of modern times. One soon develops an affection for the sleepy Valentino who died at eighteen in an atmosphere of religious conflict which recalls our own Edward VI; one needs also the beetle's-eye view for minor objects—gold sandals or gold toe caps—and a respect for mere quantity. Regalia with innumerable spare parts, boats, beds, thrones, games, dolls, crowns, amulets, jewelry of all kinds, huge gold chambers, gesso ceilings, life-size guardians with golden spears lead one up to the two great coffins, the larger somewhat ungainly, the next more lifelike and finally to the deeply moving death mask with its withdrawn pearly eyes and full young lips, its striated headdress of gold and lapis lazuli. The colors of blue, green, beige, and gold seem ideally suited for this highly finished art where bird or insect or flower have settled down into rigid winged forms which cram the maximum of dogma into their conventional roles as necklace, diadem, or earring.

The museum states the problem which remains with us all the way: here is a civilization which is both the parent of humanism and its worst enemy, creator of personality yet concerned only with permanence. Brought up in Greece and Rome, how can we manage to like it? "The Egyptians by their study of astronomy discovered the solar year and were the first to divide it into twelve parts. . . . They were the first to bring into use the names of the Twelve Gods which the Greeks took over from them, and were the first to assign altars and images and temples to the Gods, and to carve figures in stone." But what figures, Herodotus, and what Gods! The academic monotony of this endless parade of animal dignitaries and bird-headed chamberlains! Not an inch of surface on wall or column without its maze of compulsive clichés, no place for originality or intelligence, no feeling for artistic invention, only magic run to seed and man reduced to an avenue of "spinggies" as the guides call them. "Like an Egyptian temple, magnificent to look at, and inside a priest singing a hymn to a cat or a crocodile," as the later Greeks put it. To which the museum answers: "(1) Patience. (2) No art is the worse for a breath of Permanence. (3) You cannot apply the standard of 500 B.C. to a civilization a thousand, even two thousand years earlier. Go to Saqqara. And if you find a religion dull, there is always a remedy. Believe in it."

Saqqara is reached by Memphis, where we first meet ancient Egypt in its true surroundings (the open air) in the form of a sphinx of rose alabaster and a fallen colossus outstretched among the palms. The step Pyramid of Zoser is the world's oldest building. It looks like the top of a mountain but a little more deliberate and by this deliberation is unmistakably human. The great Imhotep was its architect and recently courtyards and colonnades have been unearthed, with every kind of column, even proto-Doric. Near by M. Zacchary Goneim is at work on his own newly-found pyramid whose base peeps tantalizingly out of the sand. One chamber has proved empty and he is now tunneling underneath it to find the true burial chamber. Unless the robbers have anticipated him. They nearly always do and every necropolis is the scene of an insect-like conflict between the Pharaoh who begins his tomb on the day of his accession and is compelled to take his treasure with him that his jaws may function in a future life, and the tomb robbers, crammed with cunning and unbelief. The God-King mines and countermines, constructs false doors, blind shafts, labyrinths of dummy passages, retires deeper into his pyramid as into an oak gall. The probing antennae pursue him, for however many builders he immolate, his own priests are not always to be trusted. The nobles put up less resistance, their tombs are robbed but contain fewer valuables while those at Saqqara introduce us to bas-relief (the most exquisite of Egyptian art forms) and present that unfailing theme of hunting in

the Delta swamps among the wild duck and the hippo, of gliding on tiny boats through the papyrus while wife and daughter applaud as the harpoon falls or the goose-stick whistles
through the air which constituted the good life for a thousand
years.

After Saqqara, what can one say of the Pyramids? That the
great Pyramid covers thirteen acres and is four hundred and
fifty feet high, earliest of the Seven Wonders of the World and
alone to outlive the other six? That the length of one side divided by half the height gives the number Pi correct to five
places of decimals? Or that, surrounded by honking cars and
Sunday crowds, they are more like two indestructible film
stars signing autographs? If only one could get them alone!

Meanwhile another Cairo awaits us, immensely dusky, dingy,
noisy, devoid apparently of all domestic architecture but possessing some of the oldest buildings of the Moslem world, the
ninth century mosque of Ibn Tulun, severe and vast, the
stretch of city wall (now cleared) dating from the year one
thousand, a Viking and Byzantine shield carved on the gate,
and the twelfth century mosque and seminary of El Azhar.
This is a dream of cloistered wisdom: the mosque includes a
forest of columns like an unspoilt Cordova surrounded by
swirling Arabesques and cufic inscriptions. The great floor
was carpeted in red by the late king, and, grouped all over it,
the candidates for law and priesthood squat around their
teachers. They wear white turbans over a small tarboosh and
come from every corner of the Moslem world and in every
color from *eau de Nil* to *noir de Balliol*. It is a place to which one
is irresistibly drawn. Old Cairo has none of the magical white
alleys, the spicy scents and splendid costumes of Morocco; it
is built of gray brick or yellow stucco and long distances must
be covered between each pleasure. The days are warm, the
nights still treacherous and after four of them I took a train of
all-white wagon-lits to Luxor. Here one must sightsee or perish; the hotel empties from breakfast to dusk as if set on a ski-
run and there is indeed talk of a *téléférique* to the Valley of
Kings. Light meters dangling, guidebook in one hand, fly

whisk in other, our noses smarting from mummy-dust, we troop into meals obedient to the gong, while like patient elephants the temples wait for us among the sugar cane. Luxor, Karnak, Medinet Habu, Dahr el Bahari. . . . "Egyptian architects wanted to erect the tallest, broadest, most solid structures the world would ever see: and they succeeded. The monuments of the Nile valley were projected as symbols of triumphant power. . . . They are the marks inflicted on nature by a race of giants, on the scale of stupendous entities brought into existence by nature herself." *(Ancient Egypt* by J. Manchip White.) And yet they are not too heavy. The impression in the great hypostyle hall of the temple of Amon at Karnak is of one of the most awe-inspiring sights in the world, especially when the stonework is etched out by moonlight. There is restraint and agility yet the huge pylons with their holes where the pennons floated, the avenues and courtyards, the sacred lake, the soaring painted capitals, the host of side chapels form a whole which reduces most Greek temples to skeletal insignificance. In such a place at such a moment Egypt pulverizes all objections. I begin to see that one must try to believe, to appreciate the supreme wager, the foredoomed bet on the immortality of the body by which the ancient Egyptians expressed their passionate love of life. Even Howard Carter admitted to shedding a tear on finding the little tutelary Goddesses whose gold wings met to protect the sarcophagus of Tutankhamen, an emotion which perhaps saved his life (for if one can believe anything, one can believe that), and with a grain of reverence one begins to notice the many small exceptions to the dull conformity of Egyptian art.

The last year witnessed four outstanding discoveries; the "solar" boat at Giza, the buried pyramid at Saqqara, the Hyksos Stele at Karnak, and the First Dynasty Tombs at Saqqara North. What are the prospects for this year? M. Zacchary Goneim is convinced that at any moment he will come on the unplundered burial chamber of his new pyramid, he may also discover the system of ramps by which the pyramids were built; the two boats will be extracted, chemically treated, and put together. It remains to be seen whether anything is inside them. At Karnak the discoverer of the new stele, M. Lashib Hababti, is just about to uncover the whole processional avenue of sphinxes, two kilometres long, from the temple of Luxor to the great temple of Karnak, now buried under thirty feet of mud and rubble. At Saqqara North, Professor Emery of London University, "last of the great excavators," has located two more tombs of the First Dynasty, of Horaha and Udaimu (or, more probably, of his Queen). This last tomb will not be excavated till December but may prove the most interesting for these great underground chambers and storehouses have revealed a perfection of architectural detail which indicates that the first rulers of united Egypt, *circa* 3500 B.C., were already a master race beside whose skills the pyramid builders seem a mere end product. Where did this "dynastic" or "master-race" spring from? According to Dr. Derby their skulls were of a different shape from those of the long-suffering roundheads of the Delta. They arise in all their glory straight out of the night of prehistory—from the deep South? The bracing North? The Yemen or Sumeria? or from some intermediate zone of acclimatization on the shore of the Red Sea? One unrobbed tomb in the great necropolis of northern Saqqara (where the early dynasty Serapeion also lies hidden) may yield the secret.

But the year is not to be judged by excavation only; in other fields the Past shows its gains and losses. An example of each: One of the most disappointing "musts" in the guidebook I found to be the temple of Luxor, urban, straggling, duncolored, a mosque bestrides its entrance whence the grave Wagnerian motif of the noonday muezzin sounds over the baked mud to stimulate a vague appetite for luncheon and a sense of duty done. Yet in this temple has originated a new school of archaeological mysticism which provides a burning topic for the visitor and a welcome insurgence of intellectual values in this world of Baedeker and "international" cooking, of mewing kite and bubbling hoopoe. Here for ten years from 1940, working by night and sleeping by day, M. Schwaller de Lubicz, an esoteric Alsatian philosopher, aided by his wife and stepdaughter, toiled away measuring stones and angles or recording inscriptions to evolve theories which were simultaneously generated by a brilliant French Egyptologist, M. Varye and his collaborating architect, M. Robichon. According to this little group the great Egyptian temples are not merely the dwelling-places of the Gods, their priests and stores and altars, dwellings frequently destroyed or enlarged by egomaniac conquerors to suit their pride and prosperity— but "constructions in evolution," symbolical of the whole relationship of the universe to man in this sacred country which was held to be a pattern of the sky. The plans were laid down in ages of transition by great sages like Imhotep (2950 B.C.) and Amenhotep to prefigure future astronomical changes as when the sun entered a new house of the zodiac after 2500 years. Then the reigning Pharaoh would have to pull down the existing temples, re-erect them on a "secret library" of old foundations, reorientate them to new axes, new materials, further courts. Thus the temple of Luxor contains the ancient idea of the Microcosm, of man's body as an image of the universe with every organ corresponding; it is shaped like a walking skeleton, the separated feet on a slant at the entrance, the knees by the colossi in the forecourt, and so right up to the skull in the Inner Sanctuary, with even the gland represented. Esoteric messages to those worthy of them are conveyed by a number of subtle suggestions; we must read each stone as carefully as a page of *Finnegans Wake* for every crack and seeming imperfection has a meaning. In the "knee court" the break in the blocks runs through the knees of the Pharaoh in relief; the legs of the colossi are exaggerated and distorted while other reliefs suggest a young prince sacrificing at the age of twelve, even as Jesus went at that age to the temple. Some stones are to be regarded as transparent, a blank space on one side being filled in by a corresponding drawing on the other, some inscriptions on one wall of a shrine correspond with drawings on the wall opposite. It becomes therefore the height of vandalism to remove even the smallest stone without detailed measurement and careful photography for even unfinished sketches or lapidary lacunae intentionally illustrate imperfect or transitory aspects of the soul. The patterns of flagstones in ramp or courtyard are particularly full of meaning and sometimes include whole mosaics where can be seen, in the case of Luxor, the same wise tutelary head. These theories are put forward in M. de Lubicz's unobtainable *Le Temple dans L'Homme* and in even rarer and earlier pamphlets by M. Varye while M. Robichon (who still works at Karnak) confines himself to collecting architectural evidence in models, photographs, and drawings. The movement was greeted with a storm of abuse ("where's your proof") when it broke ground in the French reviews *Critique* and *Mercure de France*. The older generation of Egyptologists, especially M. Drioton, were appalled while M. Saint-Fare Garnot wrote, *"Le débat ouvert dans les colonnes de votre périodique a été institué par un incompétent, devant un tribunal d'incompétents."* Alas, M. Varye, the best qualified of the three, was killed in a motor accident in 1951, but his ideas have been admirably developed. "Egyptology was born and developed in an age of extreme rationalism. The ancient Egyptians have been regarded as a materialist people, yet is it possible that so great a people could have been so dully materialist, so devoid of philosophy, of speculation?" (Smart.) These new theories at once found support among poets like Jean Cocteau yet continue to be fiercely attacked by specialists who find M. de Lubicz's numerological arcana particularly provoking. "Man in antiquity progressed only in proportion as he turned his back on myths of every origin in the light of Hellenic rationalism," roundly declared M. Papadopoulo, editor of *La Revue de Caire*.

I should like to assist my readers to a conclusion. One must bear in mind that a materialist two thousand years hence could live for a very long time with a Japanese garden without appreciating the symbolism of its design; on the other hand "seek and ye shall find" has dangerous consequences. M. de Lubicz both baffles and stimulates, like a Baconian, and when I visited the temple with his book, the "golden number" eluded me and wall and column seemed as incoherent and uncommunicative as ever. Yet when I am with M. Robichon light breaks in and one is inspired by the minutiae of his own inspiration.

Take the statue of Sekhmet. M. Robichon claims that it exudes a mineral magic which causes compasses to deviate and diviners' rods and needles to go haywire; one part of the statue vibrates, another is warmer than the rest; the crook of her tall wand, covering the solar plexus, is particularly radioactive. Yet the same statue, like the Portland Vase, has been smashed to pieces by an Arab guardian who was convinced that it was bewitching him and this time the dread Lion-Goddess could offer no protection. Many of the measurements seem fanciful but M. Varye's principle remains correct, that we must revalue the great discoveries of nineteenth century archaeologists by the humbler light of our present understanding of psychology and mystery religions. M. Robichon's contribution to the monumental *Karnak* which has just appeared and M. de Lubicz's new and weightier volume (not yet published) should bring fresh evidence. Equally exciting should be the new work on the inscriptions and texts from the tombs of Tutankhamen by a philologist, M. Piankhov. *"Le temps va ramener l'ordre des anciens jours."*

I mentioned also a loss; a better word would be disaster. The scheme which is dearest to the new government is that of the High Dam above Assuan with thirty times the capacity of the present one, which at a cost of two hundred million pounds is to bring enormous advantages to the country. It will increase electric power and permit heavy industry, make Egypt independent of the reservoirs in Equatoria, add 700,000 feddans for the cultivation of rice, be 300 feet high, "and bring prosperity for 500 years." It will take ten years to complete but the waters will be rising after two. The whole Nile above Assuan will become more of a lake than it is already, hideous as only a reservoir can be, and stretching for 150 kilometres into the Sudanese province of Dongola. Korosko, Derr, and Wadi Halfa will be submerged with all the Nubian temples including Abu Simbel which rises within the tropic, near the Sudan frontier.

I decided I must go there, braving the three-day journey on the Sudanese river steamer, with its fiendish parody of English cooking and "life on board ship." It was worth it. The steamer, by now festooned with small brown flies, reached Abu Simbel in the late afternoon; a sickle of sandy beach with a squatting mimosa in flower, desert everywhere, and the cliffs of pale scintillating powdered brick, orange into rose, from which the four colossi of Ramses II, each sixty-six feet high, beam in tremendous welcome. As we climb up, the thighs tower above us and the smaller colossi of his graceful daughters: someone has scribbled impertinently on one of the legs; it is in archaic Greek. At eye level the usual frieze of pinioned captives stagger by, loose-lipped Negroes on the one side (a frontier courtesy), and intellectual Semites on the other, for this is a supreme assertion of Egyptian power, the outpost of her grandeur, dominating the Blemmyes and the dusky imitation pharaohs of Meroe and Napata. Within are two more rows of colossi and the receding vaults of the temple proper, all painted and decorated in what was then permanent darkness, hollowed out of the solid rock. The aspect is both radiant and mysterious, magnificent yet full of grace; the designs are somewhat coarse but often brightly colored and illustrate the oft-repeated battle of Kadesh like a staff-college lecture. In the Cairo museum are two delightful small obelisks from the little outside temple to Ra and, carved in the same glistening sandstone, a row of baboons whose hands were upraised to the rising sun, a giant scarab and the King baboon as leaders. Now falls the brief unpaintable twilight, the green glow forsakes the towering figures and the frieze of cobras above, glitters and disappears as two rows of Nubians and Sudanese form on the sand for evening prayer, butting the earth as in Egyptian paintings. The gangplank lifts, the paddles grind and carry us on beneath the Southern Cross to the fleshpots of Wadi Halfa. (Excellent hotel.) After a glimpse of the second cataract, northern limit of crocodiles, realizing that if I go any further I shall have to buy a hat, I grab a plane for the return journey.

Abu Simbel is unique: it is in the same class as the Pyramids, Lascaux, the Pantheon, the Double Cube at Wilton, and the Temperate House at Kew, and so I advise all those who love what will certainly perish to make the journey. Although some shake their heads and say the dam will never be finished—"Egypt is Egypt," or "The Sudanese will object,"—and others talk of the UNESCO mission, of a dam within a dam or a large-scale replica to be made for a museum, even of the good to Philae which will result, I would count on none of it. What chance has one temple against 700,000 feddans of rice and some munition factories?

So let the pilgrimage be organized that the world may file past in the next two years and say good-bye. . . .

From Wadi Halfa to Cairo one flies for eight hundred miles over a desert which pales gradually from orange to off-white. Not a bush, not a blade, except when we cross the green ribbon of the Nile or the liquid blob of the Fayum. In many places the desert comes right down to the river, in others the oxen toil at the waterwheels under the palms as from time immemorial.

This valley represents a civilization which in times of strength expands like a stomach to engulf Syria in the north, the Sudan to the south. When it is weak the organism dissolves into small separate kingdoms, which ultimately reunite and begin a new process of northward and southward expansion. Such is Egyptian history. The present is a moment of expansion, but it remains to be seen whether the strength is there. The Sudan is welcomed as a long-lost brother, the Arab League brings in the north, Cairo is to become the moral capital of Islam and of Africa.

The rulers of this freak of geography which is Egypt have always to face the same problems, arising from overcrowding in the fertile strip and from centuries of foreign domination: poverty, ignorance, ill-health, corruption, and inertia. The present regime is a military-socialist movement which has grown out of a league of eight hundred young officers who vowed to end corruption and restore the dignity of the Army. They kept their secret for four years, a miracle in the East, and seized power without bloodshed. Effective power resides in three members of the Council of the Revolution, which has attacked corruption and inertia by enforcing reforms long promised but never carried out. Since agreeing to leave Suez and the Sudan, the British are treated as warm friends though American capital is much in evidence and many Germans are employed. The real losers are the Turkish land-owning class whose power and prestige are gone for ever; for almost every Egyptian is now conscious that the country belongs to him, and the measures accomplished could not conceivably be reversed.

The improvement in education, social services, medicine, land, housing, and irrigation must gladden all who use their eyes. It is difficult to see how any other group in the country could have provided the drive and energy to set all this in motion. There is certainly a faint smell of Fascism (the slogan is "Unity, Work, Discipline"), but it is mitigated by peaceable intentions, by a desire to retain the maximum of good will and a tendency to proceed cautiously by careful planning, trial and error. The rulers intend to go out of uniform, re-establish the Army (carefully purged) as a nonpolitical body, and set up two new parties, Republican and Socialist, to safeguard the revolution and return to democratic ways. Turkey is the model, and Turkey has certainly progressed from an enlightened military dictatorship to a democracy in a very few years. Egypt is now almost normal for tourists, while foreigners who live here claim that they have not felt so safe for four years. However, the effects of anti-imperialist propaganda are still felt, and it is not advisable to venture into the villages or poorer quarters without a dragoman or member of the Tourist Police.

The personal popularity of the Prime Minister is astonishing: "The best ruler Egypt has had for a thousand years," my dragoman told me. "Sixty percent good, forty percent bad" was a more liberal admission. . . . Too much censorship, too much military impatience, distrust of the middle class, ignorance of administration, too many heavy sentences summarily imposed by the courts, an increasing anti-Semitism, and a tendency to postpone indefinitely the drafting of the new Constitution. Yet on the whole an atmosphere very like England in wartime, of puritanism and moral fervor, Beveridge and brigadiers, together with an English feeling that such a state of things is not permanent, that no one—not even the ruler—wants it to last, that, the revolution won, humor, charm and tolerance will again predominate.

Yet how much good is being done! Consider the Nile, vibrating with sunlight, flecked with tall feluccas, hazily blue against the sugar cane and palms. But the whole river cries "Hands off," the *Guide Bleu* advises us not even to trail a finger, for here and in all the neighboring canals and water holes reigns the *bilharzia*, one of the most ingenious maggots devised by nature for the undoing of man. In some delta villages up to ninety percent of the population suffer from the debilitating intestinal disease (found even in mummies) which it inflicts, and hookworm is nearly as common. Typhoid, tuberculosis, malaria, elephantiasis, and purulent ophthalmia also take their toll; and as for past treatment of them, it must be remembered that sixty percent of the population is illiterate, that few doctors would practice in the villages, and that hospital beds number two per 1,000 as against sixteen per 1,000 in Switzerland.

The "simple fellah" believes, like his ancestors in the days of Herodotus, that Nile water is good, a sovereign remedy, while filtered water causes impotence. He does not associate malaria with mosquitoes, nor mosquitoes with their free-swimming larvae. Insecticides have to be thrust upon him, but they are becoming more and more popular, while a religious campaign to enforce the Koranic precept against polluting water helps to eliminate *bilharzia*, even as a better disposal of sewage and garbage helps with ophthalmia and typhoid, or slum-clearance with the ravages of tuberculosis.

Combined medical and welfare centers are being set up in more and more towns and villages, bringing midwives and information officers, medicine and loudspeakers, and new schools are being built out of the fortune from the confiscated royal estates. The acceleration in all these essential forms of progress has advanced under the revolution from, as it were, ten to thirty miles an hour, and at last the money and the will-power are forthcoming in co-operation with the peasant, who is beginning to own his wonderful land.

For the traveler how unique is Egypt! Where else can the tourist be offered such perpetual winter sunshine, such huge and extraordinary monuments or such a collection of beautiful buildings as are to be found in medieval Cairo? Yet there is something sad about it; the gulf between the traveler and the native—the gulf of language, of habits, of religion—is too wide; and the hotels, with the exception of the Semiramis in Cairo, have a melancholy all their own. There is a sunset *cafard* which the evening's amenities can hardly dissipate; after the long, heavy dinner nothing to do but contemplate the list of prohibited gambling games—Harakiri, Zoukov, Ascenseur—and creep to bed. The main stream of tourism still flows from Cairo to Beirut rather than down to Luxor and Assuan.

When I look back I think with most joy of my second visit to the Cairo Museum, of the Mosque El Azhar, older than Cordoba, and of the theological students squatting on the royal red carpets beside their teachers under a forest of columns, of many charming talks in Cairo, of Taha Hussein, the blind writer, whose ambition it is to edit a really good Arabic translation of the complete works of Shakespeare, of my delightful mentor from the Ministry of Information, a leading authority on Oscar Wilde and flying saucers, of the giant shrimps and fresh limes, of the oasis of the Coptic Museum.

Yet always I return to Assuan, one of the most beautiful places I have ever seen, to the tombs on the brick-red slab of desert, the sailing boat depositing one, at the violet hour, on Kitchener's Island, most lovely of tropical gardens, where every tree is new and must be learned from labels, the bulbous emerald trunk of *Chorisia Speciosa*, the yellow-flowering *Markhamia* from Uganda, the *Belmoriana* from Lord Howe Island, the Indian "Butter Tree," and the hoary mimosa to which all the white ibises of the river come skimming home to roost with joyous croak and clatter in the green and ashen twilight.

Kitchener's Island, the perfect garden, Assuan Dam, the

largest and loveliest of waterworks . . . they are relics of our art and altruism for which we receive scant credit. One day they will go the way of the lines of Suez or El Alamein or of the Edwardian novels and proconsular memoirs which sleep like papyri behind the locked grilles of the hotel library.

England Not My England

The love affair of which these extracts form a record is in a closing stage, even at the moment where they begin. Indeed, it had already lasted twenty-three years, and for the seven before this diary opens been dangerously articulate. Actually we have selected only the lover's vows and recriminations to his country from a batch of other declarations he made during the same period to literature, autumn, and even life itself. Only in autumn, in fact, does he seem happy, and for the rest of the year his country, unwilling to be desired merely for its climatic accidents, takes a cruel revenge. "The course of true love" is more than applicable to this *passion malheureuse* whose every phase seems to echo the complaint of Martial: "*non tecum possum vivere, nec sine te.*" Finally, Paris seduces him; with all his passion turned to hate he runs away, and the affair ends on a note of benign disillusion that is perhaps more cynical than any wrath could ever be. Like most lovers, the author appears fractious, embittered, egotistical, and not always inclined to be sincere. Well, there it is, and we cannot help feeling that if things had been different, if there had been a little more patience and understanding on both sides, if he had been more industrious with his pen, and his country more generous with her money, we might still see them billing and cooing together. Alas for him and his Lesbia, it seems that this was not to be; now Mr. Punch, a few Georgian poets, gossip writers, and lady novelists woo the cool green Motherland—who yields herself, however, only to Mr. Galsworthy. Does she ever regret—we try sometimes to imagine—her odd-eared lover? Is the wound incurable? The breach—we wonder muzzily—the whole thing over? And somehow we cannot help feeling that it isn't; but then, in this country, we usually feel that.

30th June 1927
Dined alone and caught boat to Caen. Leaving England felt like losing a limb.

22nd July 1927
I have no ambition, but will a horror of being stationary, a panic fear of keeping still, make up for it?

27th July 1927
Bad lunch on Dover boat and dreary crossing. Oh, the superb wretchedness of English food, how many foreigners has it daunted, and what a subtle glow of nationality one feels in ordering a dish that one knows will be bad and being able to eat it! The French do not understand cooking, only good cooking—this is where we score. Pleasant journey up to London reading newspapers; a gray and windy day. Arrive at Victoria and feel like Rip van Winkle, but with a vague sense of home-coming and security at being back again. All foreigners are frightful, and Europe is crawling with them.

29th July 1927
Asked Desmond about himself, and he spoke of his life at twenty-three, he told me he was as idle as I was and eventually it made him ill. I said I knew the feeling.

2nd to 4th August 1927
I ought in fairness to announce that these two days by the sea I have been distinctly happy.

3rd August 1927
Perfect summer's day, which seems the flower of all the summer days in history and makes England incomparably richer than Greece. Went out after dinner and walked down to the shore, where the cat followed me. There were some men

cutting up a log of driftwood. The sky was rose and the sea pale green, and though the hills of the Island and the lights of Fawley were clear, there was a thick mist on the shore, through which the men at the timber loomed large as I walked along with the cat over the pebbles. Came back and called up an owl. Bonfires on the air, horses in the mist, the boy scouts singing and their tents glowing in the dark. The black cat very lively on the garden wall, and the light in a bedroom window shining out over the fields. It seemed terrible to be going to London, even in a month, on such a day.

3rd September 1927

Depressed, unhappy, and apprehensive. This fag-end London.

8th September 1927

My thoughts run to depression as a child to its mother. Not to be born is best, or being born, to live at Cadiz.

17th September 1927

Lovely, unexpected, hopeless summer's evening. Resolve: to live more and more in the present, cultivating especially intensity and inconstancy in personal relations, to break free, so far as loyalty permits, from all unions that chain one to the past, while retaining them in so far as they provide a commentary, otherwise to fall in love as impermanently as possible with whoever is nearest, to study life not death, the present not the past, the actual not the literary. Only by giving the whole of myself to the moment can I make it give its best to me. A rapid series of unbearable partings is the best proof that one is living—to live in the present is the most provident of all ways of life, for by that alone can one create a valuable past. *"Pas de recherche sans temps perdu"*—no chronicles without wasted time.

20th September 1927

Depression over. Here and now I recant like Stesichorus: life is thrilling, valuable, wholly adequate, and enough. This spurt of the senses; this welling up of the mind; the magnificent power of expenditure and recovery; the accumulation of richness and depth like a symphony whose orchestra grows always fuller, whose melodies begin to develop and repeat themselves always with a greater promise and a new implication, are finer than anything that can be deduced about them; are not adorned by any tale. Life has no moral, and the moral of art is that life is worth while without one.

I am just twenty-four and dangerously happy. For once I feel ambitious and desire and believe in my chances of fame. I want to give lavishly to everyone, to enrich life as it is enriching me—granted but the vitality to enjoy life, I will give it everything that has made it enjoyed. Till then, spare me ὦ τὸ φθόνερον.

As I wrote this I found the pages of Logan's diary in the 'nineties, left in at the end of a blank notebook: "Venice. Church at twilight. Candles. Singing, Per i poveri morti. People die. I shall lose them, no more hear their voices. Let us cling to the best, forgive, not notice. I too shall die: this color and this warmth will pass from me. Let me treasure the right things, see this world brighter for the frame of death." The same pleading, the same appeal as mine. The rhetorical cry of all youth to all life, to be allowed merely to love it, to love the sphinx that breaks her lovers, to feed the hand that bites them, the indifferent hour.

27th September 1927

Converted to Paris through finding a Spanish cabaret where flamenco is sung, and by the lovely spacious autumn light and the contented people. A living crowd, while in London all the faces are dead.

To be obtained before I am twenty-five: £1000 a year, a book published, a Spanish mistress, some fame, more friends, a knowledge of German, and a visit to Cadiz.

When I was going through a bullying phase at Eton I made Buckley write a weekly essay for me on Wayne, Milligan, Eastwood, and other boys. At first he disliked these essays as much as the subjects, but soon he grew conceited over them and resented any criticism. I can't attach any moral to this or discover why it cropped up in my mind.

London, 10th October 1927

I get happier and happier—autumn intoxicates me. So does London. Richer, deeper, and more delicate, what can life hold in store? I find it gets harder and harder to read or write: I tremble on the verge of plain material hedonism though still retaining the capacity to moralize about it; the senses continue to feed the mind though nothing else does. The sun shines through my window, the air is fresh and cold, and the bell rings to take me down, to lunch alone off beer and a cold partridge, before going for a walk in the park. Life alone is worthy of being worshipped, and with the highest blend one can bring to it of scholarship and vitality.

15th October 1927

Long quiet evening alone, dining off tea, and digestion very bad. I must go to Cadiz in the spring and live and write there: London is too dangerous.

1st November 1927

Depression, literary and physical. Literature is a dead form. Avoid literary people, they go round and round like water running out of a bath, dregs that never can forgive each other. Avoid tea tables; envy and affectation are within you, but you can at least avoid tea tables. Sulk through life and in sulky places, Russia or the untidiest parts of South America. Possess nothing but lumber, store everything in houses, but do not live in them. Find the most confidently material civilization and see how it behaves. Scheme of life, make money, drop writing, go long voyages, hang round life: shadow it, worry it, bore it, only come back to England when you have learnt to miss it. Take notes and fix moments, but leave the task of setting them in order to your old age—if you can die young with nothing finished, you do well to do so.

On a base of profound and wary disillusioned indolence stands all my hope of tolerating death.

17th November 1927

Damn life, damn love, damn literature! In other words, damn journalism! Live out of London, drop journalism—yet to quit one made impossible by loneliness, the other by finance. Make £1000 a year, make pots of money out of a novel! Too soft for journalism, too rough for literature, I should be wretched abroad, bored in the country—what can one do? Trust to the ultimate creative effort of my own impatience? O for Old Buffer, I for ink-slinger, G for Jesus, A for Agag.

"What's the Latin name for parsley?

What's the Greek name for swine's snout?"

March 1928

General sense of depression and disgust, with usual horror of literature. Last days in London characterized by financial needs, desperate anxiety to get abroad, and deepening passion for low life. Spent every evening exploring London; one should be able to live at least three lives concurrently, and heaven knows how many in rotation. In a complex age, why not be complicated? Resolve: to associate with all the people I am afraid of most.

June 1928

Back in England; feel nothing but an intense disgust at its stupidity. Fatuous newspapers still fussing about the Prayer Book. The wireless with its children's corner, reports of tennis matches, lectures on the composition of the cricket team, on the searchlight tattoo. Absurd music, jolly, idiotic, or merely oodly. Miss Ivy St. Helier beginning: "Don't be afraid, I'm not highbrow"—nor is she. All actors and actresses with their frightful genteel Balliol and Tottenham accents. Miss Gladys Cooper married to a gentleman at Dorking. She drew a blank for her profession, dodged the crowd, and gave some money to a charity. "He's all right, he's a gugnunc." Really, the most deplorable country, Americanized without America's vitality or variety of race. And this absurd fuss about Shaw and Galsworthy. Assets of England: the climate, the countryside, the children, the presence of a few kindred spirits in rebellion, the country houses, the fact that I can speak its language, that it is in easy reach of the Continent.

The problem is not how to attack the Jewish-American gugnunc world, but whether there is any ideal of equal activity that we can put in its place. At present it absorbs almost all the vitality of the Western races, and no half-timbered sanctuary, no pagan rockpool, can be substituted for it. Again, since it is at its worst in America, it is from America that the rebellion will come—we are all too soaked in tradition and culture, and not sufficiently aware of this to create anything outside of them. Saving the countryside must make it a museum.

Tatters of rain streak from a dishcloth sky. Soon England will be a slagheap city in a rubble field, stogged bottles in the dingy grass, burdock and peeled hoardings stretching down to a litter of boots and halves of empty grape-fruit cast up by a bathwater ocean on an insanitary shore.

Why not let the countryside be finished, instead of propping it up in this long agony, this imbecile position between death and life?

October 1928

Back in London after five weeks in Spain. General dissatisfaction and distress. Unpleasant sense, not only of being just where I was this time last year, but of being practically just where I was the year before. As homeless, futureless, hopeless, and unestablished as ever. Shall I live in Paris or the country? I am also less interested in literature, if anything, and not really so interested in life, no sign either of the flow of natural high spirits that I had last year. I suppose my happiness is a difficult crop that requires sun, rain, soil, manure, and tending to make it flower at all.

10*th October* 1928

By some seasonable miracle I seem to be falling in love with London and recapturing the same exaltation that I attributed merely to youth last year. To feel this jungle come to life all round one in the evening, the same October mists, fires, lights, wet streets, blown leaves, to plunge into its many zones, not knowing what one will discover, and to return with a growing sense of confidence and power as a new street or a new district falls beneath one's rule, is to feel a true explorer, or rather is to combine the intimacy of a wooer with the excitement of an adventurer; to run my fingers through the town's soft pelt, to caress the lax pulsating city as rashly, as apprehensively, as a Greek might approach an Amazon, or a small spry leopard, male of some great cat.

1st November 1928

General disgust, especially with literature. Same as this time last year, only feebler.

2nd November 1928

Terrible *envie* for Paris. The cafés, the lights, the crowded warm interiors, the wasters, the artists, the drunks, the sense of liberty and rebellion, the cold transition, on the Boulevard, from afternoon to evening.

5th November 1928

Almost as depressed and dissatisfied as this time last year, my life seems in every way to have retrogressed. Poorer, older, idler, stuck in the same house, the same groove, with even fewer friends and considerably less curiosity. Resolve: to be more of an artist and a Bolshevik, to write a lot and go to Paris and live in Montparnasse, if not in love or otherwise adequately detained here by December 1st. *Envie* for Paris continues severe. "The slow gradations of decay."

November 1928

One cannot really love London. It is disappointing in every way. A foggy, dead-alive city, like a dying ant heap. London was created for rich young men to shop in, dine in, ride in, get married in, go to theatres in, and die in as respected householders. It is a city for the unmarried upper class, not for the poor. Every writer and artist must feel a sense of inferiority in London unless he is (like Browning or Henry James) a romantic snob—or else fits into the Reynolds-Johnson tradition of

Fleet Street, Garrick, good burgundy, and golf. Arnold Bennett is the English Bohemian. Of course, there are Bohemians, but they have to be smart ones, otherwise they are afraid to show themselves; without a quarter, without cafés, their only chance is to get rich and fashionable and give cocktail parties. In Paris they have a quarter assigned to them, and are lords of it. They aren't much better as artists, but they are freer, happier, and harder-working, and live in an atmosphere where great art is more likely to arise.

The more one sees of life the more one is aware how hopeless it is without art to give it meaning. "To love life in all its forms" is like loving pumice-stone in all its forms, or journalism. Life is only in exceptional cases worthy of being loved— to love life is to have the curiosity to search for the occasions when life is lovable—or rather the enterprise to create them.

And in London they are few.

Moment of happiness in Yeoman's Row. Yellow sunlight falling through the panes on golden cushions and a glass of wine; reading in the armchair, far cries of children playing.

Fear of life, hate of self, general misery and intermittent self-pity these last few days. "*Quando ver veniet meum.*" "*Sombra soy de quién murió.*" Culmination of misery on Saturday night, lost a five-pound note at a bad revue—the most unlovable mug in England. Feel ill unless I drink, and depressed when I do. Wild fits of mawkish gloom, "genteel canine pathos"—the world whips only those who look as if they've just been whipped.

> O douleur, O douleur, le temps mange la vie,
> et l'obscur ennemi qui nous ronge le coeur
> du sang que nous perdons croît et se fortifie.

December 1928

A wild month, intoxication of London as before.

1929

With a deepening sense of guilt, failure, loneliness, and insecurity, I greet the New Year.

General reflections.—Read and written far too little: increased confidence, however, and aptitude for life. Deterioration in general highmindedness; a year of social success, amorous enterprise, aesthetic Bolshevism and physical, moral, and emotional falling back.

January 1929

> "Thou hast led me like a heathen sacrifice
> with garlands and with sacred yokes of flowers
> to my eternal ruin."

Resolve: To be altogether more advanced and intelligent, to have more friendships and fewer affairs, to write and read more than I eat and drink, to revisit Paris and write a prize novel.

"We have no precedent for an English intelligentsia. The flower of our civilization is a certain splenetic enterprise, an instinctive dignity in living, an absolute grasp of the material splendor of life—a young buck tilting down St. James's Street, a clean old man in a club window, a great writer married to an earl's daughter, a country gentleman reading Keats —these are the fruits of our mind and upbringing, these are the images we should preserve. Writing is a lapse of taste rather than a crime: it is explicit and hence in opposition to our character and our climate."

Back from Yorkshire appalled at my enjoyment of a week in the country. Enjoyed the countryside under snow, the warm house, the tobogganing, the shoot, the smell of cartridges, the heavy winging and thud of falling birds on the smoky evening air. Standing in the wet woods listening to the beaters tapping and whistling; watching the farm cart full of birds bowling home over the park. Oh, the joy of lingering over port and brandy telling dirty stories with men in pink coats while it snows outside! The grim, rich, game pie England of eighteenth century squires, brown woods, and yellow waistcoats.

Abroad, I was at least interesting to myself—in London I can't be even that. I exist only to celebrate my sense of guilt.

1st February 1929

Back in London, miserably depressed. Persecution mania,

sense of solitary confinement. Finally decided London unendurable and packed up in the middle of dinner and left. It was raining as I fled to St. Pancras. The train was a red Midland express; huge drays kept coming down the platform, I lit my cigar and played the gramophone. It was one of the most pleasant solitary journeys I have ever made. The train slid through Barking and the wet stations of the East End: I played slow foxtrots in my empty carriage and felt that at last I had become a real person again. It was very wet and windy at Tilbury. I stood on deck and watched the lights along the Thames. I had a perfect moment as the boat moved out. The wind was cold and the water choppy, all the passengers were below and I saw the pilot dropped. As the little tug shot away from the ship in an Ionic curve like the prong of a boathook I had an exquisite sense of the finality of leaving, of which that seemed a definite symbol. It was very rough and I reached Dunkirk in icy cold, pitch dark and freezing. In the train this became a beautiful winter morning, and with no remorse I played a flamenco record to the rising sun.

July 1929

Landed at Newhaven. Depressed at being back in England. The countryside so dirty, sky and fields the color of corrugated iron. Everybody so weak and knock-kneed, a race of little ferrets and blindworms. England is a problem: parts of it so beautiful, a few people in it so intelligent, yet never can I manage to fit in. The intelligent ones are so stranded, such detached and *défaitiste* observers; the extraordinarily nice people, of whom there are probably more than in any other country, are also extraordinarily stupid; the "amusing" ones so dull. I hate colonels, but I don't like the people who make fun of them. Those who conform become impossible, and those who rebel rebel only toward a continental snobbery instead of a "county" one. A wave of retrograde and stupid conservatism seems to be sweeping the country. There is no place in England for a serious rebel; if you hate both diehards and bright young people you must, like Lawrence, Joyce, or Aldous

Huxley, go and live abroad. It is better to be *depaysé* in someone else's country than in one's own.

Disgusted by the crowd at Brighton. "So dull, so dead, so
woebegone," hardly a soul in holiday clothes: they might be
waiting on a tube platform. Women all dowdy, men undersized and weedy. Pathetic voices and gestures, newspaper fed
ignorance, wistful cannon fodder larvae that trail around
whining out their day's ration of bromides as if at any moment
somebody was going to hit them. No trace even of charwoman
Cockney or Dickensian vulgarity either—just little ferrety
robots squeaking round an empty bandstand. Oh, the stupidity of the old regime and the silliness of its detractors! Yet for
this Mr. T. S. Eliot changes his brown passport for true blue!

16th July 1929

Went for a long walk to Lulworth Cove. For an instant, on
the lonely crest of the downs, above an old house that sloped
down through a semicircle of beechwoods to the sea, I had a
moment of love for my country, just as we may suddenly prepare to forgive someone who has deceived us before the memory of their infidelities swarms in on us again. As we walked
farther, however, I remembered not so much the beauty of the
downs as the awfulness of the people who wrote about them:
Kipling's thyme and dewponds, Belloc's beer, and Chester-
ton's chalk, all the people writing poems at this moment for
the *London Mercury*, and two tiresome undergraduates who
discuss culture at the inn. They gaze, between mouthfuls of
tomato, at the Victorian lithographs round the parlor: *Caught
Napping*, *The Love-Letter*, *Their First Quarrel*, *The Story of a
Brave End*. "Pretty serious!" grunts one to the other. "Terrible," grunts the culture specialist. "*Glubet magnanimos Remi
nepotes*," I thought, undeterred by a burst of exquisite woodland ride between the cliffs and the valley. Peter was more
loyal to the Motherland, but talked exclusively of Villiers de
l'Isle Adam all the way. We reached a cottage by the sea for
lunch. Peter flattered the landlady and praised the bread and
cheese rather professionally. For this, to my joy, we were
charged two shillings each, and I maintained that one couldn't

be robbed more if one was a foreigner. I asked if I could bathe from the rocks without a costume. "There be bobbies' eyes from here to Weymouth," she said. Eventually we got to Lulworth Cove through a maze of complacent military reminders that a fatal accident had occurred in 1927 "through a pedestrian using the path along the cliffs when the red flag was flying." From Arishmell the sound of church bells was wafted down the petrol-scented English lanes past the carefully thatched cottages.

> O God, to hear the parish bell
> in Arishmell, in Arishmell!

Lulworth Cove was like a flypaper. People in every direction, and twelve charabancs parked across a space for building lots. "I wish I had a camera," I cried, and Peter answered: "I wish I had a machine gun." At that a miracle happened, the helpless bitterness with which he vainly protested seemed to snap something in my head, and I felt the relief with which one passes an old flame and feels "that face can never trouble me again." The deformed and swarming trippers, the motor-car park, the wooden bungalows and the tin tea-sheds seemed a heavy joke at which I could look on with ironic detachment. I felt suddenly quit of everything: my sense of possession, in regard to England, had been finally scotched. Besides, even if it is beautiful, I thought, from my point of view (that of finding things to write about) this countryside, except for a few still unchronicled phases of winter, is virtually dead. "The country habit has me by the heart," wrote someone trying to find a fresh approach to that Grantchestered old trollop—this England—or, as the papers archly call it, "This England of ours." I thought of all the ardent bicyclists, the heroic coupleteers, the pipe-smoking, beer-swilling young men on reading parties. The brass rubbers, the accomplished morris dancers, the Innisfreeites, the Buchan-Baldwin-Masefield and Drinkwatermen, the Squires and Shanks and grim Dartmoor realists, the advanced tramp lovers, and, of course, Mary Webb. I thought of everyone who was striding down the Wordsworthian primrose path to the glorious goal of an O.M. "The country habit has me by the heart," I chanted to the

Lulworth trippers, and in an usher's voice of mincing horror *"procul o procul este profani"*—but it was my friend, not they, who fled.

Went down to the cove for a bathe. Warm sunny evening. Walking back (the grace of childhood still irradiates the "walk to the sea"), I met a man with a motor caravan. Stayed and talked to him and his wife and daughter. Green beds spread in the open, a book lying on the grass, some pails, and his wife cooking porridge. He had spent his life in the East and had just retired. Walked up with them to the vicarage garden, where they were to do country dances. A few children, one or two village women and farmboys, and a couple of bustling ladies with muddy red faces and fringes of graying hair. They danced on the grass to a gramophone. "Now come along—if all the world were paper—siding, turn, slips, take your partner and swing!—if all the world were paper—too slow—too slow—too slow!" The village women pant seriously, the spinsters dance briskly, giving directions from a little book. I gingerly take part, put out to find myself also among the prophets; the Anglo-Indians skip with experience and the children stare. The girls are breathless and light-footed, yet heavy with a kind of rustic materialism, their faces and figures are gauche with adolescence, like unfinished statues left in the marble. They grin and call to the children in thick sweet Dorset voices. "Now Newcastle—now gathering peascods"—or is it "picking up sticks?" The plaintive music so naïvely vicious, so innocently sophisticated, floats out on the evening. "We want only the best for 'Clergyman's Farewell'—it's very difficult—single hey, turn, slip, siding, now be careful, double hey, grand chain!" I walk away up the road, the distressful notes of "Clergyman's Farewell," the young voices, sad slice of wan little England, pursue me over the fields. A sheep-dog is sleeping by the pond, and outside the inn some boys are playing cricket with a stone. The sun westers brightly over the folded plateau, and every flower and every weed, the air, the downs, the gray cottages, unite with the distant archaic music to cry "Saul, Saul, why persecutest thou Me?"

A mood of final emancipation came to me the next morning.

I leant against a long wall underneath a window, when suddenly a voice began to thunder from inside. "Very important. Causal conjunctions. We went very deeply into this last week. Read it out." "Causal conjunctions," quavered a choir of young voices. "Quippe, qui, and quoniam take the indicative." "Quippe, qui, and quoniam," bellowed the usher, interrupting them, "take the indicative." The rasping voice sounded like the cry of a wild animal, as if one had passed on the top of a bus by the Zoo, but the uncouth language blended perfectly with the summer scene outside. "Take this down—take it down, will you," the roar continued. "Conjectus est in carcerem—he was thrown into prison—quod patrem occidisset—on the grounds that he had killed his father—qui eo tempore—who at that time was flying into Italy—in Italiam refugiebat. RE-FU-GI-EBAT," he thundered, and the pedagogic rhythms floated out into the sun and along the dusty hedgerows. "Conjectus est in carcerem," mumbled the scribbling pupils; "quippe, qui, and quoniam," they chanted; "causal conjunctions," till the words were lost above the Isle of Purbeck, a drone above the drone of bees.

One of My Londons

Once or twice a month, like an old trapper clinging to his peltless round, I revisit London to correct a proof, drink oysters with a publisher, prospect an auction room or favorite book shop. I stay, if at all, but one night for I am usually depressed by the stale air and listless shuffle of the street, the monumental tawdriness of lettering and lighting, the quicksand of vague faces—and nothing, I find, comes up to the moment of arrival, the taxis of Charing Cross, the stucco of King William Street or glitter of Saint Martin's—unless it be the lamplit curve of the river when the train trundles homeward over the bridge.

One blue summer twilight, however, I was passing by a mews flat in Knightsbridge where two window boxes were in flower above a painted portico. A tall well-dressed young man with a baby in his arms stands on the darkening step; the door is opened by a laughing girl in nothing but a bath-towel, silhouetted against the light in the hallway. In that moment I have unwillingly lived myself into this couple; I was there when they first met at a cocktail party; I know that weak, longhanded young man, his cruel charm and mannered voice and his incurable unrest: I see this naked girl bubbling with hope in her pale summer frock, keen on the arts, angry with mother, stabbed suddenly by desire and maternal anguish as she accepts her first whiskey from him. And I am aware that the Past has yanked me back, that they are one with innumerable couples I have known, with all the trapped young *couche-tard* fathers and honey-headed girls determined, as they pile into the little car at weekends, to make the best of things

98

while the drink bills and the garage bills and the tailor's bills
pile up after them until that terrible quarrel at the nightclub,
when first she wipes her lipstick from another's mouth and his
wallet bulges with treason. . . . And another day, while crossing Bedford Square, I am doubled up with nameless and immediate anguish, blackened with fear—and forced to run for
sanctuary to some old dusty counter and efface myself among
Victorian prints, the collected works of Lamartine or the un-
saleable *Picciola*. And then I remember Petronius: "An old
love pinches like a crab." It is my discarded mistress who has
nipped me, the great city reminding one that no indifference,
however ingrowing, is proof against a casual jab from her non-
descript sting-ray buildings:

> *Tout l'affreux passé saute, piaule, miaule, glapit*
> *Dans le brouillard sale et jaune et rose des Sohos*
> *Avec des "all rights", et des "indeeds", et des "hos! hos!"* . . .

London is the capital of prose, as Paris of art or New York
of modern living and most of this good prose is concerned
with dandies or with slums or with fog: sometimes the dandy
goes slumming and sometimes, taking advantage of the fog,
the slum-folk sneak up on the dandy. The London I like best
is the one I can find in books where it lies embalmed between
1760 and 1840, the dandies still outnumbering the slums and
the fog as yet barely invented.

This London takes shape with Rochester and Etherege; in
Congreve, Pope, and the "Journal to Stella"; it comes into its
own with Boswell; Boswell and Casanova who both set out to
conquer the city in 1762 and who themselves are conquered
by love, if love be the proper term for Louisa and La Char-
pillon. And now comes the golden age of the dandies, the
London of Chesterfield and Horace Walpole, of Selwyn and
March, of Fox and Sheridan, of Alvanley and Brummell, of
White's and Brook's and Almack's, Devonshire House and Al-
bany. Brummell fled to Calais in 1816, a few hours after his
appearance at the opera—when his famous note: "My dear
Scrope, Lend me five hundred pounds for a few days; the
funds are shut for the dividends or I would not have made this
request. G. Brummell" had received its infamous reply: "My

dear Brummell, All my money is locked up in the funds. Scrope Davies." The Beau's life was written by Captain Jesse who met him in his old age at Caen and who also edited the Selwyn correspondence; four volumes of absorbing small talk from the later eighteenth century. As a cure for anxiety and worry and for that nameless sickness of the inner eye which views the contemporary world in monochrome, I would suggest a prolonged immersion in these irresponsible letter writers, in the strong, calm flow of London's eighteenth century whose eddies broaden into the Regency, with Harriette Wilson, Greville and Captain Gronow to complete it, and some of Mr. W. S. Lewis' admirable documentation, such as his *Three Tours Through London* to fill in local color.

The dandy's world is friendly, formal, and heartless, occluding the imagination, and if the cure in that direction should not go deep enough, I would propose a visit to the more spiritual London of the Romantics, to Hampstead and Highgate and Islington in the days of Keats, Coleridge, and Lamb—or a compromise may be sought in the drawing room of Holland House of which we possess such complete descriptions by Greville, Macaulay, and Talfourd.

> It is scarcely seven—and you are seated in an oblong room, rich in old gilding, opposite a deep recess, pierced by large old windows through which the rich branches of trees, bathed in golden light, just admit the faint outline of the Surrey Hills. Among the guests are some perhaps of the highest rank, always some of high political importance, about whom the interest of busy life gathers, intermixed with others eminent already in literature or art, or of that dawning promise which the host delights to discover and the hostess to smile on. All are assembled for the purpose of enjoyment, the anxieties of the minister, the feverish struggles of the partisan, the silent toils of the artist or critic, are finished for the week; professional and literary jealousies are hushed; sickness, decrepitude and death are silently voted shadows. . . . Every appliance of physical luxury which the most delicate art can supply, attends on each; every faint wish which luxury creates is anticipated. . . . As the dinner merges into the dessert, and the sunset casts a richer glow on the branches, still, or lightly waving in the evening light, and on the scene within, the harmony of all sensations becomes more perfect; the choicest wines are enhanced in their liberal but temperate use by the vista opened in Lord Holland's tales

of bacchanalian evenings at Brook's, with Fox and Sheridan, when potations deeper and more serious rewarded the Statesman's toils, and shortened his days, until at length the serener pleasure of conversation, of the now carelessly scattered groups, is enjoyed in that old, long unrivalled library in which Addison drank and mused and wrote; where every living grace attends; "And more than echoes talk along the walls."

It was nourished on such fairy tales (though with appetites more approaching those of Boswell and Casanova) that I came to live in London at the age of twenty-three. I had been taken on as secretary by Logan Pearsall Smith who had the idea of trying to endow a form of literary scholarship for a young writer by giving him a few pounds a week to live on while preparing a masterpiece and while assisting his employer by gleaning for the various anthologies which punctuated his leisure. I still carried some old debts from Oxford and my salary was soon pledged far ahead. I had also a weakness for taking my friends out to dinner at the Ivy, which has hardly changed at all in a quarter of a century; at the Berkeley which has changed considerably; at Boulestin's which was then a small pink paradise in Leicester Square or at the Tour Eiffel (the most expensive) which has quite disappeared, all turtles turned. Desmond MacCarthy gave me the novels to review for the *New Statesman* and I went to live with an Oxford friend who had gone into journalism. We rented an Edwardian cottage studio in Yeoman's Row, Knightsbridge, full of high-backed Italianate furniture and cardboard Spanish ironwork.

Drowsy hour or so in the empty house, sit in my future arm chair and read idly while somebody strums on a piano and the slum children play outside; a heavy sullen evening of imminent rain. Enjoy the children's voices and the sad thudding of their ball against the high windows. Explore the house and love it. Fondness for the strange furniture and garden outlook. Queer intimacy of possession in the empty house, a feeling of *Childe Roland* and that I would write well here. Take a taxi to the Board of Trade and wait about in the rain for an hour and a half in the hope of seeing A. No sign of her and with a curious sense of dreamlike fatality I plunge southward into Lambeth through a green and streaming urban sunset. At last I come to Charnwood Street lapped in obscurity and glaucous twilight with girls who laugh at me from upper windows. There is no answer to the bell and only a baby's crying greets me as I stand by the milk bottle outside the door. . . .

October 3rd, 1927.—Long quiet evening alone. Digestion very bad, dining off tea. Read Maurice Baring's letters from his Russian friend. He writes: "Any person taking a special interest in me is a frightful burden from which I flee in terror. I had always a disgust for men who want a woman to wash their soul's dirty linen for them and tell them the soul itself is pure. Marivaudage—Looking in woman for something she hasn't got and which you haven't got, begging where you should be giving, which leads to unceasing hesitation, and not knowing which is, after all, the right one. If you want inspiration from a woman, you must change her as you change your buttonhole; if you want to make her satisfied and be satisfied with that, marry her and turn philister. But be clear about what you want."

More unpleasant than filing one's bills is the effort of facing all the people I have thought I was in love with, permanently, since the summer. N. whom I hate, P. who is a bore, S. whose shares go neither up nor down, A. whom I have forgotten altogether, L. who is only eleven, and now R., but six years older, unawakened, stolid, last of the line of fair-haired, competent Dorian maidens about whom I feel so passionate and poetic.

October 7th.—R.'s mother came to tea on Thursday: Delicious, exquisite, and alarming. She said that she didn't believe that children really began to live till their parents were dead, that she had had a happy childhood because her mother and father were happily married, that all her sisters and she had made happy marriages, and that she was sure happiness in childhood was based entirely on that; she talked of the unhappiness of youth and how unnecessary it seemed, her daughters were not as happy as she. She spoke of the importance of money to marriage and as she was leaving said: "We must find you a rich wife!"

Philoctetes' farewell to his island is the most Elizabethan thing in Greek. The more I review novels, the more I read the classics, the only literature that is complete, that satisfies every need, and provides a decent privacy where one can understand oneself and be alone. I suppose I have had as much enjoyment from Tibullus this year as from any other author.

October 10th, 1927.—I get happier and happier, autumn intoxicates me, so does London, so does Yeoman's Row and the slum children and the evenings spent *à l'ombre des jeunes filles en fleur*. It becomes harder and harder to read or write. Dinner with the Berensons in Lady Horner's house, which is full of books and pre-Raphaelite portraits, all somehow a little wrong. B. B. looked more pained and beautiful than I have ever seen him, but very old, Isaiah as a French Academician. His temper was bad at the beginning of the meal (soup, fish, partridge, ices,

champagne, and port). He said life consisted of a double rebellion, tragic and comic, the one a revolt against death and
oblivion from which sprang all works of art and love, the other
a revolt against the law of averages which made people try to be
different from others and discover new forms of old age or marriage or writing. He said "Bloomsbury" had not got beyond the
comic rebellion, Roger Fry had adopted his own early principles and never got beyond them, Eliot was a thin and squeaking
Matthew Arnold and "Bloomsbury" a kind of dandyism only
compatible with youth. He said Europe was not decadent, neither was England, the only decadence was that of the Roman
world from the first to the fifth centuries A.D., and that decadence could never occur as an isolated intellectual phenomenon as it was primarily physiological and therefore, since
physiologically even England was unchanged, there could be
no true decadence.

In art also, he went on, people were still looking for new
forms, while decadence consisted in doing bad work in old
ones. America wasn't decadent either, the real danger to England was not Americanism, but civil servants, Tchinovnik—
the spirit which had ruined Russia, the spirit of Keynes in the
Nation.

Mrs. Berenson said Oscar Wilde was the only person of his
time whose eyes did not travel on to look for someone more
important when he spoke to you. She met him once five times
in a week and the last time he said, "I can't possibly sit next to
you, you have heard all my conversations for this week and I
have nothing more prepared. Is there any one of them you
would like to hear again?" "Yes, the one about Evolution," said
Mrs. Berenson, and he went through it but so perfectly that it
all seemed to arise from her own replies. B. B. said one could
review books for a limit of two years without becoming a hack.
I complained of my material happiness, that I enjoyed life so
much at present that I had no ideas at all beyond a vague meditation about physical things. He told me not to mind. "Ideas
will come," he said, "but youth will go."

Wednesday.—Bob Boothby, his mother, and Nina Seafield to
luncheon. I like her and she asked me to a cocktail party.
Boothby asks me to dinner. Write an offensive letter to R.
which may do some good and go round to Nina's. She has red
hair, blue eyes, an attractive stubby figure, a lovely stammer
and gasping kind of speech. Bob is there, and offers me a job;
exciting. Back and dine out with Patrick at his club. Ring up R.
to hear her voice and write to her again. Mrs. Fitz's, and a
lovely girl called Lola; French, very young and attractive.
Back, still desperately in love with R., to a late bed.

Thursday.—Dinner with Bob Boothby and Gladwyn Jebb at
the House of Commons, excellent dinner, liked them both. We
hear the new Prayer Book thrown out, most exciting. Walked

back with Gladwyn, it was agreed that henceforth I should be a cad and a careerist.

Thought of R. glows like an electric toaster.

Friday.—Lovely letter from R., hope springs again. Walked round to Elm Park Gardens but the house was dark. Hours and hours of watching but never a light. Thought of Swann and Odette and felt like my own ghost.

Κἀγὼ γαρ προθύροις νίσσομαι ὑόμενος.

Saturday.—Failed to ride with Nina owing to the snow. Lunch with Logan and we go afterward to Battersea Park. See a good eighteenth century church with tomb of Bolingbroke. Logan said Holland House must have been terribly dull. He had met in his youth one of the old survivors of that world where the conversation used to consist of long monologues which displayed your general knowledge and reading (in the case of the survivor, Aberdare, his topic was the route of Alexander's Indian expedition) while all the other old gentlemen sat around like croquet players, waiting to cut in at the first cough.

He said there were three illusions everybody passed through: falling in love, starting a magazine, and thinking they could make money out of keeping chickens. Back and wait ages for R., go in and out into the snow again and change and re-change my tie. At last she comes and we discuss our situation, not arriving at any settlement beyond the general relief of being able to discuss it. R. very lovely and boyish, wearing a yellow skirt that matched my cushions; brown-faced, green-eyed, tender and jovial. Her sister came to fetch her and we all went to Westminster in the tube and walked to South Kensington through the snow. Feel infinitely happier after seeing her. On to Nina's for dinner. N. very attractive and Gilbertelike. On after to the Café Anglais, drink R.'s health several times, back late and write to her in the small hours.

Tuesday, December 20th.—Wrote my article in the morning. Very cold day. Lunch at the Traveller's with Gladwyn. Send off article. Go on to tea with Hilda Trevelyan. George Moore comes, impressive and fussy. He said no good literature had ever come out of a salon. Logan said, "What about Proust?" George Moore (triumphantly) "Who wrote that?"

Home to dress, then dine with Leigh at the Ivy. He is charming, and afterward I go to North Street to fetch Nina. Thrill in the drawing room, the candles, the log fire, the dull light on my top hat, the taxi waiting outside in the snow, then Nina's footfall on the stair and delicious roucoulement of greeting. On to Lady Cunard's, carol singers drear, dance with Nina and talk to Patrick and Brian Guinness. Snobbish thrill at sight of the Prince of Wales walking alone up the wide staircase and shaking hands at the top with Maurice Baring and Diana Duff Cooper. Enjoy the rich patina of the evening, the lovely women and vacant faces of the extroverts, the expression of envy on

Clarence Marjoribanks' face as he asked me to introduce him to Nina, and the fatuous air of luxurious abandon on Lady Cunard's as she danced with the Prince. We sat next to him at supper.

The storm brewed over the week-end and the main fact out of a mass of complication and rumor is that R. and I are at all costs not to meet or write again.

March, 1928.—General sense of depression and discontent, with usual horror of literature and hopeless uncertainty over R.
> . . . "clene out of your minde
> Ye han me cast, and I ne can nor may
> For al this world, with-in myn herte finde
> T'unloven you a quarter of a day" . . .

The *soif* for life has greatly intensified so that to dine out every evening is not enough and has to be contrasted in a sequel among the centers of vitality; nearly every day I street prowl. Cultivated people are shrimps in a rock pool from whom I can learn nothing.

Rotherhithe.—Good docks and bridges but very little life, a few pubs, some wooden houses, continuous smell of lice which makes one feel abroad.

Limehouse.—Gambling dens suppressed. Met a Chinaman in Pennyfields who offered to show me round, he was reading a book on psychology. Touching to see the English waitress writing out Chinese ideograms on bits of paper and learning fresh ones from the proprietor. When she got one right, she smiled foolishly and threw it on the fire.

Shadwell.—Love Lane disappointing. Ratcliffe Highway, where there were a thousand brothels in 1890, is no more. Good market in Watney Street, best in evenings. Embankment lovely.

Wapping.—Good high street, wharves and water stairs. Here I saw that strange, nocturnal goatish clergyman stoop around an alley, blinking at the unaccustomed light from the bonfires (Guy Fawkes Day) that crimsoned his long white beard.

Whitechapel.—Much the best part of East End, especially side streets off Commercial Road (markets) and Leman Street, Wentworth, Old Montague streets, on the Stepney side. Here is Latin gaiety, crowds and music and color, rows of cars standing outside obscure cafés, and an excellent band and a tiny dance-hall. The Jewesses are amazingly attractive, a mass bloom seems to emanate from them in large quantities and they appear to walk up and down the street all night. Men dingy and undersized. Even when English themselves, these girls all deeply dislike the English, and the foreigners' good manners and capacity for passion are everywhere well-spoken of.

Soho.—New Compton Street. Café opposite Greek restaurant entirely full of Negroes. Very crowded, good grenadine.

Wardour Street.—Chinese restaurant with marvellous waitress, seventeen, father West Indian, mother German, name Lydia.

Hopkins Street.—Café apparently always full of crooks, sinister, open all night.

Desperate anxiety to get abroad, away from R.'s world; deepening passion for low life. Live in Green Dragon Court, Hop market, Southwark.

Lily: "Oh! I do like Piccadilly, don't you? I could never stay away from it long. Once I went to live with a man, a nice man he was, too, he had a flat in Earl's Court and I stayed down there three months. Well, one day he sent me up West to get some things and I got to Piccadilly about six o'clock. When I saw the lights and everything I was happier than I'd ever been. 'I am not going to lose this again,' I said, and so I never went back. I left all my clothes down there, and everything else, too. I don't know what he must have thought. Well, I got a fiver that night and I walked into Maxim's with it and when the waiter came up I ordered two bottles of champagne. Well, when I'd drunk them I noticed a woman with a red dress on, sitting with a man opposite me, so I said, 'You ought to give me that red dress, it would suit me much better.' I suppose I was a bit tight but I just said it to make conversation and she flew into a tearing rage. 'Take this woman out, she is drunk,' she said to the manager. 'I'll show you whether I'm drunk,' I said, 'I've paid for this and I've a right to have it,' and I hit him on the head with a champagne bottle. Oh! there was an awful row. The band stopped and all the dancing and a detective came and threw me out and they said I'd be arrested if I ever put my head in there again. But I don't mind, I never cared for Chinamen. Well, goodbye; they say the first man you meet after midnight on Hallowe'en means something to you—not that you're quite the first."

Palette for 1927. Autumn.—Brown and gold—brown curtains and chairs of Yeoman's Row, gold tiles in the fire, the green leaves through the lattice windows, then yellow leaves, then black stems of trees. The lights of Brompton Road, the newsboys outside the tube station as I come back from the *New Statesman* to the gramophone, the warm light, the evening paper and a late tea. Drinking with Patrick on idle Sunday mornings, going to the Film Society, dinners alone at the Ivy, theatres alone in the yellow fog. When I say suddenly, "autumn," I first see nothing but brown and gold, then I see three pictures rolled into one, the brown fur rug on my sofa, the two gold cushions, R.'s brown dress against them, her golden face and hair, a glimpse of the trees through the drawn curtains, a wild excitement in the air—still brown and gold the picture changes, a cold wet afternoon by Battersea bridge, R., slim,

golden, slant-eyed, in boy's felt hat and brown jumper, looking
down the road and tapping with one foot on the curb—the
swirl of the gray autumnal river, the wet embankment, the
waiting figure against the trees of the park, her marsh-green
eyes and yellow hair. Windy twilight in the Fulham Road, the
roar of buses, the November dusk, walking away from Elm
Park Gardens in the eddy of fast-falling leaves from plane and
elm crushed close on the rain-swept pavement: swirl of the De-
bussy quartet matching the wide curve of the road and the depression in my heart: walking on this windy evening, the lamps
just lit and wet with rain, alone along the broad street, brown
street with lights of gold.

Except for poverty, incompatibility, opposition of parents, absence of love on one side and of desire to marry on both, nothing would appear to stand in the way of our union.

Even after twenty-five years I cannot read the jottings of this
vanished youth who bears my name without discomfort. Insecurity and the only-child's imagined need for love have
stamped him and I remember every detail of his unhappy
courtship; the two lovely sisters who captivated the two newly
installed young bachelors, the marvellous promise of that autumn, the mischief-making false friend, the apprehensive
mother and the furious father who so easily separated us.

And this mined area round the Brompton Road is but one of
my Londons, even as Chelsea and Bloomsbury and Regent's
Park have other danger zones and trip wires. When the last
war broke out, I happened to rent the same studio in Yeoman's Row and to sleep in the room where twelve years before
I had experienced so many emotions, such maiming of heart
and pride, where I had discovered London and the blessing of
mixed society and had fallen in love and been frustrated—but
never was the Past recalled to mind—for it is too subtle to
operate in such a fashion, and we may haunt the scene of our
triumph or disappointment with perfect impunity until—in
one split second—the sky darkens; the figure in the bath-towel
who could have been R. opens the door to the young man that
might have been me; there is a moment of recollection, and the
Past strikes; the long-buried voice or gesture loom, adumbrat-
ing relentlessly the pangs of human loss—apprehension of
beauty and awareness of loss—which constitute the sour-

sweet juice of Time: "Darkness and lights: tempest and human faces," as De Quincey dreamed, "and at last, with the sense that all was lost, female forms—and clasped hands and heartbreaking partings and then—everlasting farewells, and again and yet again reverberated—everlasting farewells."

The best attitude to such London apparitions used to be a visit to the Sherlock Holmes Museum which has been withdrawn, for too long a time, to America. The reproduction of Holmes' study with his unfinished breakfast waiting, the invisible gramophone playing street music, with the sound of a hansom cab arriving, of a newsboy crying the victory of Omdurman, dismantle our personal time bomb and carry us back into a male society which protected us even before we were born. If such a mystical experience be not available, then let us visit some splendid tradesman of the old school; a tailor, a wine merchant, a bootmaker, a vendor of fine silver, of old china, fishing rods or saddles. If we owe them all money, it won't work, and we must try a good barber. I know of one who used to shave the Aga Khan in his bed without waking him. But best of all is the interior of a club, with a copy of *Country Life*, an arm chair and some anchovy toast since clubs were designed expressly to keep the demon at bay, and so here again we are back with the dandies whose leathery faces sneer down at us from their engravings. But even clubs have their perils, such as electric fires and waitresses; some careless old members have a habit of dying in them and one can be stricken down in a sullen moment while contemplating the accumulated selfishness of so many elderly lonely people. London is dangerous; it is a place for the strong and methodical, for the brute and the bank manager; but for the sensitive who are allergic to social sheen and waste, to apathy and ugliness, who have lived so long and behaved so badly, who used to think once of all the fabulous houses that they might be lucky enough to enter and now, with Samuel Rogers (last ornament of Holland House) "find a walk through the London streets like a walk in a cemetery"—for us, there is nothing to beat the 7.15 from Charing Cross, the thundering girders of the bridge and the funeral bake-meats on the diner.

II
LIFE & LITERATURE

Distress of Plenty

"Nothing odd will do long," said Dr. Johnson, "Witness *Tristram Shandy*," and such is the awful finality of this judgment that one re-reads Sterne almost with a sense of guilt, though indeed no author's reputation has so often survived its own obituary. In his own lifetime he was almost the only writer to alienate both Goldsmith and Johnson on the one hand, and Gray and Walpole on the other, and it is easy to see how the spectacle of the sleek and winning divine arriving in London to reap the success of his annual instalments must have irritated both the hard working critics of Fleet Street and the fastidious company at Strawberry Hill. Walpole, however, was hardly fitted to condemn Sterne as trivial, and Johnson was unaware of the lesson we learn from Proust, that in years of silence and dissipation a style can mature and an outlook ripen as easily as in a long apprenticeship to letters. Sterne in this respect comes near to his master Cervantes, and his scarcely broken silence of twenty-five years is probably, besides the vigor of his style, responsible for the dense and exasperating character of his mental undergrowth. Walpole was also the first to shy at Yorick's dead donkey and to perceive the terrible flaw which dominated Sterne's sensibility, the habit of luxuriating in emotion he thinks creditable, which turns his sympathy to self-congratulation and sets a smirk on all his tenderness. It is this fault that tainted the effects which Sterne intended to be his finest, as if he had skimmed the cream from comedy and pathos and found it turn overnight. And perhaps the word "sentimental" would not have lost caste so early had not his work exposed so completely its luxurious self-delight-ing nature. It is this latent insincerity, and not the mischievous indecency by which Coleridge was offended, that has made so many enemies for Sterne and turned nearly every biographer into an apologist. "I blushed in my turn, but from what movements, I leave to the few who feel to analyse," writes Yorick, and a little afterward "I burst into a flood of tears—but I am as weak as a woman and I beg the world not to smile but to pity me." One can see that he knew fairly well how the few who feel would react, and it is this irrepressible itch to commend himself, while deploring self-commendation, and to exploit his own humanity which has brought him the wrath of Thackeray, which made Coleridge call *The Sentimental Journey* "poor sickly stuff" and Leslie Stephen anxious to blot out even the Recording Angel's erasing tear.

Certainly *The Sentimental Journey* contains Sterne's most inexcusable lapses, yet in its conception as a book of travel it is absolutely right, though far from being the "quiet journey of the heart in pursuit of nature" that it styles itself. The irresponsibility, the exhilaration, and the frank independence of all its judgments (how right to call the French too serious) make it, however, through all its digressions, a real presentation of movement. Sterne was refreshingly seasick; wild with excitement even in Calais, he wished to find the French gallant, and did so. He could repeat "So this is Paris. Crack! Crack! Crack!" as inanely as any traveler rejoicing at the pall of respectability that was lifting from him, he would neither "disdain nor fear to walk up a dark entry," he would be swindled with a good grace rather than witness his host's disappointment, and though he describes but little scenery, he is still friendly to the scantiness which he has created; he seeks for adventure and avoids his compatriots, he ignores the Alps, he understands the French while remaining English, and, what is rare in a book of travel, he enjoys himself, even at a time when Dr. Johnson noted "that there has been of late a strange turn in travelers to be displeased."

Yet Sterne was not a man of deep feelings, and since his profession of sensibility requires him to appear so, there follow his flatteries and exhibitionism and the ill-concealed

self-satisfaction that rewards a well-spent tear. His "dear sensibility," however, that lachrymose goddess, was but a Roman
sense of *pietas* run to seed, and the final quality of Sterne as a
humorist lies in his wide sympathy, when not overstrained,
for every creature that is fulfilling its function, or in finding
speech for gaping and inarticulate "blind mouths" and enjoy-
ing human beings as they are. It is this Latin warmth that
links him, apart from style, to Rabelais and Cervantes, and in
a lesser degree to Shakespeare, and even Voltaire. Sterne was
as fitted as anyone to enjoy the shepherd with his "cold thin
drink out of his leathern bottle," but the temptation to make
capital out of his own emotions renders him unworthy of their
perpetual company. Within his limitations, however, his
world is one of the most wayward and serene of all Utopias,
and if the quality of his work is taken from the French, its
material is as undoubtedly English, the England of peaceful
fanatics, and gaunt unpersecuting bigots who have taken refuge from the fogs of the world in the most outrageous sanctu-
aries of their teeming minds, and who seem to spring up in the
peaceful country as naturally as teazels and to live here as happily as rare animals in private parks:

> This strange irregularity in our climate producing so strange
> an irregularity in our characters doth thereby in some sort make
> us amends by giving us somewhat to make us merry with when
> the weather will not suffer us to go out of doors—that observa-
> tion is my own—and was struck out by me this very rainy day,
> March 26th, 1759, and betwixt the hours of nine and ten in the
> morning.

This "winter's dream when the nights are longest" seems a
better summary of *Tristram Shandy* than all the many prefaces,
and justifies as well the whimsical and desultory method of
Sterne's writing, which leaves the reader "many an entangled
skein to wind off in pursuit of him through the many meanders and abrupt turnings of a lover's thorny tracts." Indeed, it
is hopeless to approach Sterne except as one who loves him,
for no one is more spoilt or more obviously ill at ease and
rattled by a hostile reader, while only a lover can really put up
with the whole bulk of Sterne's digressions, or endure with
patience the "simple propositions, millions of which are every

day swimming quietly in the thin juice of a man's understanding," and the majority of which certainly deserve to remain there.

When this is once said there is no further fault to find, and the reader can for ever bid farewell to Walpole irate beside the dead donkey or Thackeray impatient with the polyanthus that blew in December, and enjoy Sterne's beauties at his leisure. The intensity that Sterne lacked in emotion he retrieved in style, and there is hardly any diction in English so perverse and yet so adequately under control. The tempo of *Tristram Shandy*, for instance, must be the slowest of any book on record, and reminds one at times of the youthful occupation of seeing how slowly one can ride a bicycle without falling off; yet such is Sterne's mastery, his ease and grace, that one is always upheld by a verbal expectancy; slow though the action moves, he will always keep his balance and soon there will follow a perfect flow of words that may end with a phrase that rings like a pebble on a frozen pond. He is continually parodying the Elizabethans and using words with a fantastic ingenuity, as when he describes the jolting diligence:

> the thirstiest soul in the most sandy desert of Arabia could not have wished more for a cup of cold water than mine did for grave and quiet movements,

or

> "Where is Troy and Mycenae and Thebes and Delos and Persepolis and Agrigentum," continued my father, taking up his book of postroads, which he had laid down. "What is become, brother Toby, of Nineveh and Babylon, of Cizicum and Mitylene? The fairest towns that ever the sun rose upon are now no more."

Death, unreal enough here, is parodied once again in the sententious homily, alike redeemed by Sterne's sure command of gesture, that Trim delivers on the same lines in the kitchen. This control of literary emotion, the quality of *Lycidas* and Gray's *Elegy*, is what is most sustaining in Sterne's work today. We can enjoy his exquisite handling of eccentricity, and appreciate Walter Shandy's search for the "north-west passage to the intellectual world," with Tristram as a heaven-sent subject for experiment; we can hear him dropping his voice to talk of auxiliary verbs and fixing his listeners as securely as did the ancient mariner; we can see all the paradox of the household living together in uncomprehending amity while their prejudices conflict as uselessly as waves on granite. But it is the strange, bitter-sweet intensity emerging from Sterne's most artificial sentences that forms his particular signature, and which allays our suspicion of him, as it does his own vaunted fears. "I have never felt what the distress of plenty was in any one shape till now," the reader can exclaim with him as he reads of Toby "cast in the rosemary with an air of disconsolation that cries through my ears," or of Sterne's days and hours "flying over our heads like light clouds on a windy day" before his book is finished and ready "to swim down the gutter of time along with them."

There is no understatement in Sterne's style; no "slow, low, dry chat five notes below the natural tone," and his beauties are lost on those who contract intellectual hay fever from fine writing; yet the dullness of the subject, as in Flaubert, often redeems the style from cloying and enables one more to appreciate the hush of a set-piece like Uncle Toby's falling in love:

> Still—still all went on heavily—the magic left the mind the weaker. Stillness, with Silence at her back, entered the solitary parlor and drew their gauzy mantle over my uncle Toby's head; and Listlessness, with her lax fibre, and undirected eye, sat quietly down beside him in his armchair. No longer Amberg, and Rhinberg, and Limbourg, and Huy and Bonn in one year—and the prospect of Landen and Trerebach and Drusen and Dendermond in the next, hurried on the blood; no longer did saps and mines and blinds and gabions and palisadoes keep out this fair enemy of man's repose. No more could my uncle Toby after passing the French lines, as he ate his egg at supper, from thence break into the heart of France—cross over the Oyes and with all Picardie open behind him, march up to the gates of Paris and fall asleep with nothing but ideas of glory . . . softer visions, gentler vibrations, stole sweetly in upon his slumbers; the trumpet of war fell out of his hands—he took up the lute, sweet instrument! of all others the most delicate! The most difficult! How wilt thou touch it, my dear uncle Toby?

There is no question of how it is touched here, and the haunting somnolence of the whole chapter (6.35) seems almost to approach the tale of Palinurus, while as a lyric it is as complete as some of the short fragments of pastoral in *The Sentimental Journey* or the longer, birdlike raptures on the Town of Abdera.

This edition* consists of *Tristram Shandy*, *The Sentimental Journey*, the *Journal*, the fragments, one volume of letters and two of sermons. It is excellently got up and as presentable as it is easy to read. The large print redeems Sterne's tortuous system of asterisks and dashes and without altering their peculiar appearance. The reader indeed plunges into Sterne's work like a prince into an artificial and enchanted forest, "hoc nemus, hos lucos avis incolit, unica Phoenix," and in a moment the path narrows and the boughs thicken, and the sounds of the hunt recede as he struggles through thickets of dusty sycamore, lost in false metallic greenness, before he emerges angrily from the tangled breaks into one of Sterne's perfect sentences that opens before him like a moss-grown ride.

* *The Works of Laurence Sterne*, 7 volumes (Oxford).

The Ant-Lion

The Maures are my favorite mountains, a range of old rounded mammalian granite which rise three thousand feet above the coast of Provence. In summer they are covered by dark forests of cork and pine, with paler interludes on the northern slopes of bright splay-trunked chestnut, and an undergrowth of arbutus and bracken. There is always water in the Maures, and the mountains are green throughout the summer, never baked like the limestone, or like the Southern Alps a slagheap of gritty oyster shell. They swim in a golden light in which the radiant ebony green of their vegetation stands out against the sky, a region hardly inhabited, yet friendly as those dazzling landscapes of Claude and Poussin, in which shepherds and sailors from antique ships meander under incongruous elms. Harmonies of light and color, drip of water over fern; they inculcate in those who stay long in the Midi, and whose brains are addled by iodine, a habit of moralizing, a brooding about causes. What makes men divide up into nations and go to war? Why do they live in cities? And what is the true relationship between Nature and Man?

The beaches of the Maures are of white sand, wide, with a ribbon of umbrella-pines, below which juicy mesembrianthemum and dry flowers of the sand stretch to within a yard of the sea. Lying there amid the pacific blues and greens one shuts the eyes and opens them on the white surface: the vague blurred philosophizing continues. Animism, pantheism, images of the earth soaring through space with the swerve of a Ping-Pong ball circulate in the head; the woolly brain meddles with ethics. No more power, no aggression, no intolerance.

All must be free. Then whizz! A disturbance. Under the eye the soil is pitted into a conical depression, about the size of a candle extinguisher, down whose walls the sand trickles gently, moved by a suspicion of wind. Whizz, and a clot is hurled to the top again, the bottom of the funnel cleared, in disobedience to the natural law! As the funnel silts up it is cleared by another whirr, and there appears, at the nadir of the cone, a brown pair of curved earwig horns, antlers of a giant earwig that churn the sand upwards like a steam shovel.

Now an ant is traversing the dangerous *arête*. He sidles, slithers, and goes fumbling down the Wall of Death to the waiting chopper. Snap! He struggles up, mounting the steep banking grain by grain as it shelves beneath him, till a new eruption is engineered by his waiting enemy. Sand belches out, the avalanche engulfs him, the horny sickles contract and disappear with their beady victim under the whiteness. Mystery, frustration, tragedy, death are then at large in this peaceful wilderness! Can the aggressive instinct be analyzed out of those clippers? Or its lethal headpiece be removed by a more equitable distribution of raw materials? The funnels, I observe, are all round me. The sand is pockmarked with these geometrical death traps, engineering triumphs of insect art. And this horsefly might be used for an experiment. I shove it downward. The Claws seize on a wing, and the struggle is on. The fight proceeds like an atrocity of chemical warfare. The great fly threshes the soil with its wings, it buzzes and drones while the sand heaves round its propellers and the facets of its giant projectors glitter with light. But the clippers do not relax, and disappear tugging the fly beneath the surface. The threshing continues, a faint buzzing comes from the invisible horsefly, and its undercarriage appears, with legs waving. Will it take off? The wings of the insect bomber pound the air, the fly starts forward and upward, and hauls after it—O fiend, embodiment of evil! A creature whose clippers are joined to a muscle-bound thorax and a vile yellow armor-plated body, squat and powerful, with a beetle set of legs to maneuver this engine of destruction. The Tank with a Mind now scuttles backward in reverse, the stern, then the legs disappear, then the jaws which drag its prey. Legs beat the ground. A fainter wheeze and whirr, no hope now, the last wing-tip vanished, the air colder, the pines greener, the cone empty except for the trickle, the sifting and silting down the funnel of the grains of pearl-colored sand.

Nature arranged this; bestowed on the Ant-Lion its dredging skill and its cannonball service. How can it tell, buried except for the striking choppers, that the pebble which rolls down has to be volleyed out of the death trap, while the approaching ant must be collected by gentle eruptions, dismayed by a perpetual sandy shower? And, answer as usual, we do not know.

Yet the relationship between the Ant-Lion and the curving beaches of Pampelone suggests a parallel. This time at Albi. Here Art and Nature have formed one of the most harmonious scenes in Europe. The fortress cathedral, the Bishop's Palace with its hanging gardens, and the old bridge, all of ancient brick, blend into the tawny landscape through which the emancipated Tarn flows from its gorges to the Garonne. Here again one wanders through this dream of the Middle Ages, by precincts of the rosy cathedral where the pious buzz like cockchafers, to be brought up by a notice on the portcullis of the Bishop's Palace. "Musée Toulouse-Lautrec." Tucked in the conventional Gothic of the fortress is a suite of long rooms in which the mother of the artist, using all her feudal powers, forced the municipal authorities to hang the pictures of her son. Less fortunate than those of Aix, who refused Cézanne's request to leave his pictures to the city, the fathers were intimidated by the Countess into placing them in this most sacred corner, lighted and hung in salons whose decoration has concealed all traces of the unsightly past.

The concierge turns proudly to the Early Work—pastoral scenes and sentimental evocations of Millet—these he likes best; they are what the Count was doing before he left his home and was corrupted by the Capital. Then come the drawings, in which emerges the fine savage line of the mature artist, that bold, but not (as in some of the paintings) vulgar stroke, which hits off the brutality of his subjects, or the beauty of those young girls doomed to such an inevitable end. In the large room beyond are the paintings, a morgue of End of Century vice, a succession of canvases in which there is hardly daylight, and where the only creature who lives by day is the wizened little Irish jockey. The world of the hunchback Count is nocturnal, gaslit, racy, depraved and vicious; the shocked Albigeois who pass through the gallery are riveted by the extraordinary picture of the laundress who checks over with the *sous-maîtresse* the linen from her Maison. As one goes from picture to picture the atmosphere intensifies, Valentin le Désossé and La Goulue become familiars, and the lovely girls blur into the dark of the Moulin Rouge, where one distinguishes a favorite figure, the long, sad, nocturnal, utterly empty but doggedly boring face of "L'Anglais,"—some English habitué to whom constant all-night attendance has given the polish of a sentry at his post.

At the end of the gallery is a door before which the concierge smiles mysteriously, as if to prepare us for Pompeian revelations. He opens it, and we emerge on a small terrace. The sun is shining, the sky is blue, the Tarn ripples underneath. Beyond the ancient brick of the bishop's citadel and the arches of the bridge stretches the landscape of the Albigeois— foothills of green corn delicately crowned by pink hill villages, which merge into the brown of the distant Cevennes under the pale penetrating light of the near-south, the transitional Mediterranean. A lovely and healthy prospect, in which fields and cities of men blend everywhere into the earth and the sunshine. One takes a deep breath, when obstinately, from behind the closed door, one feels a suction; attraction fights repulsion as in the cold wavering opposition between the like poles of a magnet. Deep in his lair the Ant-Lion is at work; the hunchback Count recalls us; the world of poverty, greed, bad air, consumption, and of those who never go to bed awaits, but there awaits also an artist's integration of it, a world in which all trace of sentiment or decadence is excluded by the realism of the painter, and the vitality of his line. In the sunlight on the terrace we are given the choice between the world of Nature and the world of Art. Nature seems to win, but at the moment of victory there is something lacking, and it is that lack which only the unnatural world inside can supply—progress, for example, for the view from the Palace has not altered, except slightly to deteriorate, for several hundred years. The enjoyment of it requires no more perception than had Erasmus, while the art of Lautrec is modern, and can be appreciated only by those who combine a certain kind of aristocratic satisfaction at human beings acting in character, and in gross character, with the love of fine drawing and color.

Not that Lautrec was a great artist; he is to Degas what Maupassant is to Flaubert, one who extended the noble conception of realism by which a great master accepts the world as it is for the sake of its dynamism, and for the passive, extraordinarily responsive quality of that world to the artist who has learned how to impose his will on it. The world of Lautrec is artificial because it excludes goodness and beauty as carefully as it excludes the sun. But it is an arranged world, a world of melancholy and ignorance (figures melancholy because ignorant, patient in the treadmill of pleasure), and so the artist drags us in from the terrace because force and intelligence dominate that arrangement. And once back, we are back in his dream, in a hunchback's dream of the world; the sunlight seems tawdry, the red brick vulgar, the palace ornate; the crowd who stand in their tall hats gaping at the blossoming Can-Can dancers are in the only place worth being.

Now I understand the Ant-Lion. It is in Nature and with a natural right to its existence. There is no conflict between them; it is an advanced gadget in the scheme which includes the peaceful hills and the beach with its reedy pools of brackish water. Nor is there any opposition between Lautrec and the landscape of Albi. Albi was the oyster, and the contents of the museum are the Pearl. The irritant? The action of a physical deformity on an aristocratic, artistic but unoriginal mind which was happiest in the company of its inferiors, and which liked to be surrounded by the opposite sex in places where the deformity could be concealed by potency, or by the distribution of money. The result, a highly specialized painter, one of Nature's very latest experiments. And yet even that peaceful landscape was the home in the Middle Ages of a subversive doctrine, the Albigensian heresy; a primitive anarchism which taught that men were equal and free, which disbelieved in violence and believed in a chosen priesthood, in the Cathari who attained purity by abstinence, while they encouraged the Count's royal ancestors to come through excess and indulgence to heavenly wisdom. It was they who believed that the human race should cease to procreate, and so solve the problem of evil, who were massacred at Muret and Lavaur, and whom Simon de Montfort slaughtered with the remark, "The Lord will know his own." And the Heretics were right. Had a revolt against procreation spread outward from Albi the world would have become an empty place, nor would such obstinate human beings who survived have been driven to kill each other for living room, victims, for all we may know, of some deeper instinct of self-destruction which bids them make way for a new experiment, the civilization of the termite or the rat.

Much has happened since the summer. Today the Maures are out of bounds, the Museum closed, and many generalizations based on incorrect assessment of the facts fallen to pieces, but (since the operations of the Ant-Lion have now been extended) it seems worth while to recall that the statements on the life of pleasure which Lautrec took from his witnesses at the Tabarin and the Moulin de la Galette, and which he so vigorously recorded on canvas, are still available to the traveler of the future, and assert their truth.

Writers and Society, 1940-3

The position of the artist today should occasion general concern were it not that the whole human race seems threatened by an interior urge to destruction. He occupies, amid the surrounding dilapidation, a corner even more dilapidated, sitting with his begging bowl in the shadow of the volcano. What can be done to help him? In the event of the defeat of England and France, nothing. We are accustomed to the idea that there is no art worth the name in Germany and Italy (although Italy possesses a high standard of taste—witness her pavilions in recent exhibitions, and a group of interesting young painters), but we are less familiar with the fact that literature and painting are becoming more and more confined to the Western democracies, the countries where wealth and appreciation survive, and where the environment is friendly. A defeat of those countries would mean the extinction of the "liberal" arts in Western Europe, as much as of liberal opinions.

But in the democracies themselves the artist finds himself tolerated rather than appreciated. Unless he is a purveyor of amusement or a mouthpiece of official cliché he is there on sufferance, and before suggestions for the betterment of his condition can be made, we must consider his ideal status in life. Just as education cannot improve until the world for which children are educated improves, so the artist cannot receive his due until the society in which he lives fundamentally revises its conception of the objects of existence. Many people would accept the idea of a benevolent world Socialism as their political aim, a world in which all the resources were available to its inhabitants, in which heat and fuel and food were as free

as air and water, in which Marx's familiar definition of an ultimate civilization, "to each according to his needs, from each
according to his ability," was realized. But this world does
nothing for the spiritual life of humanity except to provide for
its inhabitants the material comfort and security which has
hitherto provided the point of departure only for the spiritual
life of the few. The final happiness of humanity must depend
on its capacity to evolve, on the use it makes of the capacity—
found only in human beings—of getting outside itself, of extending human consciousness to include the perception of
nonhuman phenomena, till it is not only aware of, but able to
transcend, the laws by which it is governed. Otherwise to
achieve a material Utopia, however difficult and desirable, is
still to doom the race to the disintegration of satiety, and to the
decay inherent in its own limitations.

There are certain types of human beings who are especially
equipped for the extension of human consciousness and for
the domination of the in-human world. They are the scientist,
the mystic, the philosopher, the creative artist, and the saint.
Of these, only the scientist receives the partial appreciation of
the world, because by subsidizing his researches the world
will grow the richer by such by-products as the aeroplane or
the telephone. Einstein and Freud, the physicist and the
psycho-analyst whose inventions were of doubtful value, were
exiled by their immediate public. These five types, the pure
scientist who uses measurement in his investigation of natural
laws, the philosopher who uses mind, the saint and the mystic
who make use of extra-sensitive emotional machinery, and the
artist with his dark lantern, form the aristocracy of a more
perfect world, in which the second order is composed of those
who, without seeking to expand human possibilities, work at
improving their condition. These would include the reformers
and administrators, the practical scientists and inventors, the
educators, the alleviators, the doctor and nurses, the practical
artists, actors, singers, journalists and entertainers, and the
men of law. Then would come the middle-men, the keepers of
order and the pillars of trade, and then the great mass whose
progress toward intelligence and happiness is the concern of

the others, and lastly the "blind mouths," the invincibly ignorant, the obstructive and destructive, the power-grabbers, the
back-street Napoleons, the incurable egoists and prima don-
nas, the gangsters, whether poor or rich.

While the greatest explorations of the world beyond our
boundaries have been made by scientists, never have writers
been so preoccupied as now with the investigation of spiritual
possibilities, and this alone justifies the artist's claim to the
respect of mankind. At the moment Wells, Maugham, Joyce,
Virginia Woolf, Huxley, Heard, Priestley, Eliot may all be
said to be working on it, and, among young writers, a deepening sense of spirituality characterizes the recent poetry of Auden and Spender. There is no escapism from a political
present in this, and the best analysis of it is to be found in the
opening chapters of Heard's *Pain, Sex and Time*, in which he
describes human beings as the prisoners in a submarine who
can only escape the fate of the unadaptable species by con-
centrating all their evolutionary energy on a dangerous and
difficult escape by a spiritual Davis apparatus. The value of
Picasso's *Guernica*, of the work of Proust, of the landscapes of
Cézanne, is to penetrate the darkness which surrounds the human camp fire, and reveal something of the landscape beyond
it. The artist lacks the training and the profound comprehen-
sion of a Freud or an Einstein, nor does he make a good philosopher according to academic standards, but his intuitive
intensity, his patient obsession, and the quality of his imagination entitle him to rank with the great disappointed Prome-
theuses of our age, those who are bent on changing the world
as inexorably as their rulers appear set on its destruction.

That is the ideal picture. And even there it will be noticed
that most of the artist-sages I have mentioned have accumulated their fame and fortune as artist-entertainers. Today the
scientist is subsidized, but the saint is expected to live by his
sanctity, the mystic on his mysticism, the artist by his popularity with his sitters, or with the twopenny libraries. Only
the entertainer receives his due, which nobody grudges him,
but which hardly compensates for the squalor and penury in
which the serious poet or painter is permitted to rot. Today

the most precariously situated in any society are that abandoned trio, the writer, the painter, and the liberal intellectual.
The intellectual is the most unfortunate, for he has no creative
power to absorb him, he is the Cassandra of our age, condemned to foresee the future and to warn, but never to be
listened to, nor to be able to profit from his foresight. Without
power and without money he has spent the last ten years
prophesying a disaster in which he will be the first to perish.
For the world has disproved the liberal axiom, that persecution defeats its object; it has been shown that an efficient secret
police, a concentration camp, or an invasion with tanks and
machine guns can silence any opposition, can stop the intellect
from questioning or the poet from affirming, and thus reduce
his historical potency to that of the Redskin or the Carib. In
any case, artists are easy to suppress; adaptability and subservience to the powers that be, a happy tropism, characterize
them as often as inflexible courage and integrity. They recant
more merrily than they burn.

What can be done to improve their position? They must,
like every defenseless minority, unite, and learn to help each
other, to present their case to the public. They must respect
their creative mission more than they do now, and they must
force their rulers to respect it, they must understand that their
position is desperate, and will become intolerable, that, outside the Western democracies, they are surrounded by enemies, while their friends are dwindling within them. Like the
Pet World, they are the first to feel the rationing and the
change in the standard of living; they will be hard hit if the
rentier class, on which many of them are remittance men, goes
under, nor is there any political party likely to come to power
to whom the artist and the intellectual are not at best but
means to be exploited.

But it is not easy for artists to help themselves. They are not
a class for whom co-operation is pleasant. Besides being envious and bitter, as are the economically underprivileged,
many often work better through an inability to appreciate the
art and aims of their contemporaries. When success permits
them, both writers and painters prefer to barricade themselves

deep in bourgeois country, like those birds which we admire for their color and song but which have divided our woods into well-defined gangster pitches of wormy territory. The artist and intellectual are a kind of life-giving parasite on the nonartist and the nonintellectual, and they are not to be criticized for being slow to combine with each other.

Therefore it is the public who must be educated, and the rulers who must be mollified; and here the artists can combine, for the smug hostility of the English is indiscriminately extended to all forms of art. In a number of *World Review* Sir Thomas Beecham brilliantly attacks the musical apathy of the nation; the attack must be sustained by artists and writers. The public must be asked to distinguish between the serious writer and the potboiling entertainer, between the poet and the prima donna journalist; the ruling class must be seduced into recognizing the importance of the great dollar-producing invisible export of our literature, not only the Mr. Chips, Gracie Fields, Peter Wimsey brands, which go wherever a bottle of Worcester sauce can penetrate, but the difficult, conscientious, and experimental work for which England and France are uniquely adapted, the delayed-action art and literature which survives indifference and slowly dominates—as Rimbaud or Hopkins have dominated—the creative minds of a generation. The idea of quality is an Anglo-French obsession; where the quality is not easily apprehended, the judges should be lenient. Here is a black list of some who are not.

Lord Beaverbrook. This nobleman injects into the jaunty philistinism of his papers a breath of the great art-hating, art-fearing open spaces. "You do not often see a writer mentioned on this page" complacently remarks an article in the proprietor's breezy biblical style. What information about art and literature there is in his papers is intelligently but stealthily purveyed by the younger gossip-writers. The popular press as a whole, when not content to ignore art and literature, fosters such absurd distinctions as that between highbrow and lowbrow, which has done more harm to both serious and popular art than any other false classification.

But there are other circles as much to blame. There are the

private and public schools which, under the cloak of a genial obscurantism, do so much to warp the talent that passes through them, and to harden the untalented in their own conceit. Then there is the Government, who, as Sir Hugh Walpole has recently pointed out, do nothing for literature, except to grant occasionally a miserable pittance for some half-starved veteran. Then there are the increasingly illiterate rich, often the descendants of those patrons who willingly gave a hundred pounds away, not for a picture or for a dedication, but to enable an artist to carry on. This practice is almost extinct, and a poet who was given a sum of money for being a poet rather than for writing copy for underclothes would be regarded as an undesirable. A useful remedy for this would be to let it be known that any benefactions already made to the arts, to the furtherance of research, or to the betterment of conditions in any form would be deducted from tax. But this implies a bureaucracy friendly to the arts, and we are a long way from it. Freud mentions tidiness, parsimoniousness, and obstinacy as the three characteristics of the Anal Type, and it is engaging that they also symbolize what is called the Official Mind.

Then there are the traitors among the artists themselves: the Publisher, with his Cold Feet; those who are ashamed of their vocation, who accept the enemy's estimate of it and become horse-painters or country gentlemen; those who clown for the philistines or who throw away their genuine talent through fear of being unpopular; or those defeatists who enjoy with Oriental relish the ignominy to which they are subjected and pretend that to starve and to be bullied by bank managers and passport authorities is part of the state to which artists are called, and which they must accept without question.

It is true that the artist is drifting into becoming a disreputable member of the lower middle classes waiting, in a borrowed mackintosh, for the pubs to open, but the privations which improve his talent must be imposed not by society but by himself—and any investigation of the artist's circumstances reveals that by far the most favorable conditions for him are neither at the top nor the bottom, but snug in the heart of the bourgeoisie, with a safe middle income, such as nineteenth century capitalism (the golden age of the remittance man) provided, and such as some other system will now have to be dragooned into paying.

An opponent particularly dangerous in these times is the near-artist, or Pinhead. Pinheads are a race apart, they are generally tall and bony, anal to the *n*th degree, but sometimes small and foxy. They are obsessed by a profound hatred of art and are prepared to devote their lives to gratifying it. To do this they occupy a fortified position, either at a university, or in an advanced political party, or as a publisher, and then proceed to castigate the artist, if from the university, on grounds of faulty taste or scholarship, if from a party, on grounds of political unorthodoxy or loose thinking. Every artist is an exhibitionist. The tragedy of a Pinhead is that he is a repressed exhibitionist, a guilty character whom a too strict censor is punishing for his wicked desire to undress and dance. The Pinhead is consequently attracted to the artist, whose generous immodest antics excite his own, but he is also consumed with envy and disgust for them. The ultimate enemy of art is power. One cannot desire both beauty and power, so the Pinhead, lacking as he does all aesthetic sense, usually obtains power and then becomes one of those Puritan commissars of the arts who see nothing in Picasso, who do not "understand" modern poetry, who examine art through the wrong end of the scientific telescope and see very little, or find no basis for it in Logical Positivism. They wear their Marxism like a hair shirt, and their triumph is when they have persuaded a painter to abandon color for abstraction, or a poet to write a political pamphlet, or to suppress a novel "for personal reasons." Fortunate is the artist today who is able to follow his invention without one of these poor bald old homo-puritan Pinheads blowing down his neck.

For the time being, the outlook is black. The painter, the writer, the liberal intellectual are in for a bad time; if they can co-operate, if they can assert themselves, if they can survive to the incredible period when nations are not afraid of each other, they will come into their own, for they have powerful allies. The working class, for instance, has not the deep-rooted animosity of the others toward artistic creation. Lawrence was not persecuted by it for his secession, but by his betters. The success of the *Penguin* library or of *Picture Post* or *The March of Time* show what a great potential benefactor an increasingly educated working class can be. Those who visited Azaña's Spain, our Lost Ally, will recall how pathetically friendly to culture were its masses, and there are many parts of the world where it is still a compliment to call someone an educated man. Even the Court is emerging from two centuries of Hanoverian apathy. Then the technocracies of the future are well disposed, the most powerful of all, the army and navy, show less of that hostility to art which is found in commerce and the Cabinet, and when the war is over they will hardly allow themselves to be quietly deprived of their influence, and handed a gratuity, as before. Revolutions do not happen in this country, but every now and then the public gives a great heave of boredom and impatience and something is done with for ever. When that happens, the artist must be on the crest of the wave, not underneath it, for art occupies in society the equivalent of one of those glands the size of a pea on which the proper functioning of the body depends, and whose removal is as easy as it is fatal.

Meanwhile the almond blossom is out, the sun shines, the streets look shabbier and the shops emptier, and the war slowly permeates into our ways of living. It is a war which seems archaic and unreal, a war in which eighty million people are trying to kill us, a war of which we are all ashamed— and yet a war which has to be won, and can only be won by energetic militant extroverted leaders who are immune from the virus of indecision. And the intellectuals recoil from the war as if it were a best seller. They are enough ahead of their time to despise it, and yet they must realize that they nevertheless represent the culture that is being defended. Abyssinian intellectuals, Albanian intellectuals, Chinese intellectuals, Basque intellectuals, they are hunted like the sea otter, they are despoiled like the egret. Our own are the last to survive. Granted the whole cumulus of error in the last twenty years, the greedy interlocking directorship of democratic weakness and Cabinet stupidity, then the war is inevitable. It is a war which dissipates energy and disperses friends, which lowers the standard of thinking and feeling, and which sends all those who walk near emotional, mental, or financial precipices toppling over; it is a war which is as obsolete as drawing and quartering; which negatives every reasonable conception of what life is for, every ambition of the mind or delight of the senses; and which inaugurates an era of death, privation, danger, and boredom, guaranteeing the insecurity of projects and the impermanence of personal relations. But there it is. We are in it: for as long as Hitler exists we must stay there. The war is the enemy of creative activity, and writers and painters are wise and right to ignore it and to concentrate their talent on other subjects. Since they are politically impotent, they can use this time to develop at deeper emotional levels, or to improve their weapons by technical experiment, for they have so long been mobilized in various causes that they are losing the intellectual's greatest virtues: the desire to pursue the truth wherever it may lead, and the belief in the human mind as the supreme organ through which life can be apprehended, improved, and intensified.

But they must also understand that their liberty and security are altogether threatened, that Fascism is against *them*. The Anglo-French artist and the intellectual are lucky to be alive. They must celebrate by creating more culture as fast as they can, by flowering like the almond blossom; for if they take a vow of silence till the war is over, or produce as little as do some of our lords of language, they will disappear: and their disappearance will provide further evidence that the human race has outstayed its welcome.

Several times a year articles arrive called "Where are our war poets?" The answer (not usually given) is "Under your nose." For war poets are not a new kind of being, they are only peace poets who have assimilated the material of war. As the war lasts, the poetry which is written becomes war poetry, just as inevitably as the lungs of Londoners grow black with soot. It is unfortunate from the military point of view that war poetry is not necessarily patriotic. When the articles ask "Where are the war poets?" they generally mention Rupert Brooke, because he wrote some stirring sonnets and was killed in action, though his poems were mostly nostalgic or amorous. They want real war poets and a roll of honor. That we lack patriotic poetry at the moment is a healthy sign, for if it were possible to offer any evidence that civilization has progressed in the last twenty years, it would be that which illustrated the decline of the aggressive instinct. This absence of aggressiveness, a danger in the war, is the healthiest of all symptoms for the peace, and makes possible the hope that, once we have had sufficient victories to remove self-confidence from our enemy, the awareness of the whole idiotic archaic process of war, with its boredom, its slaughter, its privations, and its general clumsy uselessness, may sweep over the world and induce people to give it up.

There is another aspect of the war and culture which it is refreshing to notice. Although there is very little new being written, there is a vast amount of old that is being forgotten. Blake told us to "drive our harrow over the bones of the dead," and such a silent revolution is happening. The vast top-heavy accumulation of learning, criticism, scholarship, *expertise*, the Alexandrian library of nineteenth century Liberal capitalism, is falling to decay. Human beings have a tendency to over-civilization, they cannot tear up old letters, they collect and catalog up to the edge of insanity. A burning of the books becomes at times a necessity; it was necessary to think Milton, or Pope, or Tennyson, or Proust, or James, bad writers, if writing was to go on. Before the war the stream of creative writing was choked with the leaves of exegesis; writers were bowed down with their intellectual possessions, with their names and dates, their sense of the past, their collection of unspoilt villages, their knowledge of cheese, beer, wine, sex, first editions, liturgy, detective stories, of Marx and Freud. It was a Footler's Paradise, a world in which, as on a long sea voyage, those came to the top who could best kill time. Culbertson, Torquemada, Wodehouse, Dorothy Sayers, Duke Ellington; the hobby dominated the art, the artists were artists in spite of themselves, or they worked in second-rate and inartistic material. In the realm of criticism the sense of the past dominated, the aunts and uncles of the great were exhumed, the load of material bore down on its inheritors, making them carping and irritable, while the ignorant but talented were forced to suffer for their ignorance, or waste their talent in catching up. The fear of democracy is the fear of being judged for what we are, instead of for what we have. Now that so many of us have no possessions, no houses or books or cars or notes, we find it less terrible than we thought. Let us also have no theories and no facts, let us forget our great names, who had so much more patience, talent, and leisure than we had, and declare a cultural moratorium. The sooner we accept the Dark Ages the faster they will be over. In the streets round this office, where the exposed green of fourth-floor bathrooms shines against the blue winter sky, an enormous Rolls Royce often passes. Each time one sees this mammoth of luxury, one wonders to whom it belongs; some fatcat of Bloomsbury? A ground landlord? A member of the Corps Diplomatique? But as it glides past it becomes transparent, and reveals on well-oiled bearings its only passenger, a neat wooden coffin. The limousine belongs to the last people who can afford it: the luxurious dead.

Invasion and You! As I write these words I hear on unexceptionable authority that the enemy is on his way, following that route, old as the seasons, by which he has brought off all his most audacious infiltrations. He landed at Europe's extreme south, the sandy scab of the Punto de Tarifa, and at once opened a pincer movement round the Atlantic and the Mediterranean seaboard, with a central thrust up the valley of the Guadalquivir. The cork woods of Algeciras, the cotton fields of Estepona, the blue sugar canes and custard apples of Almuñecar were the first to be penetrated, and in the west he reached that botanist paradise, the Sierra de Aracena and the Sierra de Monchique, at the same time as he encircled, on the east, the Contraviesa and the Gadór. The villages with their moorish walls, their goats and their aloes, surrendered on the hilltops. Soon after fell the provincial capitals, Huelva, Cadiz, Seville, Granada, Almeria, Málaga, Jaen, and Córdoba, all of Andalusia along the river, till the green corn sprouted on the white soil, the Sierra Morena became a creaming waste of cistus, and New Castile and Estremadura were threatened, until even the places with the coldest names, Fregenal, Tembleque, Javalambre, surrendered, and the Duke of Frias betrayed his title. And what has happened in the Peninsula will happen in France: the country is ripe for it, all resistance is undermined, the asphodel blossoms are frothing over the Eastern Pyrenees, the catkins are on the willows, the poplars of the west are covering with new green leaves their balls of mistletoe, the chestnut buds and the outdoor tables have climbed to the Loire. At the longest we have only a fortnight to prepare against the malice and ingenuity of our hereditary enemy, the unsound, unprogressive, uneconomical, unpatriotic, unmechanized, nonbelligerent Spring. "Make no mistake about it," said a High Official who is in his free time a Military Spokesman, "Spring will try us hard, but, buttressed in this island bastion, we will withstand him. The enemy will use gas. 'Aires, vernal aires,' 'Banks of violets,' 'Delicious South.' We have a filter for all of them. 'April is the cruelest month.' Green grass, blue sky, white clouds, primroses; everything will be tried that may distract our attention and sap our resolve. Don't look at 'em. Wear dark glasses. Stay put. What did Gamelin say to Ironside? 'Pas bouger!' Stay put!" "And bacteriological warfare?" "Ah, yes, Spring fever, glad you mentioned it, very important. When you get that pushover feeling, that false sense of well-being or euphoria, 'young man's fancy,' desire to receive or bestow affection, to crowd roads and railways, to change domicile; don't give way. If it gets too strong, consult your Mr. Sensible. And remember, now as always: win the Spring is win the war. We know what short shrift was meted out to the guzzlers in restaurants, now is the time to punish mental and emotional guzzling. We have got the measure of the food-hog. We must destroy the daydreamer, the memory-hoarder, the escapist, the beauty-wallah, the reading man. Then and then only, bastioned in this island buttress, will we be totally conditioned to total war, and when victory is ours, when the war has swept the world, when nobody anywhere gets more to eat than the poorest Spaniard or the most starving Chinese, when nobody can read or write, when nobody has anything, nobody wants anything, nobody does anything except work, work, work—when we've got the race war, the class war, the age war, the sex war, going simultaneously, when we look back at today as the happiest period of our lives, and when happiness is recognized everywhere for what it is, a dull and dishonest evasion of necessary pain; when we have reduced humanity to its lowest denominator—then the sacrifices we have made in conditioning ourselves against the daffodil and the blackbird will not have been worthless. Good morning. Stay Put." "Good morning. Go to it."

It is sad on a spring evening to walk through the bombed streets of Chelsea. There are vast districts of London—Bayswater, for example, or Kensington—which seem to have been created for destruction, where squares and terraces for half a century have invited dilapidation, where fear and hypocrisy have accumulated through interminable Sunday afternoons until one feels, so evil is the atmosphere of unreality and suspense, that had it not been for the bombers, the houses would have been ignited one day of their own accord by spontaneous combustion. Behind the stucco porches and the lace curtains the half-life of decaying Victorian families guttered like marsh gas. One has no pity for the fate of such houses, and no pity for the spectacular cinemas and fun places of Leicester Square, whose architecture was a standing appeal to heaven to rain down vengeance on them. But Chelsea in the milky green evening light, where the church where Henry James lies buried is a pile of red rubble, where tall eighteenth century houses with their insides blown out gape like ruined triumphal arches, is a more tragic spectacle. For here the life that has vanished with the buildings that once housed it was of some consequence: here there existed a fine appreciation of books and pictures, and many quiet work rooms for the people who made them. Here was one of the last strongholds of the cultivated *haute bourgeoisie* in which leisure, however ill-earned, has seldom been more agreeably and intelligently made use of. Now when the sun shines on these sandy ruins and on the brown and blue men working there one expects to see goats, and a goatherd in a burnous—*"sirenes in delubris voluptatis"*— pattering among them.

Meanwhile the bombs, which have emptied so many drawing rooms, have also been blasting the reputations made in them. Our literary values are rapidly changing. War shrinks everything. It means less time, less tolerance, less imagination, less curiosity, less play. We cannot read the leisurely wasteful masterpieces of the past without being irritated by the amount they take for granted. I have lately been reading both Joyce and Proust with considerable disappointment; they both seem to me very sick men, giant invalids who, in spite of enormous talent, were crippled by the same disease, elephantiasis of the ego. They both attempted titanic tasks, and both failed for lack of that dull but healthy quality without which no masterpiece can be contrived, a sense of proportion. Proust, like Pope, hoaxed his contemporaries; he put himself over on them as a reasonable, intelligent, kind, and sensitive human being, when his personality was in fact diseased and malignant, his nature pathologically cruel and vacillating, his values snobbish and artificial, his mind (like a growth which reproduces itself at the expense of the rest of the body) a riot of alternatives and variations, where both the neurotic horror of decision and the fear of leaving anything out are lurking behind his love of truth.

For Joyce there seems almost less to be said; Proust's endless and repetitive soliloquies are at least the thoughts of an intelligent man, while those of Joyce reflect the vacuous mediocrity of his characters; both relive the past to the point of exhaustion. Both are men of genius whose work is distorted by illness, by the struggle of one to see and of the other to breathe; both seem to us to have lacked all sense of social or political responsibility.

Yet we must remember that the life which many of us are now leading is unfriendly to the appreciation of literature; we are living history, which means that we are living from hand to mouth and reading innumerable editions of the evening paper. In these philistine conditions it is as unfair to judge art as if we were seasick. It is even more unfair to blame writers for their action or inaction in the years before the war, when we still tolerate in office nearly all the old beaming second-rate faces, with their indomitable will to power, and their self-sealing tanks of complacency.

It would not be unfair to say that the England of Baldwin, MacDonald, and Chamberlain was a decadent country— "Cabbage Land," "Land of lobelias and tennis flannels," "This England where nobody is well"—its gods were wealth and sport; from any unpleasant decision it flinched in disgust; though assailed by critics from the right and left, it still wallowed supinely in a scented bath of stocks and shares, race cards and roses, while the persecuted, who believed in the great English traditions of the nineteenth century, knocked in vain at the door.

Since Dunkirk we have seen the end of the political and military decadence of England. Whatever residue of complacency, sloth, and inefficiency there may be left, England is now a great power, and able to stand for something in the world again. When the war is over we shall live in an Anglo-American world. There will be other great powers, but the sanctions on which the West reposes will be the ideas for which England and America have fought and won, and the machines behind them. We had all this in 1918 and made a failure of it. The ideas expired in the impotence of Geneva. The machines spouted Ford cars, Lucky Strike, Mary Pickford, and Coca-Cola. The new masters of the world created Le Touquet and Juan les Pins, fought each other for oil and reparations, blamed each other for the slump, and wandered blandly and ignorantly over Europe with a dark blue suit, letter of credit, set of clean teeth, and stiff white collar. Fascism arose as a religion of disappointment, a spreading nausea at the hypocrisy of the owners of the twentieth century. It is important to see that fascism is a disease, as catching as influenza; we all when tired and disillusioned have Fascist moments, when belief in human nature vanishes, when we burn with anger and envy like the underdog and the sucker, when we hate the virtuous and despise the weak, when we feel as Goebbels permanently feels, that all fine sentiment is ballyhoo, that we are the dupes of our leaders, and that the masses are evil, to be resisted with the cruelty born of fear. This is the theological sin of despair, a Haw-Haw moment which quickly passes, but which fascism has made permanent, and built up into a philosophy. In every human being there is a Lear and a fool, a hero and a clown who comes on the stage and burlesques his master. He should never be censored, but neither should he be allowed to rule. In the long run all that fascism guarantees is a Way of Death; it criticizes the easy life by offering a noisy way of killing and dying. The key philosophies which the world will need after the war are, therefore, those which believe in life, which assert the goodness and sanity of man, and yet which will never again allow those virtues to run to seed and engender their opposites.

The greatest discovery we can make from this war, the one without which no Renaissance is possible, is what human beings are really like; what is good for them, what standard of living, what blend of freedom and responsibility, what mixture of courage and intelligence, heart and head makes for progress and happiness. We find out what we need by having to do without what we think we need. All words and ideas must be tested and built up again from experience. When we have learned what kind of life we want, what kind of man should live it, a Renaissance becomes possible. Here are some conditions for it.

An artistic Renaissance can only take place where there is a common attitude to life, a new and universal movement. By the time Anglo-American war aims have crystallized from the philosophy behind them, this should be in existence. But no political movement can have the art it deserves until it has learned to respect the artist. The English mistrust of the intellectual, the brutish aesthetic apathy and contempt for the creative artist must go. Bred of the intolerance of public schoolboys, the infectious illiteracy of the once appreciative gentry, the money-grubbing of the Victorian industrialists and the boorishness of the Hanoverian court, our philistinism (which also expresses the English lack of imagination and fear of life) should be made a criminal offence. There can be no dignity of man without respect for the humanities.

A Renaissance also requires a belief in spiritual values, for materialism distils nothing but a little rare dandyism, an occasional Watteau, and that will not be enough. The most sensible cure for materialism is a surfeit of it, which postwar science and economics should assure us. Yet we cannot get such a spiritual revival until the religious forces and the spiritual humanistic forces come to terms together, as did the Basque priests and the Spanish Republicans, as have Bernanos, Maritain, and the French Left. This is the hardest bridge to erect, but it will have to be done, and should not be impossible; for our civilization is impregnated with Christianity even where it seems unchristian; the foundations of our beliefs are those of Christianity and Greece, however those beliefs may have become distorted.

Regionalism, after the war, must come into its own. There is already a Welsh Renaissance in being; there is activity in Ireland and Scotland. Regionalism is the remedy for provincialism. Only by decentralizing can we avoid that process which ends by confining all art to the capital, and so giving it a purely urban outlook. England is one of those mysterious geographical entities where great art has flourished. We have the racial mixture, the uneven climate, the European tradition, the deep deserted mine-shaft. We must reopen the vein.

The greatest danger, let us hope, to the artist in the England of the future will be his success. He will live through the nightmare to see the new golden age of the West, a world in which no one will be unwanted again, in which the artist will always be in danger of dissipating himself in the service of the State, in broadcasts or lecture tours, in propaganda and pamphlets. As in ancient Rome or China, or modern Russia or U.S.A., the artist will have a sense of responsibility to a world-wide audience, which he must control. But that should be the only temptation for him in what will at last be a serious world, a world in which the new conquerors avoid the mistakes of the old and bring to the opportunities of victory the wisdom and dignity that they learned in defeat.

War journalism and war oratory have produced an unchecked inflation in our overdriven and exhausted vocabulary. Dictatorial powers to clean up our language should be given to a Word Controller.

The first act of the Word Controller (Mr. Shaw would be a good choice) should be to issue licences (like driving licences) to all journalists, authors, publicists, orators, and military spokesmen. Without such a licence it would be a criminal offence to appear in print or on the platform. The licences of all those found using the words *vital*, *vitally*, *virtual*, *virtually*, *actual*, *actually*, *perhaps*, *probably*, would then be immediately cancelled. This surprise action of the Word Controller would at once eliminate most journalists and politicians, and all military spokesmen. These words should be unmolested, and protected, for several years. The words *democracy*, *liberty*, *justice*, *freedom*, *jackboot*, *serious consideration*, *island fortress*, *love*, *creative*, and *new* should be suspended for six months, and the licence endorsed of anyone found using them. Lists (constantly brought up to date) of forbidden clichés with a scale of fines should be posted on every notice-board. The Word Controller, at any rate during the few hours of office before his powers turned his head, would be non-political. His aim would be to reshape the English language to its original purpose as an instrument of communication, and an invention for expressing thought. Thus the expression "The town is virtually surrounded" would become "The town is, or is not, surrounded," "vital necessity" would become "necessity," and a scientific machine for weighing words would demonstrate that while such terms as "coronary thrombosis" are as full of content as when first minted, other verbal coins are worn too thin for the public slot-machine and must be withdrawn from circulation. As he became more autocratic and more like other controllers he would find out that there is a connection between the rubbish written, the nonsense talked, and the thoughts of the people, and he would endeavor to use his censorship of words in such a way as to affect the ideas behind them, or, rather, he would give priority to statements of fact over abstractions, and to facts which were accurate rather than incorrect.

Applying himself to art, the Word Controller will remark that no great literature can be made out of the split-mind which is now prevalent. The unadulterated aggressive instinct creates its art; the detached and meditative attitude is also valid, but blended they destroy each other and produce the hotchpotch of standardized, lukewarm, muddled propaganda through which we are floundering. An artist must be in the war or out of it. He must go to America or to Ireland or to prison if he wants to write, or else fight and read the newspapers: the moment he becomes undecided, well-meaning and guilty, he is Hamleted out of service as a writer; however much he concentrates on the Atlantis of the past, or the Utopia of the future, he will be made to suffer in the present. For we live in an imperfect world: history punishes the ignorant and the mistaken: the wicked are left to punish themselves.

In the times in which we live a writer should not be able to put down more than two or three lines without making it obvious whether he has anything to say. The Word Controller, by banning the verbal camouflage of those who doubt, who twist, who are on the make, or who hope for the best, would clarify propaganda and leave literature safely where it belongs, in the hands of the very sane, or the very mad.

We are all prisoners in solitary confinement: when at last we give up trying to escape through mass emotion or sexual union there remains for us only the wall alphabet in which we tap our hopes and thoughts. Nobody should learn this alphabet who can abuse it, who jerry-builds the English language as if it were the English countryside, who wastes the time of his fellow prisoners by tapping out stale rhetoric, false news, or untranslatable messages, and so brings a perfect achievement of civilization into confusion.

What are the three characteristics of Puritan verse? Poverty of imagination, poverty of diction, poverty of experience—the characteristics, in fact, of Puritan prose and Puritan painting. If we examine an imaginary poet, for example, John Weaver, "whose austere verse, eschewing all tricks and facile solutions, so clearly depicts the dilemma of the intellectual in the period of *entre deux guerres*," we find that, of any age between twenty and forty, he is "the child of professional parents, was educated at a major university and a minor public school, has Marxist sympathies, and is at present trying to reconcile communism with religion, pacifism with war, property with revolution, and homosexuality with marriage." He will have been published in *"New Verse, New Writing*, and *New Directions*, and will have produced one volume of poems [I am quoting from the Introduction] called *The Poet's Thumb*." "John Weaver is most actively interested in politics and took part in several processions at the time of the Spanish War. Indeed, his particularly individual imagery discloses an extreme awareness of the contemporary situation.

> Come, Heart, we have been handed our passports,
> Love's visa has expired.
> The consulate of Truth is closed
> And virtue's signature no longer valid,

and many other poems show that he was among the first to await, like MacNeice, 'The Gunbutt on the door.'"

For an interesting fact about Weaver is that, though several years younger than Auden and MacNeice, he is completely dominated by them. He imitates their scientific eroticism, their Brains Trust omniscience, without the creative energy of the one or the scholarship of the other, just as he assimilates the fervor of Spender and the decorum of Day Lewis into his correct, flat, effortless, passionless verse. And it is Weaver, now at an O.C.T.U. or in the Air Force Intelligence, who is responsible for some of the badness of war poetry, who used to write "Comrades we have come to a watershed," and now talks about "Love's tracer bullets," even as his brother Paul, who once painted ascetic winter streets for the East London Group, is responsible, with his fossilized landscapes of tanks and hangars, for some of the badness of War Art. An element of Puritanism is always present in a good artist, but in a minute quantity. The Puritan poet of the thirties has been all Puritan, he has been afraid of life and repelled by it, and so has acquired no experience to digest; caught in the pincer-movement of the dialectic, he has picked up the modern vice of arrogant oversimplification, nor has he developed his imagination by reading or travel. As a person he is incomplete and therefore as an artist sterile, the possessor of a desiccated vocabulary which is not his own, but which he has timidly inherited from his poetic uncles. Auden and Spender made use of this vocabulary to chasten the Georgians, and, having served its purpose, it should have long been discarded. Such poets as John Weaver, who exist rootless in the present without standards or comparisons, are doomed to swift extinction, for the war has proved a godsend to bad artists, allowing them to make honorably, and for their country's good, that surrender to normality which in peace-time is only accepted after a long and terrible struggle.

There will always be poetry in England: it is the concentrated essence of the English genius, distilled from our temperate climate and intemperate feelings, and there will always be critics who claim that it is dead. But poetry is going through a bad patch. The sophisticated intellectual poetry of the twenties is exhausted. Poetry was taken down a cul-de-sac to get away from the Georgians, and now it has to find its way back. The academic socialism of the thirties was not strong enough to revive it, we are waiting for a new romanticism to bring it back to life. This will happen when the tide of events sweeps round the lonely stumps on which our cormorants have been sitting and gives them a fishing-ground—for one of the difficulties of John Weaver has been the isolation of his mood from the uneasy fatuity of between-war England, and another, the hitherto sheltered, unwanted, uneventful character of his life. Now that events have caught up with his prognostic and he is no longer out of step with the rest of the population, his work will be deepened and simplified.

This process is only just beginning. As an industrial nation we lag behind: our factories are not the largest, our generals not the wisest, but as an ancient civilization that is not neurotic, where thought once more is correlated with action, and which fights for its beliefs, we should, in those invisible exports like poetry and fine writing, be in a position to lead the world.

The death of Sickert, unhonored, almost unnoticed, reminds us that we live in a philistine country. Camden Town, Dieppe, Paris, Bath, Brighton, Venice, the places he loved and painted, recall to us that art once was international, that the greatest English painter could yet stem off from the art of France and Italy, could be as English, and as Continental, in the piazza of St. Mark's, or a South London music-hall; by the Porte Saint-Denis, or by a brass bedstead off the Tottenham Court Road. Looking at his best pictures, such as the French and Venetian landscapes shown at the Redfern in 1940, or the *Granby Street* shown recently at the National Gallery, we are conscious not only of superb technique, but of the sacred moment, of the absorption of the painter in what he sees, which by talent and patience he is able to communicate. It is the communication of this sacred moment which constitutes a work of art. The vision might be insane, like Van Gogh's, or ponderous with sanity as in Degas or Cézanne, but it existed. Our tragedy is to live at a time when it does not. In a continent which is exterminating itself, a country which is socializing itself, a world that is destroying its standard of living, the existence of the great artist, the free personality, of the solitary smouldering creative figure whose thought and imagination challenge eternity, becomes more and more precarious. If we want great art after the war we must restore the freedom of Europe to our artists, and also guarantee them economic security. The defects of War Art arise through the personality of the artist being shrunken by being fitted in to the military structure, and by his being denied the freedom of Europe, and so cut off from the masterpieces of the past. The sacred moment which the artist is too self-pitiful to communicate or too shallow to perceive has vanished.

As the war goes on, intimations of the kind of world that will come into being after the war become clearer. It will be a world in which the part played by the English will be of supreme importance. In fact, one might say that the whole of English history, tradition, and character will be judged in the future by how we rise to the occasion of the postwar years. England will find itself in the position of one of those fairy tale princes who drift into a tournament, defeat a dragon or a wicked knight, and then are obliged to marry the king's daughter and take on the cares of a confused, impoverished, and reactionary kingdom. That kingdom is Europe, the new dark continent which must perish if it cannot attain peace and unity, and which is yet in a constant eruption of war, economic rivalry, and race-hatred.

England is the weakest of the three great postwar powers: unless it has behind it a strong, united Europe it must be overwhelmed by America, either involuntarily or in a tug-of-war with a Communist Europe and Russia. If England fails to unite Western Europe it fails as a world power, if it succeeds and can hold a balance between American Capitalism and Soviet Communism, defending Western Europe from the reactionary imperialism of one and the oppressive bureaucracy of the other, it will prove itself the greatest and wisest middleman in History. To achieve this, England must resurrect that political wisdom for which it was once famous and produce a scheme for Europe which will incorporate the socialist idealism of Russia with the humanist individualism of America and which will lead toward the gradual atrophy of European race-hatreds and nationalist pretensions. Every European war is a war lost by Europe; each war lost by Europe is a war lost by England. When the struggle for our lives is over, the struggle for our standards of living will have only begun, and our standard includes the liberty to go where we like, stay where we like, do what we like and pay how we like.

To achieve and deserve this leadership will require courage and wisdom, with an appreciation of the complexity of European affairs and a sense of trusteeship for the European spirit which we are still far from possessing. But Europe is more than a political concept, it is still the chief breeding-ground of ideas, the laboratory, the studio, and the reference library of the world's art, science, and imagination. If England is to help Europe, it must assume the cultural as well as the moral and political protection of Europe, it must restore liberty of expression, economic security, and mental audacity to the world of art and ideas.

This is a most difficult task, because England—the only country in Europe where a man may still paint or write very much what he likes, and find a market for it—is nevertheless a philistine country. Worse still, the philistinism is an essential factor in the national genius, and forms part of the stolid, practical, tolerant, pleasure-loving, responsibility-taking English character. There is no other civilization in the world so old, so mellow, so wise, and so polite which can yet so happily dispense with respect for learning, love of art, or intellectual curiosity. The French are saturated in these things; the Americans worship culture even though they are inclined to do so for the wrong reasons; the English, to whom will fall the task of restoring paper and ink and paints and canvases to occupied Europe, dissipate their aesthetic instinct in ball games, card games, dart boards, and football pools. Even the culture of England in wartime is a most haphazard affair.

A visit to the French Exhibition at the National Gallery (the best picture show since the war started) brings the problem closer. Why is not English painting better? Why do we raise Sargent instead of Renoir, Munnings instead of Degas, Pre-Raphaelites instead of Impressionists? The climate of the Ile de France is hardly different from that of Southern England: many of the scenes chosen by the Impressionists are not in themselves beautiful; their gardens are inferior to English gardens; their tall, red-roofed villas almost as ugly as ours; their magical light is not peculiar to the Seine valley. What have they got that we lack?

Can the question be answered sociologically? The art of the Impressionists and their followers is the supreme flowering of bourgeois society. Many of the Impressionist painters were well-to-do people; they were not only secure in their patrons, they were secure in their investments; all through their lives several of them never had to worry about money. This is not all-important, but it is a great addition to a sense of vocation. They were also secure in their aesthetic philosophy. They believed in devoting a long life to the worship of beauty and the observance of Nature. Politics, society, family were all represented, but they were not the important things. There was a certain Chinese humanism about them; they loved their friends and painted them admirably in their favorite surroundings, they enjoyed, in moderation, the good and simple things of life, they were not ashamed of man's place in Nature, nor of urban civilization with its alcoves and café-tables, nor of old age with its arm chairs and book-shelves. If the highest expression of their art is such a landscape as the Renoir of Argenteuil, a vision of watery paradise, or the Seurat of a wood or the Pissarro of La Roche-Guiyon, there are two smaller pictures which perhaps betray more of their secret. One is a tiny Manet of a dark bistro-interior, which reveals all the poetry of city life; the other is Vuillard's portrait of Tristan Bernard in his garden. The garden is hideous—grass with a flinty rose-bed against the brick of a Normandy villa—and the bearded poet is rocking back in it on a cane chair. The effect is of a civilization as sure of itself as a poem of Li-Po or Po-chüi. One sees immediately that the English could not paint like that because Kipling or Meredith or Henry James would not rock about so irreverently—because the English imperialist bourgeoisie, though just as stable as the French, had that extra moral and mercenary conscience, had too much money, too much sense of duty, and so could never give off such a light and heavenly distillation as Impressionism. Whistler and Sickert succeeded because they were not English, and at the price of a Harlequin defence-mechanism which never left them.

When we restore the arts then to Europe, we can do one of two things: we can attempt to restore to bourgeois civilization sufficient order and stability to enable the cream of art to come to the top, or we can develop a civilization which will permit a new art to arise. If we adopt the second course instead of try-ing to put back the nineteenth century Humpty-Dumpty on the wall, then we must radically change our attitude to art here: we must give art a place in our conception of the meaning of life and the artist a place in our conception of the meaning of the State which before they have never known. Never again must our artists be warped by opposi-tion, stunted by neglect, or etiolated by official conformity.

The danger is that the State will take over everything; the State everywhere has discovered its inexhaustible source of wealth—the working hours of the individuals who compose it. In some countries the discovery is a few years old, here it is only two—and woe betide us if we had not made it—but more woe still if we cannot unmake it, if we cannot break the tyranny of State, here and everywhere else, after the war, or never again will we have an hour to call our own. Being a small State-owned country we will have to work twice as hard to compete with the large State-owned countries, like some wretched Cock-house at school whose members never dare break their training. For the State-owned nation will have nothing in common with the dream of international socialism, since it will always be in total competition with the others, and therefore have to ration and overwork its members while taxing both their work and their earnings. Its weapons will be propaganda, bureaucracy, and a secret police with every man his own informer. For every child born there will be one to spy on it—for life. Our dossiers will open with the first words we say! And this will continue till a revolution is made and world Stakhanovism succumbs to the cry of "Liberty, Ine-quality, and Inefficiency."

The effects of State control are already apparent in art.

We are becoming a nation of culture-diffusionists. Culture-diffusion is not art. We are not making a true art. The appreciation of art is spreading everywhere, education has taken wings, we are at last getting a well-informed inquisitive public. But War-Artists are not art, the Brains Trust is not art, journalism is not art, the B.B.C. is not art, all the Penguins, all the C.E.M.A. shows, all the A.B.C.A. lectures, all the discussion groups and M.O.I. films and pamphlets will avail nothing if we deny independence, leisure, and privacy to the artist himself. We are turning all our writers into commentators, until one day there will be nothing left for them to comment on. "A great work by an Englishman," wrote Hopkins, "is like a great battle won by England. It is an unfading bay-tree." How true that is today, and how tragic if *les lauriers sont coupés*.

This year we celebrate the centenary of Henry James, a man who, if he had never written a novel, would be considered the first of short story writers, and if he had never written a short story, the noblest of letter writers, and if he had never written anything would by his talk alone be known as a great man. Today he is more than that, for he has become the symbol of a certain way of life, a way that is threatened not only by the totalitarian enemy but by the philistine friend, and yet a way which in an unpropitious age has helped masterpieces to be created and artists to live; the path of what James called "the lonely old artist man," who is so easily destroyed and so quite irreplaceable.

Thirteen years ago Edmund Wilson, in his *Axel's Castle*, attacked this outlook. He criticized all the great individualists—Joyce, Proust, Valery, Yeats, and Mallarmé—on the ground that they had carried the investigation of the ego to a point at which it had become unbearable, and he asserted that the great literature of the future could only arise from a corporate and socialist view of art as the expression not of the individual but of the mass. This literature has not yet arisen, and ten years later, in *The Wound and the Bow*, Edmund Wilson seems to have returned to the conception of the artist as an isolated wounded figure, as different from the social realist as is a huge lightning-stricken oak from a Government conifer plantation.

It is difficult to prove that any age has been propitious for the artist; Socrates was condemned to death, so were Seneca and Petronius, Dante was exiled, the age of Louis XIV was one of both civil and religious persecution; the nineteenth century, as the lawsuits against Flaubert, Baudelaire, Hugo, etc., show, was not much better; and in the twentieth century there are whole tracts of Europe where to be a writer is to invite a firing-squad. "Silence, exile, and cunning" are the artist's lot, and, exquisite though his happiness will be when his public, educated at last, mobs him like a film star, we may be wiser to assume that, for our lifetime, "silence, exile, and cunning" it will remain. For this reason it is necessary to keep the memory of these giants like Henry James and Flaubert, or Baudelaire and Mallarmé, always before us, even if we never read them, for they are the saints of modern bourgeois art, whose virtues—sensibility, intellectual courage, renunciation, and consecrated devotion—emanate even from the mere storing of their books in our rooms. They are sacred relics which we need not too often disturb.

The tragedy of our civilization is that a specialized education has segregated an advanced artistic minority from the main body as with a tourniquet. In the interests of the masses (and therefore by his logic, of art), a Communist may be willing altogether to wash out this "advanced" literature and, from a level open to all, to make a fresh start which, with an educated proletariat, might lead in fifty or a hundred years to a new and happy art made by artists as integrated in the State as were the builders of medieval cathedrals in the Church. But anyone who does not accept the overriding authority of the proletariat must feel that, since art has advanced so far, even if down the wrong turning, it is too late to turn back. In relation to his public the artist of today is like the spelaeologist of the Peak or of the Causses of Southern France; he walks at first with his companions, till one day he falls through a hole in the brambles, and from that moment he is following the dark rapids of an underground river which may sometimes flow so near to the surface that the laughing picnic parties are heard above, only to re-immerse itself in the solitude of the limestone and carry him along its winding tunnel, until it gushes out through the misty creeper-hung cave which he has always believed to exist, and sets him back in the sun.

On Re-reading
Petronius

I first read Petronius when I was at school and though I had no idea what most of it was about, I had two editions by the time I left, two more a year later and two more since then—yet it was only the other day I read him for the first time since that elm-heavy summer thirty years ago. I was perfectly right. It is a very great book.

Not great—magical perhaps is a better word and, what is even rarer, it is a humane book. Imagine that nothing at all survived of our literature but one or two poems and histories and a long novel like Proust's of which but a few disjointed fragments reached posterity and formed the only record of how we talked or loved or ate or felt about poetry or painting or friendship or money. Imagine a few remarks of the Duc de Guermantes or some head waiter as all that was known about our pronunciation, together with a dinner party at Mme Verdurin's coming down intact and a crepuscular glimpse of Swann and Odette, Marcel and Albertine. How our posterity would pore over every sentence! Yet, though in Petronius we possess a fragmentary Roman Proust, how few have studied him; how little known to generations of boring novelists is the secret of his rapidity of style, of his visual clarity, biting dialogue, intellectual fastidiousness or of the haunting fugacity of the picaresque—that art which keeps characters on the move from waterfront to waterfront, brothel to palace, adventure to adventure. "I dimly saw Giton standing on the curve of the road in the dark and hurried towards him." Thus we are introduced to one of the principal characters. The analysis of such a book could help many young writers to give movement and montage to their characters, the lilt of transience which is the breath of readability.

There are at least four Petroniuses whom for convenience we have rolled into one: (1) the historical Petronius of Tacitus, (2) the author of the *Satyricon*, (3) the author of the prose fragments and (4) the writer of some separate poems. The fragments (preserved by grammarians) indicate that he came from Marseilles, a place, as Tacitus said, "where Greek refinement and provincial puritanism meet in a happy blend" but the fragments are all dated very much later and one of the puzzles about this extraordinary book is that it would seem, even in antiquity, to have been very little known. The *Satyricon* itself tells us nothing about the author except that he is looking at low life from a standpoint which is above it and that he is very interested in a poet who must be Lucan. Trimalchio tries to sing a song by Menecrates whom Nero greatly admired. The Petronius of Tacitus is a historical figure, the artist in extravagance, the dandy who idled into fame and who after being an efficient proconsul in Bithynia became the arbiter of Nero's pleasures until he aroused the jealousy of Tigellinus. When he found the plot against him had succeeded, he committed suicide at Cumae, "the finest death" according to Saint-Evremont "in all antiquity." "The reflection arises at once," writes his editor, Mr. Michael Heseltine, "that, given the *Satyricon*, this kind of book postulates this kind of author."

We have then a picture of a great nobleman such as haunted Versailles or perhaps like Charles II's Lord Rochester, of a poet and lover of low life who finds time between governing Asia and amusing his Imperial master to write an enormously long work of which we possess fragments only of Books 15 and 16. There may have been twenty-two like the *Odyssey*. He belongs to a strange world: to the little group of writers who effected the transition between the Augustan age and silver Latin. The next generation, Tacitus, Suetonius, Juvenal, Martial, the younger Pliny and Quintilian came through the tunnel of the terror into the prolonged sunlight of the Antonines but our group all come to violent ends. Seneca, Petronius, and Lucan were forced by Nero to kill themselves,

Persius died very young and the elder Pliny perished in the eruption of Vesuvius. As far as the arts are concerned, the Rome of the Julio-Claudian emperors was only at the very beginning of decadence. There is nothing *fin-de-siècle* about Petronius, rather an enormous gusto. What was the *Satyricon's* real subject? Is Trimalchio's banquet a parody of Nero's entertainments or is it written especially to amuse him together with the hostile criticism of Lucan? Is it a *roman à clef?* I think myself that, like James Joyce's *Ulysses*, it had something to do with Greek literature; the fragments we possess all deal with Greek-speaking cities, especially those which are on or near the sea. There are lecturers called Agamemnon and Menelaus, a charmer named Circe with a maid called Chryseis. The four main characters and a great many minor ones have Greek names and a theme runs through it like a parody of epic doom: The Wrath of Priapus. Encolpius (whose name means "cuddlesome") is the narrator, a young man with literary ambitions and all the physical graces; high-tempered but quick to forgive and with a deep and constant affection for his young companion Giton and some kind of tie with a rival, Ascyltos, who might be described as a neurotic hearty. There are also men of learning who gravitate around the three adolescents and several insatiable ladies of fashion. Though the tone is homosexual, the *Satyricon*, as Saint-Evremont remarked, is the only classical work where *galanterie* appears in the relation of the two sexes as in the delicious exchange of letters between Circe and Polyaenus. Encolpius has been in trouble at some time: "I fled from justice, I cheated the arena, I killed my host," he moans, and Ascyltos calls him "a filthy gladiator who was kicked out of the ring, one who strikes people in the dark." He has robbed a shrine of its sacred images and he is constantly profaning the mysteries of Priapus who punishes him by a psychological impotence which he remedies with difficulty only to infringe the sacred rites once more. When the story opens we find him near Naples at Cumae; later on, the three learned scallywags sail round to Croton on the instep of Italy. Fragments allude to Marseilles and Egypt and there is a reference to a quarrel in the Porch of Hercules which indicates

Rome. Encolpius, I think, was an Epicurean: Epicurus is mentioned as "divine" and as the "very father of truth." And when Encolpius has to take another name he chooses Poly-aenus, a disciple of Epicurus while only an Epicurean could proclaim "at all times and in all places I have so lived that I have spent each day as if it were my last." I think we were meant to appreciate a conflict between the sunny reasonable sceptical attitude of Encolpius and the Dark God whom he provokes and the God's priestesses with their superstitious rages and horrible medicines.

The novel is written in alternate passages of prose and verse which produce a peculiar effect rather like a staccato recitatif which leads up to an aria but the verse arias are not as memorable as the prose recitatif; they are less tense and vivid; good minor poetry and nothing more. I would like to give an example of the prose which holds, I think, something of the magic of this novel. Encolpius is speaking:

> I came into a gallery hung with a wonderful collection of various pictures. I saw the works of Zeuxis not yet overcome by the defacement of time, and I studied with a certain terrified wonder the rough drawings of Protogenes which rivalled the truth of Nature herself. But when I came to the work of Apelles the Greek which is called the One-legged, I positively worshipped it. For the outlines of his figures were defined with such subtle accuracy that you would have declared that he had painted their souls as well.
>
> I cried out as if I were in a desert, among these faces of mere painted lovers, "so even the Gods feel love. Jupiter in his heavenly home could find no object for his passion, and came down on earth to sin, yet did no one any harm. The Nymph who ravished Hylas would have restrained her passion had she believed that Hercules would come to dispute her claim. Apollo recalled the ghost of a boy into a flower, and all the stories tell of love's embraces without a rival. But I have taken for my comrade a friend more cruel than Lycurgus himself."
>
> Suddenly, as I strove thus with the empty air, a white-haired old man came into the gallery. His face was troubled but there seemed to be the promise of some great thing about him; though he was shabby in appearance, so that it was quite plain by this characteristic that he was a man of letters, of the kind that rich men hate. He came and stood by my side. . . .
>
> "I am a poet," he said, "and one, I hope, of no mean imagination. . . ."

"Trimalchio's supper" is rather top-heavy for the book as we possess it. I think the important character is Encolpius and he has to be kept in constant motion. What a prose writer he is—of a fine lady's tears "when this designing rain had ceased." *"Tam ambitiosus detumuit imber"* and his Existentialish reflection on the drowned merchant, who happens to be the only virtuous character. "Make a fair reckoning and you find shipwreck everywhere" *(si calculum bene ponas, ubique naufragium).*

Petronius died in A.D. 66 and Herculaneum was engulfed in A.D. 79. There was just time for the *Satyricon* to find its way into one of those libraries in the "Sirenland" which its author loved. If the world cared anything for literature, we might live to see a sustained effort of the United Nations to excavate all that the lava has buried—buried yet not always burned—and perhaps then the missing volumes will turn up. I know that I would sacrifice any cargo the space-ships bring back from Venus or all the minerals on the moon for a sight of those rolls in their charred cases, and for a few more episodes of these aesthetes in adventure. In the picture gallery Eumolpus said that in an age that worshipped drink, sex, and money there could be no more great art; people would no longer take the trouble to write well and would rather earn a gold ingot than own an Old Master. Like many whose gaze is fixed with longing on the past, he was apt to find himself looking into the future.

The Elegiac
Temperament

One of the unsolved mysteries of poetry is the life cycle of its
various forms. In our time we have seen the sonnet and the
iambic blank verse line totter and possibly fall; the last century
watched the heroic couplet get into difficulties and suddenly
fade away. Two facts seem to have some bearing on what happens. A great poet can exhaust the possibilities of the meter
which he chooses; one age may find one meter appropriate to
it which a succeeding age will reject. The blank verse iambic
and the sonnet belong to all periods, but Milton, Keats,
Wordsworth, Tennyson, may be said to have pre-empted
them from less talented aspirants; the heroic couplet is a meter
suited to the temper of the eighteenth century only to be rejected by the nineteenth.

But the lifetime of such meters has been but three or four
hundred years, a mere fraction of the life of the hexameter
from Homer to Claudian or of the elegiac couplet, longest
lived of them all. Sixteen hundred years divide the Greek couplet of Mimnermus from Cometas and the same huge span
links the first Latin elegiacs of Catullus with the spate of his
imitators in the Italian renaissance. The hexameter may well
be the "stateliest measure ever moulded by the lips of man";
the couplet has proved the more enduring. Often have I fan-
cied, though this kind of statement can never possibly be
proved, that the rise and fall of the elegiac couplet bears some
relation to the waves breaking on the Greek islands with the
retreating backwash that follows. "The surge and thunder of
the *Odyssey*" has been celebrated—what of the less positive assertion and milder withdrawal of the Mediterranean sea? It is

not impossible that listening to this eternal susurrus awoke in these island peoples an instinctive poetry of flux and reflux expressed in the alternation of the long and sonorous with the short and melodious line. *Litore sic tacito sonitus rarescit harenae*—"so on the quiet shore does the sound of the wave-swept sand grow fainter." Certainly a preponderating quantity of all elegiac poetry has been about the sea. The cruel and calm rhythms of the great mother, so vivid in the many Greek epigrams on seafaring, on headland shrines and drowned sailors, provide an immense stock of metaphor even where the subjects are largely pastoral or amorous in content.

I believe that the elegiac meter is unique in this, that alone of all verse forms it has produced a certain character type. When we compare the true masters of elegiac poetry, leaving out those who employed the form only for epigrams, we find distinct resemblances between Theognis and Mimnermus in Greek, Tibullus, Propertius, and Ovid in Latin, or Meleager, the Syro-Greek who immediately preceded them. All these poets consider physical love as the particular end of their existence and the majority have proclaimed their creed defiantly. Literary fame comes a close second, a fame which is achieved through a mixture of love and learning. All in addition suffer from profound melancholy and nostalgia. Many profess an inclination for the simple pastoral life (and an aversion to the military) though generally they spend their time in Rome. They are unhappy in their love affairs and invite deception and infidelities for which they blame the cupidity of their often ill-chosen mistresses, rather than admit their own inconstancy. They are addicted to alcohol and to rich patrons, while showing unexpected flashes of malice, envy, and cynical understanding. All are terrified of old age, prone to self-pity, obsessed by death, and apt to die young. They are in fact poets whose character is inferior to their talent and this, perhaps, is what keeps them out of the first rank with Horace, Catullus and Vergil, or the Greek tragedians.

They are *poètes maudits*, dandies ingrown into their pose, and if thus committed to the second rank, then their genius and their air of modernity, with perhaps that vein of stoicism which was never far from the surface in the ancient world, keep them very high in it. As long as people will wish to hear about love and the pleasures of the country, and while young lovers "long to talk with some old lover's ghost," and while the old keep an ear for music and a warm corner for grace, then these boasters will retain exactly the immortality to which, living, they laid claim. We all know the charming lines that a late Victorian addressed to Mimnermus in Church; I do not know how familiar it is that Sainte-Beuve put Tibullus in a sacred position among writers and that his ideal of happiness was to read Tibullus with a young girl in the country. And there was another French critic—or was it the same one?—who remarked that "every elegiac spirit is a scoundrel."

When we come to the situation of the Latin elegiac poet a complication appears. The Greek elegiast formed part of an accepted tradition, his Roman successor had to borrow the meter, transpose it into Latin and make it popular; he had also to borrow Greek mythology and make that his own, and he had even to justify to Roman eyes the somewhat discreditable stance of the elegiac amorist. This inclined him to be self-conscious and to appear somewhat of a pedant, flattering Caesar or giving a mythology lesson when he should have remained in wistful wanton mood. Erudition, the literary vice which a rich culture imposes on its poor relations, mars all the Latin elegiasts, including, alas, Catullus. In fact the tragedy of Latin poetry is the onus of its debt to Greece; it is as if no English poetry could survive except that which derived from the French. I do not think we are enough aware of the super-human and exhausting effort which the Roman poets made to create a native poetry out of Greek idiom and mythology. Only two hundred years separate the extreme limits of good Latin poetry between the birth of Lucretius and the death of Martial, while the golden age, the age of Catullus, Vergil, Horace, Tibullus, Propertius, Ovid, is compressed into one lifetime between about 60 B.C., when Catullus was twenty-four, to Ovid's banishment in A.D. 8. In that time, especially in the ten years at the center of it, all Greek culture was absorbed and regurgitated. The masterpieces of Latin poetry made their appearance—and the rot set in. The Latin ode almost vanishes with Horace; the magnificent tapestry of the Vergilian hexameter, the smooth narrative brilliance of Ovid's, the grace and *brio* and sadness of the elegiasts make their hail and farewell.

The appearance of Tibullus on this stage was of the briefest. He was an impoverished young squire whose life was largely passed in the little court of Messalla, a Roman nobleman whom he loyally followed on one military expedition; he died aged about thirty-five in 19 B.C., the same year as Vergil. He was of a gentle, lovable disposition, handsome and careful of his appearance. He certainly won the esteem and friendship of Ovid, and probably of Horace. He loved two women: the first called Delia (her real name was Plania) and who was apparently married, but unfaithful both to her husband and to him; and the second Nemesis, who was probably a courtesan. The secret of his appeal is that he was a quietist, like our own poet Collins. There is in him an exquisite taste, a sincerity, a freshness, which avoids the traps his successors fell into—one might compare him with Watteau as opposed to Pater or Lancret, with Propertius as Boucher, Ovid as Fragonard or Greuze, but such comparisons are waste of breath. Mackail dismisses him in a terrible sentence—"He stands easily at the head of Latin poets of the second order. In delicacy, in refinement, in grace of rhythm and diction, he cannot easily be surpassed; he only wants the final and incommunicable touch of genius which separates really great artists from the rest of the world." His poetry has a strange gaiety, a colloquial simplicity, yet it is also melancholy and affecting. Those four lovely lines to Delia:

> *te spectem, suprema mihi cum venerit hora,*
> *te teneam moriens deficiente manu.*
> *flebis et arsuro positum me, Delia, lecto,*
> *tristibus et lacrimis oscula mixta dabis*

> May I behold you when my last hour comes, and dying, clutch you with my failing hand. You will weep, Delia, and when they lay me on my funeral pyre you will give me kisses mixed with tears

echoed round the ancient world (Ovid quotes a line in his memorial poem) like a stanza from Gray's elegy. But there was another side to Tibullus: a passion for the simple rites of the peasant's religion; for spring festivals and harvest-homes. In this way he is like our own Herrick and Marvell.

Propertius was born somewhere about 50 B.C. at Assisi; it is nice to think that he may have had some Etruscan blood. (He mentions their "ruined hearths" with feeling.) He was destined for the Bar but deserted it for poetry. He was tall, pale, thin, delicate, vain of his appearance. Today we should perhaps call him a masochist, he boasted that his vice was to be perpetually in love. That was the whole pattern of his life, his only function, and he reveled in his terrible subservience to the body of his beautiful mistress. No other wars for him. The one deep passion of his life was for a courtesan called Cynthia. Her real name was Hestia; she was tall and fair, with long hands and a lovely walk.

> *fulva coma est, longaeque manus et maxima toto*
> *corpore . . .*

He constantly refers to her as *docta puella*, a learned girl, and tells how in a low voice she would recite his verses or dance, play and sing for him. She was violent in temper, jealous, revengeful, unforgiving, fond of money, unfaithful (though perhaps not more than he was), and died in great misery. They had several long quarrels and we are inevitably reminded of the relationship between Jeanne Duval and Baudelaire. Seen at this distance they appear as a lonely and ill-starred couple of life-long lovers and combatants, and yet for all their tale of shared death-beds, Cynthia was as far from Propertius as Delia from Tibullus when the end came. When he was a very young man Propertius published his first book, *Cynthia*; the first two lines are a revelation:

> *Cynthia prima suis miserum me cepit ocellis*
> *contactum nullis ante cupidinibus.*

> Cynthia to my great undoing first ensnared me with her eyes—
> though no other passion had ever touched me.

His whole genius as a poet, his cast of mind as a lover, flowers in one marvellous poem:

> *Scribant de te alii, vel sis ignota licebit.*

ludet, qui sterili semina ponit humo.
omnia, crede mihi, tecum uno munera lecto
auferet extremi funeris atra dies.
et tua transibit contemnens ossa viator,
nec dicet, cinis hic docta puella fuit.

Let others write of you or let you be forgotten, let him praise you who will plant seeds in a sterile soil. Believe me every gift of yours is consumed on a narrow bed when the black day comes and the traveler who spurns your bones as he goes on his way will never cry "this dust was once a learned girl."

Propertius is quite unlike any other Roman author who has gone before. He is tempestuous, oriental as his master Meleager, and like his other master, Callimachus, often intolerably erudite and brilliant. He burst on the world at the age of twenty-one with a complete mastery of the Greek elegiac meter, and he gave to his Latin a glassy and metallic radiance that had never been seen before. The critics called it *Blanditia*, enchantment, and found it irresistible. Consider this ravishing and so Greek texture, drugged with lovely names, compact of learning and lubricity—it is the beginning of his third poem. This is Butler's translation:

Like as the maid of Cnossus lay swooning on the desert strand whilst the bark of Thesus sped swiftly away, or as Andromeda, child of Cepheus, sank into her first sleep, freed at last from her hard couch of rock, or as the Thracian maenad, no less foredone by the unending dance, lies sunk in slumber on the grassy banks of Apidanus, even so, meseemed, did Cynthia breathe the spirit of gentle rest, her head propped on faltering hands, when I came dragging home my reeling feet, drunken with deep draughts of wine, and the slaves were shaking their dying torches in the gloom of night far spent.

Qualis Thesea jacuit cedente carina
languida desertis Gnosia litoribus:
qualis et accubuit primo Cepheia somno
libera jam duris cotibus Andromede:
nec minus assiduis Edonis fessa choreis
qualis in herboso concidit Apidano:
talis visa mihi mollem spirare quietem
Cynthia, non certis nixa caput manibus,
ebria cum multo traherem vestigia Baccho,
et quaterent sera nocte facem pueri.

The reading of this first book of Propertius is an outstanding literary experience. One is altogether enraptured by this strange gusty music, by the glimpses of Greek mythology, of drunken quarrels and heavenly reconciliations, of the moon gliding across the window over Cynthia's bed, of her basking among the sun bathers on the beach at Baiae, of a group of weekend guests, wine glass in hand watching the fast skiffs and slow barges drift under the woods along the Tiber, of Propertius battering in vain at the locked door of her whom he called his mother and sister, his only home and parent, while the little cold breeze of early dawn blows across him as he lies outside; a moment he will often recall with feeling. Among his loveliest lines are those which describe the pool of the nymphs where Hylas was sucked under.

> At last the children of Orithyia, Pandion's daughter, retired discomforted, and Hylas, alas! went upon his way, went to be the wood-nymphs' victim.
> Here beneath the peak of Arganthus' mount lay the well of Pege, the watery haunt so dear to Bithynia's nymphs, o'er which from lonely trees there hung dewy apples that owed naught to the hand of man, and round about in a water meadow sprang snowy lilies mingled with purple poppies.

> *Iam Pandioniae cessit genus Orithyiae:*
>   *a dolor! ibat Hylas, ibat Hamadryasin.*
> *hic erat Arganthi Pege sub vertice montis*
>   *grata domus Nymphis umida Thyniasin,*
> *quam supra nullae pendebant debita curae*
>   *roscida desertis poma sub arboribus*
> *et circum irriguo surgebant lilia prato*
>   *candida purpureis mixta papaveribus.*

The remaining three books of Propertius, though stored with fine things, lack the magical impetus of the first.

His last poem, a magnificent ode of consolation to his friend Paullus, was put into the mouth of his wife who had just died and shows that Propertius was learning to feel and live for others—he had burst his bonds and thrown off his stifling neurotic obsession with lust and glory. In the poem the dead wife asks her husband to look after the children, to hide his grief from them, while they in turn must not mention her in front of their new stepmother, if he remarries, nor do anything which may upset his old age if he stays single. Enough for him must be the nights he wears out with his memories of her—*sat tibi sint noctes quas de me, Paulle, fatiges*—the dreams in which she seems to confront him again. And when he talks to her image, he must breathe every word as though to one *responsurae*, who "was about to reply."

On this query we leave him, on this doubt about human survival which was all that the Roman world permitted itself in the rare moments when it went beyond a flat negation. He himself died, probably of consumption, in 15 B.C., aged thirty-five, and prematurely gray, he tells us, and old. He left a splendid posterity—this antique Baudelaire—yet one cannot read him without a sense of despair, not on his personal account (he writes too well for that) but from the appalling gloom and emptiness of the late pagan world. What an intolerable ennui surrounded them when once they lost their religion, when the shining deities, Zeus and Apollo, Pan and Dionysos, Artemis and Athena, Orpheus and Hermes became empty symbols; how quickly youth passed, and how little consolation to those whose temperament was extravagant were the Stoic's grim courage or the Epicurean's frugal caution! Only the worship of the Emperor, the germ of totalitarianism, remained open to them, or the private religion of the Mistress, the sacred *egoisme à deux*, with its tears, sighs, scenes and ecstasies, its multiplication of deceit and its dread of old age. All poets who have made a trial of it have ultimately found sexual passion liberating as a means only, not as an end. *Sunt a pud infernos tot milia formosarum.* "So many thousands of beautiful girls have gone to the grave." A great love is a great doom, an unconscious method of self-destruction and the foreboding, as of *Tristan* or *Pelléas*, which haunts the couplet is no accident.

> *Sic nobis, qui nunc magnum speramus amantes, forsitan includet crastina fata dies.*

Propertius, for all his learning and passion, is condemned to the monotony of his own limited personality, a monotony which is precisely that expressed by the elegiac meter. He was a weary and precocious adolescent in a tired world—for I think it is beyond doubt that the unlimited indulgence in promiscuous sexual intercourse from the earliest age had a more deleterious effect on the constitution of the pagan body than wealth or luxury or wars, and thus assisted the insidious progress of oriental religions. The Romans of the Empire, through physical excesses, were stunting the growth of the spirit. A change had to come. There is a line from a poem long attributed to Tibullus which was scrawled on the plaster of a house in Pompeii as the molten pellets were raining down. I do not believe this referred to a mortal Delia any more than Valéry's *Tes pas, enfants de mon silence* . . .

> *Tu mihi curarum requies, tu nocte vel atra*
> *lumen* . . .

Thou art the repose of my troubles; even in night's darkness thou art my light.

In Quest of Rococo

One can describe a passion only in terms of passion. Many years ago I noticed that certain works of art brought tears to my eyes. Lines of Horace, Dryden, Rochester, Pope, the last paintings of Watteau, Mozart's *Voi che sapete* while in the summer of 1938 two small buildings—Palladio's Roman theatre at Vicenza and the Amalienberg pavilion outside Munich—were added to my list. What had they in common? Perfection or the ideal of perfection—a lyrical conception of humanity, a response to all that is transitory and fugacious, a calligraphy of farewell. I have, of course, been more deeply moved by that art which springs from the tragic sense of life, I have been fissured by romanticism, spellbound by Baudelaire or Wagner yet I have come to believe that there exist also an unselfconscious gaiety, an acceptance of human limitation quite as significant as the romantic protest and no less congenial an incubator of works of art. The Amalienberg, a royal huntman's bagatelle which Mr. Sacheverell Sitwell calls "a supreme monument of the period," was the first rococo I had seen, for of my youthful visits to Potsdam and Dresden I have no clear recollection. Here in that round room of blue and silver with its long mirrors and hanging chandelier was a poetry of living, a revelation of intimacy and delight that I had not thought possible.

> *Ci-gît, dans une paix profonde,*
> *Cette dame de volupté*
> *Qui pour plus grand sûreté*
> *Fit son paradis en ce monde.*

So familiar are we today with the rococo that it comes as a

surprise to learn that the cult is very recent. To love and understand the first half of the eighteenth century would seem a prerogative of the present.

"Rococo is a term applied specifically to a type of ornament, style or design belonging to the reign of Louis XV and the beginning of the reign of Louis XVI. In general, it applies to everything that is old and out of fashion in the arts, literature, costume, manners, etc. 'To like the rococo,' 'to fall into the rococo,' 'that is very rococo.'"—*Dictionary of the Académie Française*, 1842.

"Rococo. A debased variety of the Louis XIV style of ornament proceeding from it through the degeneracy of the Louis XV. It is generally a meaningless assemblage of scrolls and crimped conventional shell-work wrought into all sorts of irregular and indescribable forms, without individuality and without expression. The term is also sometimes applied in contempt to anything bad or tasteless in decorative art."— *Chambers*, 1882.

The first allusions to the new style referred to it as "*goût moderne*" or "*goût du siècle*" (Blondel, 1738). The expressions "Pompadour," "Rococo," came from the studios and were first used by Maurice Quai in 1796-97. In 1828 Stendhal writes: "Bernini was the father of that bad taste called in the studios by the somewhat vulgar term Rococo." Victor Hugo is the first to admire it: "The belfries of the Cathedral [in Nancy] are Pompadour pepper pots . . . the square of the Town Hall is one of the gayest, prettiest and most complete of any rococo square I have ever seen . . . it is a marquise of a square" (1839).

In 1836, the word appeared in English, in 1843 Burckhardt uses the term in Germany whose art historians have slowly succeeded in stripping it of its pejorative meaning. Since it is now international I am in favor of keeping it, not of bringing forward the French *rocaille* which is apt to create a false distinction, being used by French apologists in order to disassociate their country from the extreme consequences of its own invention. *Le style Louis XV* is more familiar but imposes an artificial chronology.

We must now face the problem of what rococo is and where

it came from. Mr. Fiske Kimball of Philadelphia has settled this question in his monumental *Creation of Rococo* (1943). He proves, I think, conclusively, that the movement begins as a breaking up of the massive baroque of Louis XIV into contrasting asymmetrical curvilinear forms, an invasion of architecture by decoration until (as in some German churches) decoration creates its own architecture. He is thus at variance with the German theory that rococo is but another name for late baroque, which came as an organic development from Italy to Vienna and Vienna to Germany. Nor does he believe that it was evolved by the Nordic "will-to-form" nor by direct observation from nature nor from the properties of new materials such as stucco and porcelain. Its genesis is in the arabesques of Bérain which Lepautre translated into decoration and which were carved in hard oak paneling around Versailles about 1699, the artists being stimulated by demands for the new Palaces of Marly and Meudon, for the King's *oeil-de-boeuf* room and chapel and for the night nursery of the young Duke of Burgundy. By close study of the original drawings and builders' accounts Mr. Kimball has sorted out the possessors of inventive genius from the hierarchy of official craftsmen: the great precursors Bérain and Lepautre who soften up the heavy baroque, Oppenordt and Vassé who lead the first attack under the Regent, Audran and Watteau with their arabesques, Pineau, Meissonier and Lajoue, the brilliant general staff of *le style pittoresque* in the victorious years 1730-35, and finally Babel and Cuvilliès. We watch the somewhat finicky *Régence* line struggling with the heavy shapes of doors and windows, furniture and paneling and gradually controlling the shape of the object itself until by the late 1730's every article in use; view and vista, palace or summer house, temple or tomb begin to be subjugated to the line of ebb and flow, to the convolutions which govern both water and the shells and rocks which are formed by it and the sprays and tendrils which drink it in.

The reaction begins after 1750 when the younger Cochin, the antiquarian Caylus and the Abbé Leblanc take up the cudgels in the name of French good taste, when the youthful

Marigny sets out on his Italian journey and returns with all
Pompeii, when Servandoni's St. Sulpice and Soufflot's Pan-
théon arise, when Gabriel replaces Boffrand and, above all,
when England is victorious in the Seven Years War (1759).
Pedantic England, led by Burlington and William Kent, had
side-stepped the rococo and gone straight from classical Palladio to neoclassical Adam (who returned from his Dalmatian
trip in 1759)—with Horace Walpole's neo-gothic as the only
deviation! The rococo was not a movement to outstay its welcome, there was no decadence, its latest achievements are
among its best; rather was it displaced by the overwhelming
reality of the new vision of the classical world which had ma-
terialized in all its simplicity and strength in Herculaneum,
Spalato, Greece and Asia Minor before the eyes of eighteenth-
century travelers. The magic of the rococo is in that it is a
European movement of spontaneous originality, a true *style
moderne* arising between two backward-looking periods, the
grandiose baroque and the academic neoclassical.

Mr. Kimball builds his case on correct dating and the personality of artists; for him it is the last years of Louis XIV
(Bérain, Lepautre) and the *Régence* (Oppenordt) together with
the decorative wood-carving of Pineau after his return from
Russia (1727) and the genius of the architect and goldsmith
Meissonier that are truly important. The hôtels de Toque-
laure, de Touilly, de Soubise and some rooms at Rambouillet
(all before 1740) form what he considers the peak. The soft
paste of Vincennes and Sèvres, St. Cloud and Mennecy,
the faïences of Strasbourg and Marseille, the tapestries of
Boucher, the lacquers of Martin, the engravings of Gravelot
and Eisen, the bindings of Pasdeloup, the silver of Thomas
Germain, the snuff boxes, knickknacks and even the whole
gamut of Louis XV furniture he sees as secondary artefacts of
the architect's creation.

He also minimizes political and economic influences although it is clear that the rococo was an explosive affirmation
of the private life, an escape from Versailles; its great phase
opens with the stage of the reign of Louis XV referred to as *les
premières infidélités*. In fact, the whole of Europe needed libera-

tion from heroics and the rococo is an art sponsored by leading personalities; the Regent Orléans, Louis XV, Stanislas of Lorraine, Frederick the Great, Maria Teresa, Madame de Pompadour (*"Reine et Marraine du rococo,"* Goncourt), Count Brühl, the Schönborns, the Wittelsbachs and Spanish Bourbons, the Margraves of Bayreuth and Ansbach which caught on immediately with the humblest of their subjects and united all in a masquerade of gaiety and pleasure terminated (as is every European aesthetic movement) by an internecine war.

Let us suppose that the imagination of some studious American is kindled by the Bouchers in the Frick collection (formerly in Madame de Pompadour's collection at Crécy) or his tapestries in Philadelphia from the oval room of the hôtel de Soubise and that he decides on a journey to learn more about the civilization that produced them. Where should he go?

He might stop off at London's Wallace collection where he can study the basic rhythms among some of the finest furniture, china, and paintings of the period. England was to the fore in three minor examples of the rococo: the so-called Chippendale furniture, Lamerie's silver and the china of Chelsea and Bow, so luxurious, fresh and countrified. London's masterpiece was the interior of Ware's Chesterfield House decorated by the best French workmen (1749) and demolished in 1934. There is however a surprising amount of stucco, often by Italian workmen.

In France he would visit the *petits appartements* at Versailles, now in course of restoration, the hotels already mentioned (especially Soubise) and various rooms, doorways, and staircases of the Faubourg St. Germain and the Place Vendôme. But Paris, despite the Place de la Concorde, is not the capital of rococo; the opposition to the style there was strong and constant. Mr. Kimball quotes from Cochin's secret memoirs: "At that time there were any number of makers of bad ornaments who enjoyed the most brilliant reputation; like Pineau who ruined all the architecture of the period with his sculpture, like La Joue, who was a rather mediocre painter of architecture and who designed some miserable ornaments which sold with the greatest rapidity. It was M. Openor, the architect,

who began the flight from the good taste of Louis XIV's reign
. . . and things went from excess to excess reaching the height
of absurdity which we know only too well."

This attitude persists two hundred years later when in his
Architecture Française (1951) M. Hautecoeur writes of the crea-
tors of the *style pittoresque* in words which might easily be applied to cubists or surrealists: "When we find some form of
exaggeration in France, we must discover its perpetrators and
these perpetrators are Oppenordt, son of a Dutchman, Meissonier, born in Turin, Pineau, who returned after a long stay
in Russia, Cuvilliès, born in Hainault or Lajoue, who was not
an architect, but a painter."

If, then, there is so little left, it is not entirely due to the
guerre aux châteaux of the Revolution but because the style was
itself revolutionary, abandoned later by the fashionable and
the conservatives through a mistaken worship of straight lines
and moderation. Only in Nancy, fief of Louis XV's Polish
father-in-law Stanislas, is there a rococo architectural ensemble, one of the loveliest agglomerations north of the Alps,
where Heré's planning is enriched by Lamour's exquisite ironwork. The situation there and in Germany was quite different
from France; the country was proud of its rococo and the
princelings were seldom in a position to redecorate, while
their descendants regarded the splendid rooms which they inherited as a symbol of a golden age. Here the devastation is
entirely due to the last war and irreparable damage has been
done in the three capitals of the rococo, Würzburg, Munich,
and Berlin. Those who find Cuvilliès' surviving work in Munich cloying or overcrowded should study the vanished decoration of the golden hall of Charlottenburg and Voltaire's
rooms in Sans-Souci, the work of the more sober yet no less
gifted Johann August Nahl. Of Hoppenhaupt's silver room in
the Potsdam Neue Schloss (removed in its entirety by the
Russians), Mr. Sitwell writes, "the boiseried rooms decorated
in silver are quite inconceivable in their loveliness; many of
the doors have a wavelike waterfall treatment which is again
echoed in some of the wall panels in two shades of gold, or
with a greenish silver that gives variety to that more conven-

tional shade of moonlight. Pictures by Watteau can surely have never found a more congenial environment."

I do not think that the ecclesiastical rococo of southern Germany can be attributed entirely to French sources. There would seem to have been some instantaneous fusion around the lake of Constance of French, Italian, and Austrian influences among the deeply religious yet pageant-loving mastercraftsmen and wood-carvers of Württemberg and Bavaria. The impulse to build or renovate large monasteries spread westward from baroque Vienna along the Danube and the Inn while the stucco-workers came up from the Ticino and the court architects returned from Paris with new books of ornament and design.

In central Germany the position is clearer. Here the great family of Schönborn, Prince Bishops who traded and mediated between Vienna and the West, controlled Würzburg, Bamberg, Mainz, Speyer, and Trèves. In 1719 Johann Philip Franz, succeeding to his estates, announced to the alarm of his Chapter that the building bug *(Bau-Wurm)* had got him. He chose as his architect a young captain of engineers who had just returned from the Turkish wars where he had visited Vienna and Belgrade. This specialist in fortifications and cannon foundries became one of the great architects of the eighteenth century, a large, generous, serene and triumphant personality. Johann Baltazar Neumann's first plans for the Residence of Würzburg were made in 1719, and in 1723 he was in Paris consulting Boffrand and Robert de Cotte. The Palace took shape from 1720-44 and included much exquisite decoration by Bossi, a card room in green lacquer, a mirror room with Chinese ceiling in gold, gray-blue, and white with a black marble chimneypiece, all destroyed by incendiaries in the raid of March 16th, 1945. The great staircase hall and three other sumptuous rooms remain. The Tiepolo ceiling in which Jupiter's envoys carry the good news of the establishment of Apollo's reign to the four continents almost makes one forget the war damage by their airy serenity. For Tiepolo (as can be seen from his "rooms" in the "Ca' Rezzonico") is the quintessence of the spirit of the rococo in painting. (It is misleading to talk about "a rococo painter" but there are clearly some artists such as Boucher, Huet, Pillement, Longhi, Devis, and Laroon who abandon themselves to the movement as wholeheartedly as the great porcelain modellers Kändler and Bustelli.)

Besides work on seventy churches, Neumann was also in charge of artillery, fortifications, waterworks, roads, bridges, factories in all the Schönborn dominions; he even held a scientific chair at the university and left behind an unfinished theoretical textbook. He also built Schloss Werneck outside Würzburg and the lovely staircase hall at Bruchsal near Karlsruhe, an apricot palace once full of exquisite rococo work by Feichtmayer, now badly damaged. Two chapels for the Schönborns in the Würzburg Residence, and attached to the cathedral, lead on to his other masterpiece, the pilgrimage church of Vierzehnheiligen (1743 onwards) between Bamberg and Bayreuth. Every aspect of this church is grand, warm, welcoming, and lovely. Twin towers of golden stone rise above the fields and woods while all within is light and harmony. Like Wies (though much larger), it is a church in which every square foot is exquisitely decorated.

Feichtmayer's confessionals suggest sedan chairs or boxes at the opera and (as at Wies) the main feature is an oval shrine with a colonnade of colored marbles built in the oval center of the church and removing emphasis from the altar at the end of the nave. This feature distinguishes those churches which are built in the eighteenth century from those which are merely renovated, for the oval form satisfies an aesthetic need of the age. Neumann is thus a link between French rococo and south German church interiors though in Tiepolo's fresco (1753) it is neither as a pilgrim nor as a court architect that he chooses to be represented but as a full colonel of artillery meditating beside his cannon.

The Goethean genius of Neumann subdivides into two in the brothers Zimmermann who came from a family of craftsmen in Wessobrunn. Johann Baptist (1680-1758) went forward in court circles as a painter and decorator and drove back from Paris to Munich in a golden coach while Domenico

(1685-1766) became an architect for the humbler monasteries, living all the time in the country at Landsberg or Wies, where he died quietly at the age of eighty-one. He was uninstructed and could hardly get his drawings correct, using wood and stucco to solve problems in stone while his more worldly brother was working with Cuvilliès on the "rich rooms" of the Munich Residence.

Yet at Gunzbourg, Steinhausen, and Wies he produced works abounding in natural genius. Steinhausen is a small pilgrimage church near Biberach in Württemberg with a ceiling fresco by J. B. The church is elliptic in shape and decorated in white, pink, beige, and pale blue; even the lettering of "Jesus" is rococo while the circular fresco of Mary as Queen of Heaven, full of green paradisal scenery, is bounded by a Versailles vision of a fountain in a glade. These upward leaping fountains (there is another in the Asam fresco of St. Maria Victoria in Ingolstadt) suggest the rococo title page of Meissonier or the imaginary ornaments of Cuvilliès and Lajoue. Yet Steinhausen is but a preparation for Wies (near Füssen), the supreme achievement of the two brothers. The outside is plain: fields, dark woods, and distant mountains (often under snow) frame the lonely scene so that the contrast within is all the more striking, a pilgrim's dream of pastel perfection. The painter to the Munich court and the rural master builder have here fused all their separate capacities. Such interiors are impossible to describe, they must be illustrated by color and diagram and then a prolonged visit must be undertaken. Wies, Vierzehnheiligen, Zweifalten, Birnau, Ottobeuren, Weltenburg—these have to be studied, then seen, then relearned over again for no words can evoke both light and space and color. J. B.'s ceiling at Wies is a Day of Judgment where all is charity and forgiveness and Christ descends on a rainbow; the whole small edifice breathes delight and serenity. After the two old brothers' work at Wies was done Domenico retired to a nearby cottage where he could contemplate his handiwork and remained there until his death.

The brothers Asam (Cosmo Damian, 1686-1739, and Egid Quirin, 1692-1750) are more famous for they too were capable of building and decorating a whole church between them, yet their work is not so well known as their name for the best of it is somewhat inaccessible. Their genius is more agitated than that of the Zimmermanns; they too worked best away from cities in the remote monastic lands that bordered on the Danube. Their youthful masterpiece is Weltemburg with its magical statue of St. George slaying the dragon and its enchanting bust of Cosmo by his brother, a Cherubino arising from the stucco while at Rohr the younger brother Egid Quirin went on to create his sensational altarpiece—a theatrical tableau of the Assumption. Osterhofen and Straubing are considered their finest late work, while at Munich their carved rococo house-front can still be seen next to the dark, damaged, somewhat occluded church they built together for St. Johann Nepomuk. The brothers are the earliest of the rococo church architects of southern Germany; they studied in Rome which must have developed their sense of theatre and began to work at home in the 1720's. They combine a brilliant invention, grace and wit with the fresco-gift of Cosmo Damian and the outstanding sculptural talent of Egid Quirin.

One more church architect must be mentioned, Johann Maria Fischer (1691-1766), who sprang from a line of Upper Palatinate masons and began to work in Munich with the Asams and Cuvilliés, then became the architect for the greater monastic orders, especially the Benedictines. In richness of conception he was the equal of Neumann and, like him, finished off his work with superb decoration. He, too, was extremely prolific and was connected with thirty-two churches and twenty-three convents, but he never became a builder of palaces, and of his life we know next to nothing. Although his designs go back to Austria and Italy and he was well versed in French art, he never traveled. His finest churches are Diessen (on the Ammersee), Ottobeuren (near Memmingen in the south of Bavaria), and Zweifalten in Württemberg. This is indeed a marvellous creation where his lofty spiritual quality combines with the dazzling stucco of J. M. Feichtmayer and the moving sculpture of Christian. The church is surrounded by hills and woods, its precinct encircled by a quiet little stream. The exterior is billowing and gracious, the inside extraordinarily rich; the pulpit drips with golden waterfalls and is ornamented with skeletons rising from the dead while greenery cascades to the serpent on its base and is faced by another full-scale model by Christian of the vision of Ezekiel in the valley of dry bones. The art of rococo here brings the whole of the great church under its genial domination. There is a throne with rococo chair and two confessionals by the entrance which must be unique; one is a stucco box carved with a swaying palm grove, the columns encrusted with vegetation while in the other the stucco is carved into a catastrophe of falling columns. Ottobeuren is on an even grander scale.

One other exquisite church remains of the mid-century— Neu Birnau, a pilgrimage church at the west end of the Lake of Constance on a hillside among meadows and orchards. Peter Thumb was the architect and Joseph Anton Feuchtmayer in charge of the stucco. The entrance doors are gray with pink facing. Inside is a blaze of color, a ceiling fresco containing a real mirror with gold busts below to catch the reflected sunshine from it and everywhere patches of green—in interstices in the scroll work or at the top of the pink altar columns where it is echoed by green plants and the green in the cracks of the honeycomb pergola above the altar and again in St. John the Baptist's outspreading tree. There are several statues of an elongated El Greco character and on a wall memorial Death has been reduced to the dimensions of a dried sea-horse while from the pulpit near by a girl's head as fresh and secular as Mozart's Barbarina looks out while from below another head peers.

The strangest figure of the German rococo is certainly Cuvilliès (1695-1768); this Walloon from Soignies was a dwarf of under four feet high. Although of French origin, he worked entirely abroad and before 1711 had become the page of the exiled Elector Max Emmanuel of Bavaria, with whom he returned to Munich from Brussels in 1715. After an apprenticeship as a military engineer, he was sent to Paris where he studied under Blondel from 1720 to 1724. In 1725 he became court architect to the Elector and succeeded Effner, the crea-

tor of Nymphenburg and Schliessheim. His books of ornaments are fertile and original variations on the themes of
Lajoue but his opportunities for realizing them on the grand
scale were much greater. Apart from work (now badly damaged) at Brühl outside Cologne, he produced three triumphant
interiors, the five rich rooms in the Residence (1730-37), the
Amalienberg (1734-39) both decorated by J. B. Zimmermann,
and the Residence theatre (1753). Both the theatre and these
rooms in the Palace have now vanished utterly. Jacob Burckhardt considered these rich rooms "the most beautiful rococo
which exists on earth, excelling in inventiveness and subtle
elegance anything I have seen." There were particularly fine
chinoiseries, a bedroom in white and gold and wine red, a long
picture gallery hung with silk and a blending of all the sea-
borne themes of French *rocaille* with German hunting scenes
and northern woods. Here the Elector Karl Albrecht dreamed
his luckless dream of Empire which was to end so tragically.
The theatre (now restored to use with most of the original
paneling) ("Rococo art at its absolute culmination."
S. Sitwell) was a vision of white, gold, and crimson, the key-
note of which was the Royal Box and four circular tiers of
boxes each with rococo ornamentation; it held only six hundred and thirty-seven people, and here Mozart conducted the
first performance of his opera *Idomeneo* (1781).

A link between Church and State is formed by the monastic
libraries whose frescoed oval ceilings, undulating bookcases,
and allegorical statuary proclaim an opulent calm where the
atmosphere is deeply religious although no detail can offend
the delicate susceptibilities of an unbeliever. St. Gall in Switzerland, Fürstenzell, Wiblingen near Ulm, Dillingen and
Schussenried in Württemberg are among the loveliest. There
are also rococo gardens like the Jardin de la Fontaine at Nîmes
and above all at Veitschöcheim outside Würzburg. Expelled
from the shrubs which are confined to high enormous formal
hedges forming a series of "*cabinets particuliers*," Nature seems
to flower in Tietz' statuary, exquisitely exuberant and robust
yet like rococo china, touching, even pathetic. Trains, trams,

gasworks, and factory chimneys, waiting greedily for the end, cluster and hoot round the alleys and the delicate grottoes.

> Unwater'd see the drooping sea-horse mourn,
> and swallows roost in Nilus' dusty urn.

One last word to those who want to study the rococo, Hurry! A style which ignored frontiers, which convoluted all it touched from a cathedral to a chamber-pot, which included all classes, whose message was movement, spontaneity, intimacy, formal extravagance and spiritual delight, which brought love and warmth for a half lifetime into gloomy interiors, which in its day was daring and contemporary and universal as no other has been since—unless we elevate *art nouveau*, cubism, and surrealism to an authority they do not merit—such a creative fire as swept through every capital from Lisbon to Leningrad, Cork to Constantinople, is nothing if not perishable and attracts to itself an undeviating hatred. Even as I write some façade is crumbling; a ceiling flakes, paneling is being stripped, plasterwork crushed, chimneypieces torn out, a Chippendale looking-glass cracks and innumerable pieces of china are thumbed and shattered—("The period of rococo may well be called the age of porcelain and without a sympathetic understanding of rococo no appreciation of the art is possible." Honey). So hurry, before the last cartouche, the fading arabesque, the final *cul-de-lampe* goes the way of Sans-Souci and Schönbornslust, Belle-Vue and Bruchsal.

> Another age shall see the golden ear
> Im-brown the slope and nod on the parterre,
> Deep harvests bury all his pride has plann'd
> And laughing Ceres re-assume the land.

James Joyce: 1

This is no time to attempt a critical estimate of Joyce. Wilson's forty pages in *Axel's Castle* (Scribners) have done that best. He has died this week, but it will be a year or two before anything can be said about him which is worth saying. In the next period of expansive leisure, when we can read again and reassess the past, he may well take the place which Henry James has lately occupied, that of the Forerunner in vogue, the fine product of a vanished and alien civilization which by its completeness and remoteness stirs the imagination and so enters into communication with its successor. Joyce was the last of the Mammoths, not perhaps quite the last, for there is still Gide, Claudel, Vuillard, Bonnard, in France, but I know of none in America and England, and by Mammoths I mean those giant inhabitants of the middle class who believed in life for art's sake, and were prepared to devote sixty or seventy years of unremitting energy and patience, all their time, all their money, all their mind to it. We see them browsing in small herds through the sixties and seventies and eighties, Impressionists, Post-Impressionists, Ivory Tower dwellers, Realists, Parnassians, their food the experience of a lifetime obtained through a giant curiosity, a private income and a deep sense of security, for their protective bourgeois coloring, their rich dark suits and stiff collars, their comfortable homes and devoted women disguise them completely and merge perfectly into the contemporary bourgeois landscape. With the turn of the century the herds thinned out, the feeding grounds deteriorated, the last war had somewhat the effect of an ice age yet the pastures which had supported Cézanne and Flaubert,

Degas and Henry James continued to nourish Moore and Yeats and Proust, Joyce, Gide, and Valéry. Now most of them are gone and the ice cap is returning with velocity.

Joyce was not a revolutionary. His life contained only one revolutionary gesture, his departure from Ireland after the final suppression of *Dubliners* (1912) which was to have been brought out in 1904. He produced a fierce poem, *Gas from a Burner* (1912), which contains some excellent hate of Ireland and left his country never to return. He then taught English in the Berlitz schools, where he was working at Trieste when the last war broke out, after which he moved to Zurich. It is odd to think that there must exist many Italians who learned their English from this lord of language, who was quietly acquiring every known tongue in his spare time. *Dubliners*, an admirable collection of short stories, was finally published in 1914. It shows Joyce torn between the realism of the "modern movement" and a decadent Celtic romanticism. In 1916/7 he published *A Portrait of the Artist* through the Egoist Press. It is a quite remarkable book, adult, sensitive, unreassuring, in which the two veins of Dublin realism and Celtic romanticism are woven into an elaborate fugue. After the publication of *Ulysses*, which was due to the courage and devotion of Sylvia Beach, he became, through a private benefaction, financially secure, and was able to live the kind of life he wanted which was that of a well-to-do high priest of art, remote from equals and competitors and not too accessible to admirers, in a luxurious apartment in the Rue de Grenelle. It was there that I used to go to see him, or else in his room at the American hospital in Neuilly, when I was writing an article on *Ulysses* and *Work in Progress*. I had read *Ulysses* with passion; it is very much a young man's book, packed with the defeatism and the guilt of youth, its loneliness, cynicism, pedantry, and outbursts of bawdy anarchist activity. Guilt about a dying mother, boredom with an actual father, search for a spiritual father, reliance on robuster friends, watery and lecherous cravings for girls, horror and delight in failure, horror and fascination for the gross calm, bitchy, invincible feminine principle as exemplified in Molly Bloom, "Queen of Calpe's rocky mount, the raven-haired daughter of Tweedie"; it was like, and always will be, nothing one has read before.

At that time there was a complete cult of *Ulysses*. Books were written about it. Stuart Gilbert provided a fascinating crib; there was a map of Dublin with the journeyings of Bloom and Stephen in different colored inks, and on "Bloom's Day" (June 16th) there was a celebration, Joyce going to the country with a few friends and admirers for a picnic, one of which was ruined by a clap of thunder for which Joyce had a genuine terror. I could not write about *Work in Progress* without having it explained to me and so my talks with Joyce ended up in my being put on to construe. "Now, Mr. Connolly, just read this passage aloud and tell me what you think it means." "It's about the Danish walls of the original Danish encampment—er—I mean Dub-b-lin—the black ford? Ford of the oxen? Hill on a fort?" "No, no, no—I refer to the three cathedrals of Dublin, Mr. Connolly, the only city, you know, to have three cathedrals." It was not quite like being at school, it was like going to breakfast, after one had left school, with one's schoolmaster. In theory you were grown up, in practice you weren't. After one difficult passage about Roman Dublin intoned by Joyce in his magnificent voice, he paused. "You know, of course, to what I refer, Mr. Connolly?" "No, not exactly." "I refer"—there was a moment of acute embarrassment—"I refer to a Lupanar." After the tutorials he would go to the piano and sing Dublin street ballads with a charming, drawling, nasal parody of the old itinerant singers. He talked endlessly about Ireland. "I am afraid I am more interested, Mr. Connolly, in the Dublin street names than in the riddle of the Universe." He was even interested in Irish cricket, and always, when I knew him, wore the white blazer of an obscure Dublin club. He was very proud of his family, and like all the Anglo-Irish, a snob. In Paris he liked good food, especially a Montparnasse restaurant called Les Trianons and going to the opera and order and wealth. Sometimes, however, he went out with Hemingway or Lewis and got drunk. He always seemed to be two men, the legendary Joyce, blind but patient, pompous, cold, easily offended, unapproachable, waiting to be spoken to, with a strange priestly blend of offended dignity, weakness and intellectual power and underneath the warm, sympathetic bawdy Dublin character. In the years to come something really important could be written about him. Revolutionary in technique, yet conservative in everything else, so deadly respectable in his life, so fearlessly sensual in his writings, so tortured with the lapsed Catholic's guilt—the *"Agenbite of Inwit,"* so obsessed with his own youth that his clock seemed literally to have stopped on June 16th, 1904, and yet so determined to create a mythical universe of his own. We will never have the time, the security or the patience in our lifetime to write like him, his weapons "silence, exile and cunning" are not ours. I hope but only for the time to read through him and one day make a study of this literary anti-Pope, this last great Mammoth out of whose tusks so many smaller egoists have carved their self-important ivory towers.

James Joyce: 2

"These letters should be read in conjunction with an authoritative biography of James Joyce"—the first words of Mr. Gilbert's excellent introduction define this book.*These are not letters which portray a man or tell his story so much as chips and shavings which fly from the machine while *Ulysses* and *Finnegans Wake* are getting themselves written. Few great writers, I feel, can claim such dedication to a self-appointed task, for, if family matters be excluded, there is hardly a line here which does not deal with Joyce's work and the mechanics of having it printed, published, reviewed, and understood.

James Joyce does not reveal or wish to reveal his character, his "sluggish, slimy, slithy, sliddery, stick-in-the-mud disposition." He flirts with no woman and unbends with no man, not a Jim is heard, not a humorous quote: only Mr. Budgen inspires a certain playfulness. This does not make his letters dull; they present an absolutely closed world into which the reader must crawl like a speleologist and watch the subterranean grottoes unfold before him until, in 1940, all grows dark again.

Mr. Gilbert stresses this formal reserve, which made Joyce even ask to be referred to as "Mr. Joyce" throughout "James Joyce and the making of *Ulysses*," and I still possess a telegram summoning me to the Euston Hotel in 1929 and signed "Joyce" which I took to be the Christian name of a girl I knew; a misunderstanding which was never cleared up satisfactorily with either of them.

* *Letters of James Joyce*, edited by Stuart Gilbert (Faber).

The whole *schema* by which Joyce lived is growing more and more unfamiliar. We live in an age when highbrows prefer music to literature, middlebrows painting, and lowbrows television, and when the prestige of the written word, the whole cultural heritage of literary "happy families" is a fading dream. Joyce, who made and kept a vow never to write prefaces or give a lecture or grant an interview, saw himself as among the great revolutionaries, a lord of language like Dante, or a king in exile:

> You must know that the Opera in Paris is considered, not without some reason, by the Paris intellectuals as beneath contempt and the spectacle of the immensely illustrious author of *Ulysses* endeavouring to hustle crowds of journalists and protesting admirers into that old-fashioned playhouse to hear antiquated music sung by old-timer Sullivan was too much.

His attitude to psychoanalysis, as far back as 1921, can only be described as irreverent:

> A batch of people in Zurich persuaded themselves that I was gradually going mad and actually endeavoured to induce me to enter a sanatorium where a certain Doctor Jung (the Swiss Tweedledum who is not to be confused with the Viennese Tweedledee, Dr. Freud) amuses himself at the expense (in every sense of the word) of ladies and gentlemen who are troubled with bees in their bonnets.

"At the expense" . . . through all his life Joyce manifested a very exact regard for money. As with all who refuse many undertakings for money, he was most tenacious in the remainder. Royalties, translation rights, serialization, small privately printed editions bulk largely in his correspondence. "Already in 1917," Mr. Gilbert tells us, "Miss Weaver had made her first benefaction . . . this was followed, in 1924, by the transfer of a large sum of money" which supported Joyce and his family for the rest of his life: the Mallarmé of English prose could give up his teaching. In the same year the first fragment from *Finnegans Wake* was published in a little magazine and the artist was well away on his journey to Byzantium; never was a subsidy so graciously given, so well-deserved, so richly spent.

The most interesting letters over the long years are to his benefactress, especially when he explains the meaning of episodes in *Ulysses* or of key passages in *Finnegans Wake*. Let us look at one: the famous first sentence whose beginning completes the last phrase of the book, "river runs"

> *brings us back to Howth Castle and Environs. Sir Tristram, violer d'amores, had passencore rearrived on the scraggy isthmus from North Armorica to wielder fight his penisolate war; nor had stream rocks by the Oconee exaggerated themselves to Laurens County, Ga, doublin all the time. . . .*

Dear Madam: Above please find prosepiece ordered in sample form. Also key to same. Hoping said sample meets with your approval, yrs trly Jeems Joker.
Howth = Dan Hoved (head) (an island for old geographers).
Sir Amory Tristram 1st Earl of Howth changed his name to Saint Lawrence, b. in Brittany (North Armorica).
Tristan et Iseult. Passim.
Viola in all moods and senses.
Dublin, Laurens County, Georgia, founded by a Dubliner, Peter Sawyer, on r. Oconee. Its motto: Doubling all the time.
Passencore = pas encore and *ricorsi storici* of Vico. 'Rearrived' idem.

And so on for another page. How Joyce must have appreciated the reviewer of this fragment in Laurens County, who exclaimed: "We and the Oconee river of all places in the world are in it, too." It has sometimes been said that Miss Weaver's subsidy turned Joyce away from the realities of life and caused his genius to run to seed or rather flower itself to death in the wastes of *Finnegans Wake;* but a study of his work shows that it was always moving in this direction, that his gift for languages was leading to an obsession with language, that he sought inspiration from the form and was always drawn by his personality to the arcane and esoteric.

A letter from Wells (much finer than his strictures on Henry James) expresses the public incomprehension once and for all. Yet neither subsidy nor vocation nor the dedicated life in the quiet Paris street can stave off the tragedies of life or the attrition of time:

> Twilight of Blindness. Madness, descends on Swift . . . unslow, malswift, pro mean, proh noblesse. Atrahora. Melancolores, nears; whose glauque eyes glitt bedimmed to imm!

His own eye troubles, his daughter's mental breakdown,

the vicissitudes of war, return him at the end to the Zurich where, in the first world war, so much of *Ulysses* was written. The wanderer, Vico-like, comes full circle.

At the end we emerge from these letters, haunted rather than dominated, pitying and wondering rather than loving this strange, arrogant, shy, kindly and meticulous scholar whose stoical reticence cannot obliterate a fundamental bitterness, even a touch of the "injustice-collector":

> I have refused scores of requests to sit to painters and sculptors, having a very profound objection to my own image, needlessly repeated in a picture or bust. In fact years ago casual glimpses of it in shop mirrors, etc., used to send me speeding away from it. I think I was right for, underfed, overworked, ill-dressed, with septic poisoning gradually undermining my health and unable to attend to it for sheer want of time and money, I must have been a dreadful spectacle.

James Joyce: 3

It is strange how many figures of the twenties, like mammoths in a block of ice, are now reappearing in their perishable completeness—in Mr. George Painter's *Proust* and Miss Sylvia Beach's autobiography (not yet available in this country), and now in Mr. Richard Ellmann's monumental life of Joyce*, which takes us in 800 pages through the fifty-eight-year span of the most sedentary of exiles. Allowing for extensive references this still leaves about fifteen large and solid pages for every year of the man's life.

I do not know whether to be more impressed by the scholarship, patience, industry, and devotion of such a biographer or to be appalled by the standard he sets. A computing machine could not have done better. I think I must be about the only person who knew Joyce not to be mentioned in it.

There is a weakness inherent in this all-embracing method of biography which depends on the filing of innumerable interviews. Too many stray visitors appear whose reminiscences are of doubtful accuracy and seriousness. These have then to be incorporated in the larger annals as if the Person from Porlock's account of his reception formed part of *Kubla Khan*.

But Mr. Ellmann is not a computing machine and he manages to evaluate most of the evidence; in fact, when he steps in with a judgment or a brief estimate of one of Joyce's works he is both penetrating and sympathetic. It is this gift of criticism held in reserve which makes his book a truly masterly biography, wise in its completeness. If Joyce be a great writer, then this is a great book.

* *James Joyce*, by Richard Ellman (Oxford).

I say "if" because I do not think it is altogether established that Joyce is a great writer in the sense in which Yeats or Proust is. There have been many times when I have thought so—when I first read *Ulysses*, when I met him, when I wrote a long article on *Work in Progress* in 1929, when I hear the recording of his wonderful voice reading *Anna Livia*, when I read the last page of *Finnegans Wake:* let us say, then, he is a marvellous writer.

But I cannot feel absolutely sure of his greatness, as once I did, because I am now less tolerant of his faults. I feel that so much of *Finnegans Wake* and of *Ulysses*, even when the obscurity has been penetrated, is fundamentally uninteresting that there must be some failure of conception or execution or both, and I think it perhaps springs from Joyce's absolute refusal to let himself mature through the spiritual struggles and intellectual discoveries of his time.

His life is one of the saddest and one of the emptiest except in so far as it was filled by the joys of artistic creation. For he rejected everything—he ignored the war of 1914 and displaced himself from Trieste to Zurich, he ignored the last war and again displaced himself from Paris to Zurich, he ignored the Irish Republic which he had called for in his youth, he ignored fascism, anti-fascism and communism, he despised psychoanalysis, he hated painting, took no interest in architecture or travel or objects, liked no music of his time except for a brief craze for Antheil and seems equally immune to modern poetry and literature. His clock had stopped on Bloomsday (June 16th, 1904). "His true Penelope was Flaubert" one might say with Pound—but Flaubert did manage to live in the present, if only through his hate—as one can see from *Bouvard et Pécuchet*.

I am not criticizing Joyce from a journalistic or Marxist point of view but I am trying to suggest that he fed his queen bee of a mind with inferior jelly and that from such subject matter it could not produce the sublime or even the comic effects which were intended. He asks too much of his ideal reader. This is perhaps an English heresy and may account for the way we lag behind America in our appreciation of Joyce (or is it our lack of subsidized theses?); and perhaps I am the only person to find the plans and keys and clues and commentaries on Joyce's books more exhilarating than the originals. Is there an immaturity in his mind and humor or a blind spot in mine? Mr. Ellmann has the answer ready:

> If we ask Joyce to bestride literature like a colossus, he will disappoint us. No generals paid him visits of homage, no one called him the Sage of Dublin. As he makes clear enough himself, in the world's eyes he began as a bad boy and ended as an old codger. There is much to rebuke him for, his disregard for money, his regard for alcohol and other conduct lacking in majesty or decorum. Yet we have to ask with Parsifal the question that Joyce also asked: "Who is good?" . . . Yet as the nobility of his heroes gradually overcomes their ingloriousness, so the tenacious craftsman, holding to his idea, gradually surmounts that roving debt-ridden scene through which Joyce kept his elegant way. . . . To be narrow, peculiar, and irresponsible, and at the same time all-encompassing, relentless and grand, is Joyce's style of greatness, a style as difficult but ultimately as rewarding as that of *Finnegans Wake*.

I have said that his was a sad life. His two profound interests, according to Mr. Ellmann, were his family and his writings. "These passions never dwindled. The intensity of the first gave his work its sympathy and humanity; the intensity of the second raised his life to dignity and high dedication"—but what tragedy can lurk in two most natural obsessions?

Poverty crippled the first half of Joyce's life, illness the second, and he died almost as poor as he had begun. Many artists, the majority even, have been poor, but there is something Baudelairean about Joyce's poverty—his feckless drunken father, his own miserable shifts and flittings, the duns, the bailiffs, the pawnbrokers, the borrowings of florins and shillings, the patched trousers, the missing dress suit, these become a nightmare of shabby-genteel bohemia—until one feels it is infectious, that one will rise from this book a poorer man than one sat down. I don't know which is sadder—the Dublin poverty and moon-flittings of Joyce's parents or his days at the Berlitz school in Pola and Trieste with his children born in such unfavorable circumstances and his books also being held up and vilified by publishers with all the prejudices of the time.

It was not till he reached Zurich, in his middle-thirties, that good fortune came his way in the shape of the subsidies which were to prove his undoing. Not but what Miss Weaver acted like a goddess of tact and goodness, more devoted than Athena to Ulysses; but the sums which Joyce required to expunge and blot out the years of want and injured pride were so rightly enormous that they required the use of all capital as income. Nor was he ever able to clear the fortune from *Ulysses* which a world-wide distribution of a classic ought to have provided.

He died suddenly of a duodenal ulcer, a poor man, and Miss Weaver paid for his funeral. She was his "true Penelope" as her name implies. All his fortune in later life was of small account compared to the troubles of his eyesight, his long, excruciatingly painful and losing fight against blindness, his many operations and the tragedy of his daughter's madness which he tried so hard to mitigate and perhaps had helped to bring on. His son's marriage also ended in disaster.

Anyone who met the Joyce family at the height of their prosperity in their apartment in the Faubourg St. Germain, must have felt there was something incongruous about the position of this highly decorative family of Italian-speaking Irish expatriates. They seemed to rotate in a social vacuum like the brilliant shadow-cabinet of a long dispossessed government.

Mr. Ellmann describes the famous meeting between Joyce and Proust in which both outshone each other in mutual ignorance of their work and Proust asked Joyce if he liked truffles. But Proust was, after all, on his home ground. If they had both known how outrageously the other overtipped, a friendship might have been formed, the Esprit de Berlitz been recognized by the Esprit de Guermantes. But though Proust and Joyce shared an aversion from happiness and made instinctively toward the tragic sense of life, the rainclouds where their genius flowered, Joyce was immune to the snobbery of our time and maintained that not one of his characters was worth a thousand pounds.

He liked nice clothes and he liked his family to have them. "Never mind my soul, just be sure you have my tie right," he said to an over-intense painter to whom he was sitting. Otherwise meals in good restaurants, white wine, champagne, and cures for Lucia took up his money. He did not want possessions. "We're going downhill fast," he told Beckett at Christmas, 1939; and Jung diagnosed father and daughter, five years earlier, as "two people going to the bottom of a river, one falling and the other diving."

Farewell to Surrealism

I

Looking back upon surrealism—for, although the movement is still active in Paris under its vigorous leader, the momentum decreases, the fissions multiply—we cannot fail to become more and more impressed by the spectacle of what was without question the greatest artistic commotion of the twentieth century and one of the few enlargements of sensibility in the last thirty years which stand to the credit of humanity.

There is a tendency to discuss surrealism and cubism as if one proceeds out of the other, but in fact there is no similarity. Cubism was a way of painting which a group of painters imposed on themselves, surrealism a philosophy of life put forward by a band of poets. The first was essentially a method of breaking up the object and putting it together again according to concepts of pictorial structure, a phase of the greatest importance in the development of such painters as Picasso, Braque, Marcoussis, and Gris, but affecting literature only through Apollinaire, and life hardly at all. The second was the attempt of a highly organized group to change life altogether, to make a new kind of man. *Le surréalisme n'est pas une école littéraire ou critique. C'est un état d'esprit. A notre époque, seule l'imagination peut rendre aux hommes menacés le sentiment d'êtres libres.* ("Surrealism is neither a literary school nor a method of criticism. It is a state of mind. In our time, only the imagination can give back to mankind in peril the idea of liberty" —Invitation to the International Surrealist Exhibition in Amsterdam.) So in discussing surrealism it is necessary to forget terms like cubist, fauve, abstract, post-impressionist—which belong to painting, as symbolist belongs to poetry—and to think of surrealism as a new interpretation of life, as the name of one of the last and fiercest explosions in our human consciousness which has been detonating since Heraclitus and Galileo. This last combustion, whose effects we are still experiencing, was brought about by a few young poets dreaming of what man ought to be. As Aragon wrote, *It's a question of arriving at a new declaration of the rights of man.*

II

Why a group? "Here's the essential thing. A group is the beginning of everything. The isolated individual can do nothing, reach nowhere. A properly directed group can do a great deal and has a good chance of getting results which one man would never be in a position to obtain. You don't realize your own situation. You are all in prison. All you want, if you are in your right mind, is to escape. But how can we escape? We must break through the walls, dig a tunnel. One man can accomplish nothing. But suppose there are ten or twenty and that they all take their turn; by combining together they can finish the tunnel and escape. Besides, no one can escape from the prison without the help of those who have got out already." (Gurdjiev, quoted by Ouspensky, quoted by the surrealists.)

III

In the beginning was the word. The word was "dada." The darkest moments of European wars are strangely propitious to new movements in art. There is an awareness of absolutes, a closing-in on the self; like those pine cones which germinate only in forest fires, the rarest talents are liberated by the deepest despair. Zürich, Swiss capital of German humanism, was the scene in 1916–17 of a strange incubation. Here, while the battle of Verdun was raging, James Joyce was quietly working on *Ulysses,* here collected the war-weary and war-desperate, displaced neutrals or refugees from conscription like the German war-poet Hugo Ball, who opened in 1916 the *Cabaret Voltaire*. In it congregated Richard Huelsenbeck, another German poet in exile; Jean Arp, Alsatian poet, sculptor, and painter; Tristan Tzara, a young Rumanian poet. The fear of extinction which dominated the group led to a concerted attempt to render ridiculous the powers which were destroying the world they knew. Choosing the word "dada" haphazard from a dictionary (according to the legend), they baptized their revolt against futility in terms of futility.

The movement had no positive quality but an exhibitionism of the absurd; being against "art" (*Art is rubbish*, wrote Jacques Vaché in 1918), its only medium was nonsense—the use of nonsense in public to discredit all forms of sense. This nihilism suited the angry despair of German intellectuals in defeat, and dada groups soon formed in Berlin, Hanover, and Cologne, contributing Baader, Baargeld, Kurt Schwitters, Max Ernst, and many others. Meanwhile a similar trend had come into the open in New York where Marcel Duchamp from Paris, Picabia from Barcelona and Man Ray, in their prophetic discontent, had published the review 291. After the war all these bands converged on Paris. The greater the ability, the deeper the disgustability—only thus can we explain the presence of such pure artists as Ernst, Arp, and Schwitters or the three painters from America in this troupe of destructive harlequins.

In Paris, Tzara and Baargeld, with their sublime dadaist effrontery, immediately triumphed; art and life were rejected as impostures equally vile. The first to rally round the invaders from the East was a handful of very young poets, just released from their War service: André Breton, a medical student, and Louis Aragon, a law student, Paul Eluard, Philippe Soupault, Benjamin Péret. (Breton himself had been greatly influenced by an isolated and undeclared dadaist, Jacques Vaché, who had just committed suicide.) In 1919 this disillusioned group had founded the magazine *Littérature*, in 1920 Breton and Soupault collaborated in *Les Champs Magnétiques* and Max Ernst gave an exhibition in Paris of his first *collages*, with Breton's introduction. All sought inspiration in three isolated and unfortunate geniuses of the nineteenth century, poets with a contempt for humanity and a deep hatred of "literature"; Lautréamont, Rimbaud, and Jarry. Both the dadaists and the young French band, however, revered the poet of the *avant-garde* and interpreter of cubism whose death was so recent, Guillaume Apollinaire.

At first the combination seemed to work smoothly, giving birth to books, magazines, pictures and, above all, to scandal-making public meetings, until toward the end of 1921 a quarrel of capital importance broke out between Breton and Tzara. Breton was fundamentally a poet who wished to facilitate the germination of new beauty from those lofty arts which the necessary whirlwind of dada had uprooted. Tzara was the destructive showman. "The true dadaist is against dada"—this terrible and logical axiom of Tzara would in the end render all action impossible. The absurd cannot engender even absurdity without some order creeping in. In dada the pendulum of European vitality had reached the extreme point of its arc, the impetus of defeat and despair had exhausted itself, and now, even as communism was replacing nihilism, capitalism beginning its recovery, Mussolini marching on Rome, insulin and the tomb of Tutankhamen being discovered, so Breton's party won. Dada abdicated and surrealism was born.

IV

Surrealism—out of respect to Apollinaire the word was borrowed from his last play-title—means the reality which lies beyond what we call real. As a former medical student who had treated the shell-shocked, Breton was familiar with Freud and, after the revelation of automatic writing which occasioned his first book with Soupault, it was clear to him that the reality beyond reality (Nerval's "supernaturalism") was the subconscious mind, the universal truth that underlies all poetry, all imagery, all desire and which Lautréamont and Rimbaud had drawn on inexhaustibly, the truth in reach of all that reason is bribed to deny. The German dada movement, however, was inclined to bolshevism and was as susceptible to

Marx as were the surrealists to Freud. The revolutionary element in surrealism was therefore two-fold: it was a revolt of the psyche, against the authority of reason; it was also an appeal to reason to liberate man from his oppressors—family, church, fatherland, boss. It embraced both Freud and Hegel, the promenade which the iron pot in the fable forces on the uneasy earthenware vessel had already begun.

The early years of the group, before the inner tensions became intolerable, can only be described as magical. The youthful surrealists possessed talent, courage, and charm: they had also experienced a revelation, a glimpse of a dream-dazzled world: "The marvellous is always beautiful, anything that is marvellous is beautiful; indeed, nothing but the marvellous is beautiful," wrote Breton. They lived only for these mystic glimpses and for each other; while the group held together, and while it was strong enough to pulverize its enemies, excommunication was a kind of torture. Meeting in large cafés on Montmartre or in the now-demolished Passage de l'Opéra, drinking Mandarin-curaçaos, whiling the afternoons away applauding at films in the wrong places, they would pass the evening in conversation, composition, confession or love, being driven on by an apostolic intoxication of liberty. To a conventional young Englishman they represented the very arcana of Paris, the spirit of insurrection arising from its most sacred flaking quarters, the dark and shabby corners which they loved—the Buttes Chaumont, Musée Grévin, Rue de la Lune—alight with their revolutionary intelligence and gaiety. I remember seeing them all one summer evening in the fun fair of Luna Park, in the blue suits and white knitted ties they affected, gathering like a band of gibbons around "La Femme Tronc," a legless, armless wonder with a charming face who was seated on a marble pedestal, signing her photographs for them with a pen held in her teeth. The brotherhood seemed to have long given up all recognized means of livelihood and to exist only for the ecstasy of the mystical experience—"eager to discover the formula and the place."

V

In this early period the poets dominated the scene. Breton, Aragon, Eluard, Péret, Desnos, Char, Soupault, and Crevel —they formed a central committee. Ernst, Miró, Tanguy, Arp, Man Ray, Picabia, were honored associates but not framers of policy. Books like Breton's *Nadja* or Aragon's *Paysan de Paris* or the poems of Eluard and Péret with their exaltati:n of wonder and hatred of humanism appeared the supreme expression of the movement. But the painters were steadily gaining in authority. They could reach a wider public and, by the nature of their work, they were less involved in political purges. They were allowed to make a reasonable income from their pictures in a manner which was not permitted to those who sought a living from their articles. As Breton wrote: "Surrealism requires from its participators that they should observe the utmost purity of mind and life . . . and is less ready than ever to accept departures from this purity which are justified by the obscure and revolting pretext that 'one must live.'"

The dissensions within the movement sprang from three causes: the attempted Freud-Marx synthesis, the dada legacy, and the economic problem. Although automatic writing had been accepted as the principal literary method of surrealism, as the secret weapon by which reason was to be overthrown and the poetry of super-reality placed within reach of all, the new vision had certain inconveniences: it became impossible to earn a living by one's books and thus some of the weaker vessels were driven into journalism, for which they were publicly excommunicated. Nor was it a weapon of much efficacy in the class struggle and one or two persistent dreamers like the sleepy Desnos and the gifted Artaud, were viciously expelled as apolitical. As under dada, the revolution came first and words were only to be used "to wring the neck of literature."

While a team of scientific researchers can devote themselves quietly to their pursuit, the surrealists had inherited from dada a taste for public manifestation. The group-spirit evolved according to the laws which govern groups: manifestos, excommunications, public penitences, secret betrayals; it was avid for notoriety and sensation and to miss a meeting was to court disaster. The surrealists were too dynamic to consider the overthrowing of reason by the unconscious as separable from the destruction of bourgeois capitalism (the society which reason had created), they refused to be called parlor revolutionaries whose activities were merely aesthetic, and therefore they handed themselves over to the Communist Party as Marxist shock troops to be employed as it thought best. The automatic writing of the poets was frequently combined with a vicious polemical style, with "humor" (in the sense of a macabre, cannibal sadistic gaiety) as the common factor of both. *Un Cadavre*, a pamphlet deriding the obsequies of Anatole France (1924), is the first of the "jokes in bad taste" with which the group achieved notoriety in the name of integrity. The swing to and from communism left several surrealists behind when Breton—unable to accept the disciplines of a party-line—veered back toward Trotskyism and the formation of an independent aesthetic and revolutionary movement.

Around 1931, the widely advertised defection of Aragon to the Communists and the entry into film making of Dali altered the balance of power. The visual arts and the exhibitions connected with them began to attract far more attention to the movement than Breton's search for his precise political position or the spread of automatic writing as "the communism of genius." Dali's eventual marriage to Gala, ex-wife of the poet Eluard, seemed a symbolic consecration of the new emphasis.

VI

The master of surrealist painting was Max Ernst. This great self-taught artist, with his bold eclectic imagination, passed effortlessly from dada in Cologne into the Freudian surrealist pantheon. The doctrines of Breton seemed especially created for him. His *collages*, arrangements of cut-out nineteenth century illustrations to provoke disquieting, ironical, and erotic

suggestions were, like so much surrealist art, essentially literary. They adapted the fantastic children's world of half a century before to the sophisticated wonder seeker. *La femme cent
têtes*, 1929, and *Rêve d'une petite fille*, 1930, are somewhat monotonous, but the *Semaine de Bonté* or, rather, the "Seven Elements" as it was subtitled, is one of the masterpieces of the
movement, a reassembling of lion-headed or bird-faced super-
men and their passionate consorts with their adventures "by
flood and field" into a sequence new, beautiful and disturbing—a tragic-strip from the Minotaur's nursery. The romantic nineteenth century was the epoch wherein the surrealists
felt most at home, and Germany the place; in the master from
Cologne they possessed a magician who could create around
some familiar feature, like the Paris statue of the "Lion de
Belfort," a new mythology of poetry, bloodshed, unrest, and
nostalgia.

The three great forerunners of surrealist painting stood in a
very different relation. Chirico, whose early work presents a
closed world of the imagination, already perfect and passing
away, a dream of urban apprehension, a haunted inner city of
squares and statues, of freight trains and grief-stricken colonnades in the last second before the explosion, this once most
surrealist of all painters, before the fact, had begun to trick
and evade, copying ineffectually his old paintings (according
to Breton) and falsifying the dates. He had seen the vision but
was unworthy and soon was drifting into the paranoiac false
classicism of Mussolini. Chagall remained a little too Oriental:
his imagination was like a peasant's fairy story, marvellous,
certainly, but without the tragic intelligence of the surrealists.
Picasso, though for a time thoroughly surrealist, had also been
undeniably cubist and would soon become—what else? This
giant fish, after reflecting a moment's glory on the surrealist
anglers, would break the net. It was not painters who were
surrealist for whom they were looking, but surrealists who
were painters.

Two more Simon Pures were found in Tanguy and Miró.
Tanguy's world was another closed private garden, an allot-
ment of poisonous plants from remoter planets, landscapes of

which it would be impossible to say that life doesn't exist in them or to prove that it does. Like many surrealists, he was obsessed by perspective and, somewhat constricted in his handling of paint, original only in the content of his dream. His world is static, as if he had secret access to an inexhaustible supply of Mars salad and Venus weed. Miró, unlike the others, is essentially a patternmaker, an artist in whom an exquisite gaiety seems to be always pouring out in an ever changing kaleidoscope of shape and color; he combines the impeccable taste of abstract painters with an irrepressible Catalan warmth and audacity. His pottery is the most beautiful of surrealist "objects," his bird-happy colors, the yellows and blues of serenity, pervade all his work.

Arp, the dadaist woodcutter, though for long associated with the surrealist movement, has strong affinities with abstract art. The group's most typical sculptor is rather the earlier Giacometti, whose imagination supplied a note of austerity welcome amid the surrealist flamboyance. His archaic personages are so etiolated by internal conflict as to seem more or less than human; his constructions appear heroic embodiments of frustration, the desire for perfection contrives to bring all his work to a ferocious standstill. His counterpart in painting is undoubtedly Masson, another rugged militant of the arts who has tried to interpret nature with a deep intuition of her violence; through the insect world, whose cruelty is too extreme to leave room for fear or hate, through the giant body whose mountain udders and pubic forests we mortals inhabit, to the cloudy clash of planetary wear-and-tear which we dimly envisage.

VII

In Masson and Giacometti, surrealism has discovered two of its most original artists with a revolutionary attitude to their mediums. It is they who supply it with some of the emotional discipline and intellectual tension which were the glory of cubism and which are lacking in the fretful doodling or weary Pre-Raphaelism of many surrealist painters. On the other side: perspective-haunted, oil-bound, conservative, even academic in their treatment, though startling in their choice of subject-matter and bold in imagination, are such typical surrealist painters as Dali, Magritte, Delvaux, Pierre Roy, and Leonor Fini.

Magritte, a very early surrealist, remains a completely literary painter who startles us by the force and universality of his dream symbols, but who gives us little pictorial quality. With Dali we reach the core of the problem: Dali and Aragon, the two geniuses of the movement, were also its two evil geniuses, the right and left deviationists, the one leading on toward salons and *succès de scandale*, Hollywood and shiny-papered fashion magazines; the other into Marxist polemic "the boring pamphlet and the public meeting," until each reached his perspective goal, an interview with the Pope, and the editorship of a Communist daily. Dali and his fellow Spaniard, Bunuel, were responsible for two famous surrealist films, *L'Age d'Or* (in which Max Ernst appeared) and *Un chien Andalou*. Man Ray, whose photography can raise the dead, also contributed *Les Mystères du Château de Dé*, a film built round the ultra-modern villa of the Vicomte de Noailles above Hyères, for this family were the Medici and chief patrons of the movement at the end of the golden age.

In the silent film surrealism had found an almost perfect medium; Man Ray, the painter and photographer who "drew in light," as Picasso described his work, made three films of increasing lyrical quality before the crisis of the *Age d'Or*; Dali's *Andalusian Dog*, in spite of some superfluous sadism, has a crystalline intensity that reveals unexplored regions of pure cinema; it becomes something far more moving than even the scenario leads one to expect. *The Golden Age* is less concentrated and suffers from an awareness of the new talking films, which the surrealists didn't have the funds to produce. It contains more shocking material; erotic, blasphemous, or anti-social (i.e. kicking the blind) than any picture ever made, but in spite of being a dithyrambic ode to physical passion, it is too disjointed and amateurish to qualify as great. It is a collection of incidents based on the theme of the world well lost for love, orchestrated by the Marquis de Sade. After the scandal which it caused, the cinematic expression of Dali's celebrated paranoia was compelled to filter down through the Marx brothers, reappearing in a much-watered form in his famous Hollywood dream-sequence for *Spellbound*.

The surrealist object was also removed by Dali from the region of pure sculpture where Giacometti and Arp were confining it and took on a more ephemeral form, as in the lady's bust enlivened with ants and a necklace of corncobs, with Millet's *Angelus* on a loaf of bread as an inkstand-headdress, which appeared, increasingly mildewed, at several international exhibitions before the famous fur tea set of Mereth Oppenheim took away the spotlight.

Although in theory the surrealist object was in reach of anyone who chose to put it together, even as poetry was available to all who could hold a pen when half-asleep, it was still the painters who produced the best: the fur-lined tea set, for instance, is not ridiculous but alarming, for there is something more horrible than one would expect about such an association, tea and cup having a deeply buried Freudian content which the fur brings up to the surface. Dali's red satin sofa, shaped like two closed lips is another uneasy-chair. The suggestiveness of so much surrealist art, based on liberating the unconscious, takes effect only on the repressed and so it is among the guilty, puritanical and bottled-up society of Anglo-Saxony that these luxurious objects find new victims. The ascendancy of what Breton called Dali's "master impulse," in 1931–6, brings surrealism nearer to the big money and the fashionable crowd. Dali's genius, so dazzling in conception, so reactionary in technique, so original yet so meretricious, is baffling even now. His most recent exhibition in Paris contains some spectacular draftsmanship, painting which seems like a triumph of color photography, and evidence of that inflation of the ego which brings this academic psychopath from the cove of Cadaqués near to Chirico, who signs his recent pictures "Pintor Maximus"—a conjuror dazzled by his own skill.

VIII

The later thirties were the period of success abroad and dissension within. International exhibitions flourished and surrealism was launched in Prague, London, New York, and Teneriffe, but in 1935 the charming René Crevel, *le plus beau des surréalistes*, and also their most intelligible prose writer, killed himself, *dégoûté de tout*; Breton's political position grew closer to Trotsky's; manifestos multiply; and the frog march along the razor's edge perceptibly quickens. The war caught the surrealists without a clear policy; their hatred of 1914–18 had brought them together, their bewilderment in 1939 now led to their dispersal. They remained for a while in Vichy France designing their Tarot pack of cards, and then gradually sought asylum in Mexico or the United States. Hating Hitler, they were threatened by Pétain; international, they detested a nationalist war; artists, they were also pacifists; revolutionaries, they yet lacked a political organization. When Jean Cocteau (the counterfeit surrealist and private enemy of the movement) was told by a young poet that he was joining the Resistance, he replied: "You are making a mistake; life is too serious for that"—which may be described as the surrealists' final attitude.

Their arrival in America may be likened in its consequences to that of the Byzantine scholars in Italy after the fall of Constantinople. From that moment "the surrealists" were disbanded but surrealism began to sow itself spontaneously. Dali in Hollywood, Breton and Masson in New York, Péret in Mexico, Ernst in Arizona, were its wandering apostles—the inevitable luxury magazine, a gelded *Minotaur*, appeared as *Triple V*; the Daliesque objects spread to fun fairs and shop windows; *Dyn*, edited by Paalen, appeared in Mexico City; Wilfredo Lam, Matta, and Gorky and the Caribbean poet Aimé Césaire were acclaimed by Breton. When the exiles returned to Paris, where reason had been re-enthroned by Sartre, they had left behind what was worst in surrealism—a flourishing commercial formula beloved of window-dressers or a façade for rich complex lightweights, for few, alas, were the disciples who had understood the astonishing galaxy of ideas which Breton had all his life so harmoniously assembled and so passionately, if obscurely, expounded—his homemade revolution: *"Changez la vie!"*

IX

For we cannot bid farewell to surrealism without a formal tribute to its founder. This much-loved, much-hated and therefore enigmatic figure, has accomplished far more than Apollinaire; he has formed and led his group of writers and artists instead of merely interpreting them; his distinguished bull-like appearance, as of a serious Oscar Wilde, with some of Wilde's dignity and benevolence and none of his vulgarity, reflects a strange mixture of qualities, the ability to lead, inspire, deceive and threaten, to criticize and create, to love and command both jealous rivals and the envious young. His own writing, with its seventeenth century fullness, at its best in *Nadja* (that hymn to Hazard) or in the valuable art criticism of *Les Pas Perdus* rather than when married to the welling, inexhaustible fountain of Eluard's poetry, achieves (as in his description of the peak of Teneriffe) an extraordinary vigour. Condemned by the logic of the times to lead his flock along the *arête* between militant Marxism and introverted lunacy, this reason-hating intellectual brought safely over as many as he could. Besides Eluard, Aragon, Péret, Crevel, Hugnet, and Gracq, one must admire his influence on many ex-surrealists, such as Paulhan, Pongé, Prévert, Queneau, and Leiris, who are well known today. His passion for art not only gave painters the feeling that their ideas were important, but inclined him toward those who were truly original rather than to the fashionable antiquarians, while he was quick to discover the surrealist content of much primitive and popular art.

Without the surrealist movement, "surrealism" might still have come into being; the unconscious would have found other aesthetic interpreters, but under Breton's guidance the synthesis between Freud and Marx was attempted many years in advance, as a parachuted battalion can attack an objective weeks ahead of schedule. A share of the faults of totalitarian leaders was not lacking, but seldom has one man's intellectual honesty, courage, and passion for beauty enriched us more. Always with the surrealists, in spite of their lapses into vulgar mystification, spiteful pettiness, or Freudian cliché, one is conscious of the dedicated life; of the whole conception of *bourgeois* living being utterly rejected for the sake of a mystical idea—*le merveilleux:* "Neither a school nor a clique, much more than an attitude, surrealism is, in the most complete and aggressive sense of the term, an adventure," proclaims a manifesto of May 1951, an adventure which has not recoiled from madness and suicide in the search for inspiration, for the vision which is not always compatible with art, which may destroy art and literature and sometimes life itself. If surrealism is to perish, it will be because the world we live in renders ineffectual the private rebellion of the individual and because the symbols and battle cries of the Unconscious—Sade, Ubu, Maldoror, Oedipus—awake no answering revolt in a generation which finds its predicament too serious even for surrealism!

They were, perhaps, the last Romantics. Despite the shapeless obscurity of so much of their writing, despite their rejection of the advances made by impressionism, fauvism, and cubism for "the rehabilitation of academic art under a new literary disguise" (as the critic Clement Greenberg has written), the world of literature and art would be—and, in fact, is—the flatter and feebler without them. They have restored to man, love-child of fatality and chance, his belief in a destiny; they have given woman back her pride and her magic; they have handed the imagery of the unconscious over to poetry and returned freedom of subject to painting, imprisoned by its own rules. To the question "What does that picture represent?" the surrealists make answer: "The person who did it."

Imitations of Horace

This* is the first volume to appear of this eagerly awaited edition, and includes some of the least known work of Pope. As other volumes will be devoted to his major poems and presumably will include a biographical sketch, a general consideration of Pope had better be left to their reviewers; Mr. Butt confines himself to elucidating as many allusions and borrowings as possible, and leaves the character of the great Borrower to be explained by others.

One would have enjoyed an account of the influence of Horace on English poetry, an influence which seems to have grown with the growth of London as a metropolitan city. For though Milton imitated Horace, as he has never since been imitated ("Lawrence, of virtuous father"), it was round the Court of Charles II that the impact of the Horace of the *Epistles* and *Satires* first made itself felt. The Horace of the *Odes* is one of the great lyric poets of all time, but the Horace of the longer poems is the poet of a clique, a clique which is always reproducing itself, and which rises constantly to power in highly civilized urban communities at the hub of great empires. Because this clique is reactionary, concerned with the eternal values of power, rank, fortitude, elegance, and common sense, and opposed to the eternal truths of genius, whether spiritual or revolutionary, Horace has made many enemies, and more than once among romantic critics appears the ridiculous statement (also applied to his disciple Pope) that nobody who admires

* *Imitations of Horace*, edited by John Butt; The Twickenham Edition of the Poems of Alexander Pope (Methuen).

him can admire poetry at all. Today the attack has somewhat shifted. Horace was a Perfectionist, and Perfection, as the imperfect are proud of telling us, is Dead. The Perfectionist is sterile, a figure, according to Mr. Day Lewis, "embalmed in a glacier."

What did the imitators of Horace imitate? It is clear from reading Rochester, Roscommon, Dryden, Cowley, that what appealed to them was sophistication, the new possibilities of personal relations, the improvement in critical values, the discoveries in Taste, which were afforded by the increased security, wealth, artificiality, and centralization of the London of Wren and of the Court of Charles II, a civilization which owed much to France, to Saint-Evremond, Boileau, Molière. They were fascinated by the mechanism of clique life, by conversation without brawls, disinterested friendship, criticism without duels, unpunished sex. They were modern in the sense in which Pepys is modern; early products of an urban culture, with a newly developed city sense, and an interest in the more mundane ethics, in friendship, or the use of riches, in the value of moderation or the follies and rewards of youth and age. In Rochester the freshness of these discoveries gives to his adaptations a vitality, a clumsy naïvety which is lacking in Pope, and which is the difference between the Londons of Charles II and George II; and Dryden, being both a lyric poet and a genius, is also a greater translator, because he comprehends diversities of the original which escape his more talented, but more limited, successor. His translation ("Descended from an Ancient Line") is one of the great poems in English. But it is not in translation that the influence of a writer is felt so much as in work indirectly inspired by him, and it is in Pope's *Moral Essays*, in his *Epistle to Lord Burlington*, or his *Characters of Women* that his debt to Horace is repaid, repaid by the depth and variety of observation, the perfection of form, and by that manliness which was the Roman contribution to poetry, and which, present for so long in English verse, has in our time degenerated into heartiness, and now disappeared.

When Pope comes to translate Horace, in spite of his enormous verbal felicity (no tight rope has been more delicately walked), one is conscious of three defects which intrude themselves. One because the heroic couplet is not the natural medium for translating the hexameter, and hence, although the colloquial and broken conversational effects of Horace are exquisitely done, there arises a certain reproach as one compares the splendid and sullen force of the original with Pope's urbane numbers. Another and graver defect is that, while we take Horace's estimate of himself on trust, we cannot do the same with Pope, for while Pope in these poems is in love with his own moderation, loyalty, and devotion to virtue, these qualities appear illusions which sharply engender an awareness of their opposite, when we compare them with the rude avowals of the original. Moreover, Horace, although eighteenth century in much of his thought, was an ancient Roman, and Pope seems too anxious to fit him, as he had fitted Doctor Donne, into the *dixhuitième* mould. On the lecherous, irritable, and prematurely bald man of genius the periwig does not quite fit, and it is his lyricism which must suffer. Thus, even as Swift translates *O rus quando ego te aspiciam*, "Oh could I see my Country Seat," so Pope makes:

> *O noctes coenaeque deum, quibus ipse meique,*
> *Ante larem proprium vescor,*

into

> O charming Moons, and Nights divine
> Or when I sup, or when I dine.

and one feels that his translation is inadequate, because it lacks nostalgia, just as his most beautiful lines are those in which nostalgia appears. Mr. Butt quotes a sentence of Addison, an epitaph on the Augustans:

> It is impossible for us, who live in the latter ages of the world, to make observations in criticism, morality, or in any art or science, which have not been touched upon by others. We have little else left us, but to represent the common sense of mankind in more strong, more beautiful, or more uncommon lights.

Yet at his best Pope leaves common sense far behind, as in his expansion of the lovely *Singula de nobis anni praedantur euntes Eripuere jocos, venerem, convivia, ludum.*

> Years foll'wing years, steal something every day,
> At last they steal us from our selves away.
> In one our Frolicks, one Amusements end,
> In one a Mistress drops, in one a Friend:
> This subtle Thief of Life, this Paltry Time,
> What will it leave me, if it snatch my Rhime?

and

> Long, as to him who works for debt, the Day;
> Long as the Night to her whose love's away;
> Long as the year's dull circle seems to run,
> When the brisk Minor pants for twenty-one;
> So slow the unprofitable Moments roll
> That lock up all the Functions of my soul;
> That keep me from Myself; and still delay
> Life's instant business to a future day.

Sic mihi tarda fluunt ingrataque tempora—if there had been a little bit more of Johnson in Pope, Horace would have been born again.

This volume includes the *Epistle to Dr. Arbuthnot*, which has always struck me as a priggish and even vindictive poem wherein Pope's inferiority complex is unhappily at work, and where, though the invective to which it rises is unique, his fragments of self-justification and self-flattery undermine the whole. In Pope, as in Tennyson, sensuality was more rewarding than a moral sense.

Mr. Butt's notes follow through the poems like a handrail in a subterranean passage, and one comes to lean on them heavily. He makes the political significance clear, and a parallel emerges with our own time, for Walpole, with his appeasement, was not unlike Mr. Chamberlain, and Bolingbroke, the lion in opposition, not unlike Mr. Churchill. Could not these lines be ironically applied to the Hero of Munich?

> Oh! could I mount on the Maeonian wing,
> Your Arms, your Actions, your Repose to sing!
> What seas you travers'd! And what fields you fought!
> Your Country's Peace, how oft, how dearly bought!
> How barb'rous rage subsided at your word,
> And Nations wonder'd while they dropped the sword!

But the appeal of Pope must always be to lovers of poetry, to those who appreciate the subtlest arrangements of which the language is capable, and they will look forward to the remaining volumes of this admirable edition, perhaps regretting that the old spelling was not preserved, but more concerned with the mysteries of versification, the technique of a great artist:

> O you! whom Vanity's light bark conveys
> On Fame's mad voyage by the wind of Praise . . .

Such lines seem all air, yet the structure is rigid, and each word has weight.

Ninety Years
of Novel Reviewing

The reviewing of novels is the white man's grave of journalism; it corresponds, in letters, to building bridges in some impossible tropical climate. The work is grueling, unhealthy, and ill-paid, and for each scant clearing made wearily among the springing vegetation the jungle overnight encroaches twice as far. A novel reviewer is too old at thirty; early retirement is inevitable, *"les femmes soignent ces infirmes féroces au retour des pays chauds,"* and their later writings all exhibit a bitter and splenetic brilliance whose secret is only learned in the ravages on the liver made by their terrible school. What a hard-boiled, what a Congo quality informs their soured romanticism! Invalided out only in February, my memory is still fresh with the last burgeoning of prolific and uniform shrubs and bushes. Those leathery weeds, so hard to kill, at first attract through the beauty of their flowers—the blurb or puff "splurging," as a botanist has described it, "its gross trumpet out of the gaudy wrapper." Wiry, yet insipid, characterless, though bright, these first-flowering blooms of Girtonia or Ballioli are more oppressive in their profusion, most reviewers will agree, than the forest giants, the Galsworthys and Walpoleworthys, whose creeper-clad trunks defy attempts to fell them.

An unpleasant sight in the jungle is the reviewer who goes native. Instead of fighting the vegetation, he succumbs to it, and, running perpetually from flower to flower, he welcomes each with cries of "genius!" "What grace, what irony and distinction, what passionate sincerity!" he exclaims as the beaming masterpieces reproduce themselves rapidly, and only from the banned amorphophallus, "unpleasant, dreary, difficult, un-English," he turns away his eyes.

Another sight for the cynic is the arrival of the tenderfoot who comes fresh from the university and determined, "above all, to be just—to judge every book on its merits—not to be led astray by the airs and graces of writing, the temptations to score off a book in reviewing, but primarily to try and help the author while advising the reader as well." "The great thing," he begins, "is never to forget one's standards—and never to grow stale." I remember very well sitting round the camp fire one night when Tenderfoot and "Goo-Goo" (who was then going native) were "doing" a book. The date escapes me, but it should be easily traceable, for I remember there was some talk of the *Mercury* falling off, and the *Criterion* getting dull.

"This book," said Goo-Goo, "has genius, and not only is it a work of genius—of passionate intellectual sincerity and emotional directness—but it comes very near to being the best novel of the month, or at least of the latter part of it."

"Although I would willingly give an earnest," interrupted the Tenderfoot, "that this is Miss Bumfiddle's first novel, she seems to be a writer of very delicate intention, and has brought to a difficult subject a restraint, a distinction, that, to my thinking, makes *Goosegrass or Cleavers* remarkable not only as a novel, which, if not of the very first order (remember my standards), does at least attempt to state the series of reactions which a young woman of keener sensibility and more vulnerable perception than the common must inevitably receive in the conflict between genius—I use the word in all circumspection—and what, for want of a better definition, we must call life. I should like, however, to suggest to Miss Bumfiddle, in all fairness—"

"*Goosegrass or Cleavers*," broke in Goo-Goo, beaming tipsily, "is modern, as the name implies—as modern as Matisse or Murasaki. It is bold, and confronts the critic in all the perishable flamework of youth—of postwar youth burning fitfully in all its incandescent ardour. Take the scene where Alimony leaves her parents:

Midway between springsummer and summerautumn falls the old-fashioned month of August-come-July—season of gross yellow moons, brown grass, and lousy yearnings. Alimony lay awake counting the slats of the blind that seemed to scab viciously across the rich broth of evening sunlight like the splayed fingers of a crucified neargod, a flayed Marsyas. She hated bed by daylight. Through the windows came the noise of the party and her parents' voices. "Now try and rush the red down to the next hoop—with luck you might perhaps push her through it. Oh dear! You should have poked her more." "But I did poke her." Alimony cringed involuntarily. To think she ever would be one with the ungainly old—and yet tomorrow was her birthday! It was hot, stifling—out in the fields perhaps. . . . She opened the introduction to a novel beside her. "A short while ago a friend of mine put into my hands an object which I had little difficulty in recognizing—Sir James Buchan and Mr. John Barrie, whom I consulted, soon confirmed me. 'Yes,' they said, 'it is a book, but only identifiable as such by a few discriminating people.'" Idly she turned the pages. "Girt slough of cloud lay cast upon the jannock mere. Weaver, be th'art there—weaver, I'm drained with love of you among the drule scrobs, though in the village they call me a hard woman." "Ah, to write—to write like that," thought Alimony—"to write like Mary Webb. But how, without experience? Out in the fields perhaps.". . . She rose and collected a few scattered belongings. Tiptoeing down the stairs, she saw it was not yet past seven. Suddenly she imagined herself tiptoeing through life, a broken stalk embalmed of this day's roses—like her own equivocal youth, now cast behind for ever. "Alimony! go back to bed." It was her mother. Something in Alimony seemed to snap. She turned, her face transfigured. "For crap's sake leave me alone, mother. I will not be run by people; all my life people have been trying to run me and all my life I've been escaping them. I damn will continue to. I guess my life is my own, even if it is a mess, isn't it? And you presume to speak to me when I have to listen to you and Poppa fighting on the lawn like a pair of alley cats. Hell and all it gripes me so I guess I could up-chuck." "Dearest mine o' mine, my own ownest, my octopet." "Oh, go sit on a tack, mother—can't you see I've had enough of it?" She flung out, past the front door, with its friendly knocker, on to the gravel, by the dining-room windows. She turned to look through them. Her birthday presents were there for the morning; on the table was the solemn cake with its eleven candles. The click of croquet balls sounded faint on the lawn. "Weaver," she sighed again; and something told her the old Alimony was dying—would be dead, perhaps, before the night was past—before even the moon of metroland had risen on the filling stations.

"A strong book," resumed Goo-Goo. "This is no work for those who prefer—"

"One has to be on one's guard, of course," said Tenderfoot, "against being too sympathetic to a writer simply because she provides a restatement of one's own problems."

"One of the few modern masterpieces," continued the other, "a book for the library rather than the linen room—for those who like to find, between a Bradshaw and a breviary, between a gold and a glister, a modern-ancient trifle that will fulfil Milton's definition of the novel as something slow, sinuous, and sexy. A work, in fact, a work of— But be it not mine to deface our lovely currency by stressing that most distressful word. Simply I will say—slowly, sinuously, but not, I hope, sexily, 'Welcome, Miss Bumfiddle! welcome, Alimony!'"

And yet, looking back on those evenings when the fates of so many unreadable books, and so many more unread ones, were brilliantly decided, I can't help feeling regret and tenderness rather than relief at being free of them. It is easy to forget the nerve strain and the nausea, the cynical hopelessness with which we strove to quench the indefatigable authors. There is something so clean and surprising about a parcel of review copies that one cannot but feel pleasure in opening them. The sense of getting something for nothing, though short-lived, is pleasant while it lasts, and the early expectations one had of discovering a new writer are perhaps less keen a pleasure than one's later hopes of being able to discredit an old one. The real fault of English fiction is that it has ceased to be readable. If novels were only this, it would matter much less that they were bad. American writers are readable; in general, a second-rate American book carries a reader along with it. He may resent this afterward, but it is desirable at the time. The English novel doesn't, and never will so long as it consists either of arranged emotional autobiography or a carefully detached description of stupid people to show that the author is too clever to be clever. But I am getting into my stride again. Meanwhile a new generation of novel-reviewers is growing up, and this thought brings me to the real tragedy of reviewing—to that ironical and irrevocable law of poetic justice which ennobles the humdrum work and allows the broken journalist to feel in his very ruin something of the divine. For all the novels that he scotches the novel will in time scotch him; like the King at Nemi, the slayer shall himself be slain. Brave and agile, the reviewer enters the ring. He rushes blindly at the red wrappers. He disembowels a few old hacks. But his onsets eventually grow futile, his weapons are blunted, his words are stale. He may go under nobly, a Croker facing his Keats; he may simply wear out in praising or abusing—(it matters not which)—the never-ceasing flow of second-rate and worthy productions—but eventually the jungle claims him.

What advice, then, would I give to someone forced—for no one could be willing—to become a reviewer? Firstly, never praise; praise dates you. In reviewing a book you like, write for the author; in reviewing any other, write for the public. Read the books you review, but you should need only to skim a page to settle if they are worth reviewing. Never touch novels written by your friends. Remember that the object of the critic is to revenge himself on the creator, and his method must depend on whether the book is good or bad, whether he dare condemn it himself or must lie quiet and let it blow over. Every good reviewer has a subject. He specializes in that subject on which he has not been able to write a book, and his aim is to see that no one else does. He stands behind the ticket queue of fame, banging his rivals on the head as they bend low before the guichet. When he has laid out enough he becomes an authority, which is more than they will. And had I stood the climate, this was what I might have been! The problem of the retiring age has long bewildered economists. Wandering, as I now do, among other finished critics, broken in health and temper by the rigours of the service, or the censure of authors, publishers, and public, I can't help wondering, in the shabby watering-places, the *petits trous pas chers* near Portsmouth or the Riviera that the retired inhabit, if we are really down and out. Can a reviewer come back? Is he too old at twenty-five? Could he find a place, with younger men, in the front lines where

they stem the advance of autumn novels—and die in harness?
I know it is foolish to dream, to think on these possibilities. I
should face facts as bravely as I once faced fiction.

> miser Cyrille desinas ineptire
> et quod vides perisse perditum ducas—

And yet these secret heartburns are only human. The other
day, languishing among the back numbers in a French hotel, I
received a letter from New York which almost gave me hope
again. "When," demanded the writer—"when will you tell
the public that Mr. Compton Mackenzie, in his last three novels, has not only recaptured the prose style of Congreve, but
also Congreve's attitude to life?" "When," I breathed—and
there were tears in my eyes—"when shall I?"

More about
the Modern Novel

Sixty books out of every hundred published are novels, nine
out of those sixty are here, three out of that nine are readable,
none out of the three worth seven and sixpence. This type of
remark is a reviewer's platitude by now. There are several
obvious but impracticable remedies. One author thinks that
novels, like poetry, shouldn't be reviewed any more. Then
only the best work would struggle occasionally into print. But
if novels are not reviewed, then the publishers complain (for
sixty books out of every hundred, etc.), and if they complain
they will not advertise, and consequently there wouldn't be a
paper left in which to review the good ones. I would prefer to
have a close season, no new novels to be published for three
years, their sale forbidden like that of plovers' eggs. And nobody under thirty should be allowed to write one—it is amusing to apply this age-canon and see how well it works out, how
little would be lost to us. But above all, I should like to see an
enormous extension of the censorship—not simply libel and
obscenity would be taboo, but whole landscapes, whole strata
of our civilization would become unmentionable. Schools and
universities, all homes with incomes of between three thousand and three hundred a year, words like Daddy, love,
marriage, baby, birth, death, mother, buses, shops—I particularly dislike both the shopping expedition ("she looked at her
list, let me see, two bars of soap, three bars of chocolate, but
already the huge store had overwhelmed her with its Oriental
mystery—it was an Arab bazaar, Eunice decided rapidly as
she paused before a chinchilla mantilla. Seven yards of demi-
rep the list continued")—and those horrible bus-rides, when

the stars are so close, and the young man treads on air ("he was getting nearer, Pimlico was a forgotten dream, Fulham and West Brompton passed unheeded—supposing she should be out? 'Fares please,' shouted the conductor for the third time. 'Fourpenny to heaven,' he answered unthinking"), and picnics, and going for walks, and conversations in pubs, and all novels dealing with more than one generation or with any period before 1918 or with brilliant impoverished children in rectories or with the following regions, which I understand are going to be preserved from novelists by the National Trust: the Isle of Wight, the Isle of Purbeck, Hampshire, Sussex, Oxford, Cambridge, the Essex coast, Wiltshire, Cornwall, Kensington, Chelsea, Hampstead, Hyde Park, and Hammersmith. Many situations should be forbidden, all getting and losing of jobs, proposals of marriage, reception of love-letters by either sex (especially if they are hugged closely and taken up to attics or the familiar seat in the apple tree), all allusion to illness or suicide (except insanity), all quotations, all mentions of genius, promise, writing, painting, sculpting, art, poetry, and the phrases "I like your stuff," "What's his stuff like?" "Damned good," "Let me make you some coffee," all young men with ambition or young women with emotion, all remarks like "Darling, I've found the most wonderful cottage" (flat, castle), "Ask me any other time, dearest, only please—just this once—not now," "Love you—of course I love you" (don't love you)—and "It's not that, it's only that I feel so terribly tired."

Forbidden names: Hugo, Peter, Sebastian, Adrian, Ivor, Julian, Pamela, Chloe, Enid, Inez, Miranda, Joanna, Jill, Felicity, Phyllis.

Forbidden faces: all young men with curly hair or remarkable eyes, all gaunt haggard thinkers' faces, all faunlike characters, anybody over six feet, or with any distinction whatever, and all women with a nape to their neck (he loved the way her hair curled in the little hollow at the nape of her neck).

Really good novels excepted, the rest fall into two kinds, English and American; the one will probably be written by a woman, the other by a man. The English novel certainly, the

American probably, will begin with childhood. This insistence on childhood is the radical defect of most ordinary novels of today. There are three reasons for this. Childhood is not in itself interesting, the great accounts of childhood are of abnormal childhoods, and the reader is now too wary to be caught with this familiar bait—which permits the novelist to meander about among the past, confident of hiding his egotism under a thin coating of squalid charm, and behind a tender appeal to the universal experience of the race. Secondly, childhoods are nearly all wholly irrelevant to any plot; memoirs, essays, poems are the proper place for accounts of childhood; at the beginning of novels they only hold up the action, while giving a very poor idea of the characters. And lastly, the novelist is usually clever, and the childhoods of the clever are invariably unpleasant, a record of grievances and snubs, of too brutal perception and too smart replies. Then the childhood theme is often introduced to show up the parents, a dreary device. Formerly the most touching feature of Victorian novels lay in such a situation as "Mother, why have those men taken father away?" "There has been a dreadful mistake, my darling, but he will soon come back, for the law will put it right." This has changed, however, to the child complaining with all the pained malice of the habitual eavesdropper of commenting brutally, with the penetration of self-pity, on the defects of the parents' conjugal relations.

The American novel will only not begin with childhood if the hero is a group hero (a family, a factory, a small town, a business, or the American nation). In these cases it usually begins several generations farther back with matter which is as irrelevant as childhood, but which yields that dazzling sequence of births and deaths which enables the book to appear an "epic." The typical 100 percent American novel has almost invariably a group hero, and is usually a monument of wasted energy, sentimentality striving after realism, and an admirable talent for description being thrown away on life that is quite unworthy to be described. This vigorous material confidence provokes many exceptions, and these in turn fall into three classes, for the romantic revolt against success in life and realism in literature has but a very narrow path of escape. If the novelist hates business, births and deaths and prosperity, he falls a victim to minority worship and writes about Indians, Mexicans, Negroes, or subject populations of America, finding in them the idealism which is his goal. If he is too reflective for those, he falls back on the past—tales of a grandmother, the old days on the farm, the novel of the orchard. If he is interested as well in style, he is swallowed up by Europe. This type of American is invariably a culture snob. These uprooted self-exiled Americans, however, are mostly taking refuge from a life for which they were unfitted rather than seceding in passionate rebellion; hence a limpness in all their work, for the soft spot that caused their failures in their native land becomes a defiant timidity when they are landed on an indifferent Europe; hence the tepid quality of the expatriate American novel, which has escaped vulgarity to become insipid instead. Many more American novels are halfway toward Europe, with a dullness about things American similar to that in caterpillars, which, when about to enter their chrysalis, go off their feed. The culture applauded in these American novels is nearly always the French literature of the end of the last century, the art for art's sake movement which reveals the timidity rather than the defiance at the heart of these emigrants religiously escaping for the sake of their style. Flaubert, Verlaine, Huysmans, Baudelaire, Pater, Henry James, and George Moore are alluded to most frequently by these intending fugitives, and a mention of one of them should place the book at once for the reader, just as that of an American real-life writer will betray the fake epic, the ruthless saga about the most commonplace world.

With the English novel we are in a different universe, the realm of the egotist, and of the most dangerous kind of egotists, those who, for self-protection, have developed the gland of charm. Having so often bewailed the glut of feminine autobiographies, there is little more to say about this except to warn the reader against the daydream which, always abused in these novels, leaves a sickening taste behind. The daydream is an immense discovery for the novel's technique, but an innate capacity for luxurious wish-fulfilment makes it an instrument to be handled with the greatest reluctance and care. The daydream should be crisp, terse, and relevant to the plot, or else an exquisite and impersonal lyric like a simile from Homer or *Paradise Lost*. When the reader experiences a muzzy and unpleasantly tipsy feeling, it means the passage is autobiographical, and probably the most trying form of autobiography, the arrangement which self-worship dictates of how something might have happened could we have it all over again. These English autobiographies, however, at least end in marriage, while the American epics seldom end at all. They are, moreover, tender, graceful, and humorous books, and their zeal for understatement saves them from the terrible American faults of style ("powerful" passages in the epic, rhetorical epigrams in the Europeanized form). The English cake is plain and edible except for the dank spots where the mildew of childhood daydreams and school friendships has left its shadowy web; while the American is either massively stodgy and commemorative, thick with icing, or, like tea cake on a railway train, cut into thin, tasteless slices, not indigestible, but a little stale. If the reader can apply this classification to the main body of novels he will need no reviewer at all; only he must keep in mind the possibility of the grace of England, the vitality of America, or the enterprise of the Rive Gauche, producing at any moment a great work.

Oscar Wilde: 1

"Oscar Wilde has been dead long enough for an opinion of him and his work to be formed without prejudice," opens Mr. St. John Ervine. His impartiality is maintained for two pages, after which, with a rapid gear change, he reaches the cruising speed of bumbling vituperation which is kept up for the rest of the book*.

An Ulsterman who has written lives of Carson and Craigavon, Mr. Ervine seems to have a temperamental and racial bias against Wilde; he combines the aggressiveness of Carson with the malice of Brookfield and yet there is something almost mechanical about his virulence, as if he feels real to himself only in moral indignation. "Hate is a form of atrophy and kills everything but itself," wrote Wilde in prison: and in this book it leads, despite some interesting dramatic criticism, to distortion and misrepresentation.

Thus, though by all accounts the disposition of Robert Ross was angelic, Mr. Ervine portrays him as a kind of monster. And of Wilde he writes: "He bragged and boasted of his success, and demanded that his sycophants should boast and brag of it too. He sneered at rivals and belittled those who produced and performed his plays. They were unworthy of him. There was always a derogatory word on his lips for someone. . . . Other writers must be mentioned, if mentioned at all, only in derision."

Now if there is one fact uniformly vouched for about Wilde it is his total absence of malice: in this respect he was almost

* *Oscar Wilde: A present-time appraisal*, by St. John Ervine (Allen & Unwin).

unique among wits. "I knew Wilde," said the late Bishop of London, Dr. Winnington Ingram, "and in spite of his one great vice—which was surely pathological—I never met a man who united in himself so many lovable and Christian virtues." As to this vice, Mr. St. John Ervine lays down the law like a Bottomley come to judgment: "Ross, Wilde, and Douglas were habitual and incorrigible liars, as all pederasts are. . . ." Bold words! But do they account for the extraordinarily long shadow which Wilde still casts from his tomb in Père Lachaise, or help us to understand the mystery of his tragedy?

Gratefully we turn back to the wisdom and charity of the present Lord Queensberry's account of the men who destroyed his inheritance, to Mr. Montgomery Hyde's admirably documented *Trials of Oscar Wilde*, and to the good humor and good sense of Mr. Hesketh Pearson. Best of all are the brief accounts of the two poets who saw beneath the mask— Yeats and Gide*. Indeed, it was in answer to Gide's disparagement of his writings that Wilde exclaimed: *J'ai mis tout mon génie dans ma vie; je n'ai mis que mon talent dans mes œuvres*— what a cry of despair from the admirer of Ruskin and Arnold, the devoted disciple of Flaubert and Pater, the poet with a first in "Greats" who knew that his art, however, successful, had taken a wrong turning and who obscurely divined that some catastrophe was required to bring him back to the world of thought and poetry.

He wanted, of course, a catastrophe that was symbolic, not real; as he said to Gide, "I must go on as far as possible. Something is bound to happen . . . something else."

It was because, underneath his mask of flippancy, he was in despair that he allowed himself to fall completely under the spell of Lord Alfred Douglas. A man of forty is not destroyed by an undergraduate except by unconscious consent. Wilde's old life, his plays, his marriage, his social success were turning to dust and ashes. The "great white caterpillar," as a lady described him, awaited he exhilarating puncture of the sandwasp, hopefully abdicating to an egotism fiercer than his own.

Douglas was a gifted and desperate young man in search of

Oscar Wilde, by André Gide (William Kimber).

a substitute father; how could Wilde know that he would be treated exactly as Douglas had used his own poor Caliban of a parent, and eventually come to reproach Douglas in almost the same terms as Queensberry had used? "You are the atmosphere of beauty through which I see life," he writes at first; and even at the end, when he is becoming what Mr. Ervine calls "a drunken sponger in the back-streets of Paris," he explains his fatal return to Douglas in a letter to Ross: "I cannot live without the atmosphere of Love; I must love and be loved, whatever price I pay for it. . . ."

Wilde's truest remark was also made to Gide: "My great mistake, the fault for which I can't forgive myself, is that one day I ceased my obstinate pursuit of my own individuality, stopped believing in it because I listened to someone else, stopped believing I was right to live like that and began to doubt myself."

I take this "someone" to be Douglas, an Alcibiades at war with society, who lured the happy aesthete of the eighties off his pedestal of wit into the gloom of the underworld and the glare of the law courts. "And I? May I say nothing, my Lord?"

"His lordship made no reply beyond a wave of the hand to the warders, who hurried the prisoner out of sight. . . ."

Oscar Wilde: 2

First let us honor that rare combination, the scholar-publisher. Mr. Hart-Davis has got together enough Wilde letters to fill 800 pages, weeded out the inessential and the forgeries and contributed a mass of footnotes both necessary and readable, including thumbnail biographies of all the recipients which are models of compression. The index is a pleasure, and I regret to say that this costly and splendid book,* fruit of so much exacting labor, is a "must" for everyone who is seriously interested in the history of English literature—or European morals.

I use the word "regret" purposely. For after reading through the whole volume carefully (including my third reading of *De Profundis*, for Mr. Hart-Davis includes the final—British Museum—text) I did regret having to give up three days to Wilde. "I have put my genius into my life and only my talent into my work," he said to André Gide; and it is in his letters that a man's life and work run closest.

But my three days with Wilde's letters are no proof of his genius. On the whole they are viscous, even oppressive, they adhere rather than delight and one is left with the impression of having escaped at last the clutches of some great greedy beetle. It is the same feeling as we get with Sade's letters. Perhaps prison, among other damage, gears people too closely to trivialities, to petty grievances about possessions. Certainly *De Profundis* is an obsessive piece of writing, a quicksand of self-pity and recrimination in which the reader is soon up to the neck.

* *The Letters of Oscar Wilde*, edited by Rupert Hart-Davis (Hart-Davis).

Of the thousand letters here printed I should say that two-thirds were about money. It is an element in the condition of authorship that a great many letters must be about money; a writer is a fisherman with many lines out who must go around giving them all a tug. But Wilde's "business sense," of which he was evidently proud (and which was really an obsession with money), caused him to expatiate at great length on royalties and percentages, while after his release from prison nearly every letter includes a request or demand and he suffered agonies from being quite penniless until some friend or publisher, often himself impecunious, could send him ten or twenty pounds: one night Wilde said that by bankrupting him Queensberry had ruined him even more effectively than by putting him in jail.

Early success had made him extravagant. Luxuries became necessities, prison was only a temporary alleviation of a psychological urge to play the king. Free again, he was like a great stranded whale, beached and blowing for his native element, the "red and yellow gold" which had once come so easily. The only way to ease such sufferings is for friends to unite and provide an allowance which is paid in cash monthly, or better still weekly or even daily, taking in return any products of the pen. This is more or less what was being done for Wilde at the end by marvellous friends like Ross, Turner and More Adey.

It seems to me that with the years we all feel more and more guilty about Wilde and the paternal system of punishment which upheld the father (Lord Queensberry) and sent the prodigal off to stitch mailbags with public howls of righteous sadism. Homosexuality, flogging, prison, capital punishment —they form one deep chord in our puritan natures.

When I last wrote about Wilde I suggested that he had himself desired his notoriety and punishment, partly out of a need for self-destruction, an instinct to free his talent from the unreality of success, partly from a desire to challenge the hypocrisies of social convention; and there are lines in the letters that support this claim:

> Why is it that one runs to one's ruin? Why has destruction

such a fascination? Why, when one stands on a pinnacle, must one throw oneself down? No one knows, but things are so.

But a reading of the letters as a whole does not support this view. Wilde was clearly bowled over by Douglas. He never expected Queensberry's retaliation and walked straight into his trap. This truth only dawned on him in prison.

> Time after time, I tried, during those two wasted weary years, to escape, but he always brought me back, by threats of harm to himself chiefly. Then when his father saw in me a method of annoying his son, and the son saw in me the chance of ruining his father, and I was placed between two people greedy for unsavory notoriety, reckless of everything but their own horrible hatred of each other, each urging me on, the one by public cards or threats, the other by private, or indeed half-public scenes, threats in letters, taunts, sneers. . . . I admit I lost my head. I let him do what he wanted. I was bewildered, incapable of judgment. I made the one fatal step. And now—I sit here on a bench in a prison cell. (To Ross, Nov. 1896.)

I think this is a true explanation. Wilde failed to understand the nature of the mutual hatred of Queensberry and his son, or how the son, by replacing his real father with the doting extravagant Wilde, was also casting him for the hated role. Was there much difference between his telegram to his father—"What a funny little man you are"—and his later message to the sick Wilde: "When you are not on your pedestal you are not interesting. The next time you are ill I will go away at once." Money incidentally also runs all through *De Profundis*. Wilde seems to think no one has ever kept anyone before.

Wilde's tragedy resulted from his need for love. It so happened that just after creating Dorian Gray he met his *garçon fatal*, then an undergraduate at Oxford who was being blackmailed. Wilde came to the rescue of beauty in distress and fell, perhaps for the first time in his life, hopelessly in love. He was on the hook, and even when he protested against Douglas's failings, his scenes, his extravagance, his petulance, the near-madness of his rages, he could not see that this invulnerable rival egotism was part of what kept him on the hook. Two kinds of desperation ran together. Wilde wrote his only real love-letters to Douglas, he was the "graceful boy with a Christ-like heart," "my immortal, my eternal love," "my sweet rose, my delicate flower, my lily of lilies, it is perhaps in prison that I am going to test the power of love . . . I have had moments when I thought it would be wiser to separate. Ah! moments of weakness and madness." "You have been the supreme, the perfect love of my life. There can be no other."

Perhaps the real tragedy of Wilde's life—assuming that prison or some equivalent suffering was necessary to the rehabilitation of his talent, as he sometimes believed—lay in the bad planning of his release. By going only as far as Dieppe and settling at Berneval he seemed on the threshold of a new and simpler existence, happy in freedom, natural beauties, and little pleasures. But once these wore off, it was the *fin de saison* and the weather became British. Wilde easily succumbed to Douglas's appeals and went to join him in Naples.

"My only hope of again doing beautiful work in art is being with you." When the friends protested at this ominous renewal he wrote defiantly to Ross, "I cannot live without the atmosphere of Love. I must love and be loved whatever price I pay for it. . . . When people speak against me for going back to Bosie, tell them that he offered me love, and that in my loneliness and disgrace I, after three months' struggle against a hideous Philistine world, turned naturally to him. Of course I shall often be unhappy, but I still love him: the mere fact that he wrecked my life makes me love him."

The Douglas family cut off Boise's allowance, Mrs. Wilde cut off his, and the poverty which neither could tolerate soon forced them to separate. Wilde's last reference runs, "Bosie I have not seen for a week. I feel sure he will do nothing [for Wilde]. Boys, brandy and betting monopolize his soul. He is really a miser: but his method of hoarding is spending: a new type."

Other lines of speculation suggested by the letters: whether Wilde's career would have been saved if he had joined the Catholic Church at Oxford, as he so nearly did; or if he had, with his double first, become a school inspector, as he tried to do. Perhaps what emerges from his letters is his fatal indifference to the real demands of a talent. No one talked more about art and artists or worked less. He mistook greed and lust and vainglory for life and allowed insincerity and affectation to seep through everything he wrote, with such fatal facility, so that he survives only through his one comedy and a couple of melodramas.

He had all the gifts of a great writer except the conscience and was behind, rather than ahead of, his time. His two letters on penal reform to a daily newspaper are models of vigorous polemical writing, without humbug, and as modern as his early letters to his parents from Italy. They show what he might have done without his exhibitionism. But then we should not have had his conversation.

Mr. Vyvyan Holland deserves a word of special thanks for allowing the letters to be printed in their entirety.

Living with Lemurs

After twenty years I have a ring tailed lemur again; my sixth. I still think them the most delightful of all pets; it is their owner, not the breed, who has deteriorated. Yet a singular doubt has grown. Are they clockwork? How do they differ from a machine?

I used to think of them as possessing an unearthly quality— ghosts; *lemures*, like their name—uncanny, primitive, remote; man's one authentic ancestor. Their plaintive cry, their eyes of melting brown under long black lashes, the indescribably forlorn and touching quality of their expression as if dimly aware of their predicament halfway between man and beast, a terrier's head on a furlined Pharaoh's body, toenails as well as claws, hands that grip fruit yet cannot peel it. . . .

And now they remind me of Arab musicians. "How unutterably sad," I said of such monotonous singing. "No—the sadness is in you," my companion replied—and indeed the musicians were shaking with silent laughter. The lemur's typical plaintive cry, for instance, which certainly results from loneliness, from any separation from the herd, is also automatically reproduced in answer to any sound of the same pitch— children's voices or the mew of a cat.

A lemur, in fact, has about six noises each with its corresponding body posture, and runs through them in regular order like the gear changes on a car. They fall into three groups.

1. EMOTION	NOISE	POSTURE
Anxiety, hunger, etc.	= short mew	= skipping with imaginary rope
loneliness, recognition	= plaintive cry sometimes prolonged to a sob	= head lifted, cheeks blown out

2. EMOTION	NOISE	POSTURE
Excitement, irritation, play	= metallic, *bdib*, *bdib*, *bdib*	= leaping, bouncing
alarm	= short croak	= stares at suspicious object, jumps to safety
anger	= high squeak	= biting, clawing

3. EMOTION	NOISE	POSTURE
Pleasure	= purring	= licking and cuddling up
sex (males only)	= nasal whinny	= tail held over head and stiffly waggled

Lemurs are inclined to bite when food (or what they consider food—i.e. eyeblack, toothpaste) is taken away from them or when picked up roughly or much against their will, or when sexually rebuffed. If the ribs or armpits are tickled they are compelled to purr, to abandon any other posture and to start licking whatever lies in front of them.

They are, I believe, affectionate and devoted to only one master or mistress whom they will follow or precede closely; yet they appear quite promiscuous, like married couples at a cocktail party. They resent all ties or dependency and have a deep-rooted love of freedom; their temperament is amiable, steadfast, sunny and mischievous. The basic play form is "catch me if you can."

This is how they play together; an impertinent tap or nip is followed by a delirious chase ending in a boxing and wrestling match. They express themselves by their agility and will reserve their longest leaps for the largest audience—they seem to like best children and the very old.

Lemurs regard cats as being germane to themselves and will immediately attempt to groom them; dogs are generally to be teased. They are almost fearless, but all dislike aeroplanes and large birds. They rely on their brilliant timing to get out of the way, will jump on the dog's rump or advance backward upon it in a manner that even large hounds find completely unnerving.

Their front teeth form a currycomb; the canines grow back like fish hooks and can give a most painful bite; in addition the males have a blunt claw inside the elbow with which they can rip and tear in moderation; all box cleverly, "southpaws" who lead at their opponents' eyes.

When a lemur is let loose in a strange room it does not skulk in corners and investigate smells, like a dog or cat, but immediately establishes a four-wall circuit until it can leap round the room at picture level. Each new leap is tested with hilarious *bdib-bdib-bdib-bing*. In these circuits, pictures, china and even quite large pieces of furniture come rapidly to grief and—since lemurs are beautifully precise and sure-footed—it is clear that they enjoy the crash and jingle of breaking glass or cascading Chelsea. Out of doors they will choose some fragile and elastic shrub and bounce up and down on it, like children on a clump of rushes. They will always answer and come when called yet show the greatest reluctance to being caught, except when feeling tired or cold.

At night they prefer to sleep in a bed, will find their way to the bottom like a hot water bottle and remain quiet for hours. They rise at dawn. They will not foul their bed but it is impossible to house-train them; any perch above ground is considered a privy.

On the other hand they can be controlled to some extent through the times when they are fed and, being vegetarians, are seldom noxious. They will consume between two and three bananas a day, one or two bits of bread or cake, some grapes or a few leaves of lettuce. They must be protected from alcohol or they become topers.

Lemurs are not greedy and spend very little of their time in eating. Sleep, play, and fur combing come first. Their coat is short, thick, and extremely soft with a smell of young kitten. They enjoy traveling and will sit for hours looking out of a railway window.

What are the limits of their intelligence? If tied to a post they immediately become hopelessly entangled and, unlike a monkey, can never unwind themselves. They will not run carrying their leash in one hand, as I have seen a monkey do, but can tug at it if it is bothering them. They altogether lack the imitative impulse of monkeys and their hands are extremely clumsy.

Matches and match boxes fascinate all lemurs though they have great difficulty in manipulating them; newly cut wood usually sets up the elbow-clawing reaction.* Their sight and hearing are excellent and they perceive everything; in fact, they may well be much more intelligent than anyone has supposed since their reproachful glance or sneer or look of love is subtle almost to the point of imperceptibility.

They never appear as if they are trying to say something—they are too self-satisfied, too much the dandy to give way to emotion. Their parting protest, however, can lacerate one with guilt.

The ring-tailed lemur *(lemur catta)* has a fairly short history. It appears in a Chinese painting of the eighteenth century and in several eighteenth century pictures, one a charming Stubbs of the Duke of Atholl's family. With the gibbon, Humboldt's woolly monkey, the sea-lion, cheetah, beaver, and otter it is in the top flight of pets; it is hardy, diurnal, clever, sensitive and devoted, reasonably clean and very easy to feed as it can be let loose for long stretches in the garden.

Before the war there was a great rush on lemurs and the French Government has now prohibited their export from Madagascar. They are preserved, like the Australian koala, in their dwindling forests. I am not sure that this is the right policy; it would be better to enclose them in various tropical and subtropical zoos where the climate suits (even an English

---

* Mr. Ivan Sanderson wrote to me that the horny excrescences release a glandular secretion.

summer day drives them into the shade) to encourage them to breed in captivity.

But breeding is difficult for human beings seem to exercise a fatal fascination; lemurs will spurn their own image to pursue the huge creatures who, like monkeys and apes, are descended from them, who once possessed a tail with sixteen rings and the lost virtue of irresponsibility.

Beyond Believing

I have reached an age at which I am sometimes asked what I believe. The question invariably confounds me. Before I can reply the mind panics as when, in a free association test, it is given the word "lake"—lake, hake, fake, crimson-lake, *"Delacroix, lac de sang hanté des mauvaises anges"*—deep sleep: and at the thought of that eternal sleep (better lake than never) I linger delectably over the word: reaction time twenty-five seconds. So, like La Fontaine, I believe in sleep: the time spent in sleep (the time when we are out of trouble) is not charged to our account but is handed back to us in later life to use as we please: sleep and its stealthy approaches: daydream, doze, siesta, garlic's blackjack; wine's persuasion; the phrase dimming on the page, the book falling from the hand; these are reservoirs of perennial youth and therefore all but sacred. "Death will come on swift wings to him who disturbs the sleep of the Pharaoh" (Inscription on Tutankhamen's tomb).

Sleep first then, and secondly—Irresponsibility. And by irresponsibility I mean the refusal to accept any obligations as a social animal, as well as a mere European, Englishman, or good citizen.

> Hippocleides, a young Athenian chosen by Cleisthenes of Sicyon as husband for his daughter. At the final banquet Hippocleides not only insisted on dancing, but even stood on his head on the table and waved his legs in the air. Cleisthenes was disgusted and cried, "O son of Pisander, you have danced away your marriage." The young man smiled and said, "Hippocleides don't care," which became a proverb. *(Lemprière's Classical Dictionary.)*

A proverb which we too seldom hear when all the talk is of

Atlas; of shouldering burdens and responsibilities, of fulfilling
trusts and missions, carrying out our obligations as a great
power, great debtor, etc., and meeting new crises, sternly facing facts. What are these facts? That modern man, and in particular, Western man, and above all, European man has
become mortally involved in a web of duties and sanctions, of
social, emotional, and intellectual obligations. Knowledge de-
sires to be known and the task of the living is to acquire it. The
past refuses to let itself be obliterated at the old pace. Consider
the London Record Office, the newspaper files of the British
Museum, the wills and codicils of Somerset House, the multiplication of microfilm: then compare for one moment the life
of man with that of an African elephant, which lives for about
the same span. How much knowledge will the elephant,
wisest of beasts, require in its eighty years? Of what to eat,
what not to eat, of where to go, where not to go.

Consider the savages who surround such elephants—pyg-
mies, Azande, and the like—they need to learn only a little
more, a few crafts and skills, hunting methods, songs and
dances, tribal traditions, witch doctors' beliefs. But an educated Western European begins to be crammed at the age of
three; he must go to school, learn to read and write, acquire
Latin and French, history, science, economics, mathematics,
draw a map of the kingdoms of Israel and Judah, know the
purchasing power of the mark in the reign of King John or the
logistics of a Roman legion; his I.Q. is graded at four-and-a-
half, endless examinations and probably two years of military
service await him, then a lifetime of ferocious competition and
financial liabilities, until, at rest in the tax-free grave (though
even graves must be kept up), he hands on the burden to his
loved ones in the form of posthumous debts and death-duties.
I have left out the particular responsibilities of each country as
the custodian of its national glories or protector of other people's; I remark only on my travels that ignorance is bliss and
that the happiest people would be the least organized, except
that no one will let them alone. I think Freud in his *Civilisation
and its Discontents* understood the root of the trouble when he
remarked that the State is more anal-erotic (mean, tidy, obsti-

nate, and grasping) than the individuals who compose it. We inherit the passions of bygone bureaucracy, we have created even in our least corrupt institutions (inland revenue, customs and excise, probate, etc.) non-human cancerous growths, benignant tumors which oppress our society. The living cannot breathe because the dead refuse to die. A packet of old love-letters turns up in the attic—a delicious theme for a novel. But I have seen such attics slope downstairs; I have watched a fine dinner party ruined as a coprolithic flow of old stamp catalogues, imperfect collections of mosses and minerals, of pedigrees of racehorses, time tables, bus tickets, score cards, or boxes of brass cowbells, Welsh postcards and legless Swiss bears, piles up against the door and pelts like a rain of lapilli on stricken host and guests, dispelling the aroma of cigars and brandy, of roses and red wine, in a dusty faecal miasma of hereditary hoarding. It is to early Christian art, according to Malraux, that we owe the first wonderful portraits of old men; the Jeromes, Augustines, and Gregorys no longer merely serene, their wise old faces furrowed with the consciousness of sin and suffering. Hippocleides must dance them away.

> The universe spells death with a small "d"
> Disdains proud "I" yet sanctions little me. . . .

The natural condition of created things I hold to be one of undiluted ecstasy. Self-consciousness is the consequence of some imperceptible deviation in biological process, a deviation spreading like a ladder in a stocking which cannot now be halted.

Very small organisms have no fear or knowledge of death which, in a cell, is synonymous with parturition, and quite large organisms have no feeling of pain. It was not obligatory that there should be any disturbance of the primal ecstasy according to whether one ate or was eaten. The plankton barges into the Whale's open jaws as the Tunnel of Love. The indifference to death of some large creatures like turkeys and camels remains otherwise inexplicable. "Man has created death" because he has watched man die. Even so, assuming that natural, even violent death could be part of our ecstasy as human beings or that our awareness of it can add meaning and poetry to life, such noble exits can be the reward only of a Sophocles or Goethe for in our time and place so full a life—the slow, simultaneous ripening and ultimate rotting of mind with body —is seldom attainable. The happiest creatures are those which live out their brief existence in instinctive harmony with the universe, unconscious of their role in it. But since self-consciousness has arisen, we must stake all on developing it to the ultimate moment when we shall have completely understood our environment, for to understand may be to change it, to find a way of reducing death (so nearly a blessing, and the source of all our dignity and tragedy) to something we can bear. Self-consciousness, which begins with the awareness of death, may end with its elimination. And here we have certain indications that we are on a likely path.

I believe in two wholly admirable human activities, guilt-free, unpunished, two ends in themselves rewarding: the satisfaction of curiosity (acquirement of knowledge) and the mating of like minds (friendship and mutual attraction) with the apprehension of beauty in so far as it be not included in the other two. It is impossible to undertake any kind of research without being perpetually made aware that the truth is plying us with suggestions, the past prodding us with hints and that if no benefits result from such assistance, it is not the fault of our heavenly helpers but of our all too human obtuseness. Who wrote *Kubla Khan?* We now know what books Coleridge had read; everything that was in his mind—but we know also how completely incapable he was, in normal conditions, of making use of such knowledge. Setting this impotent polymath to a constructive task, forcing an entrance into his cranium, the divine ecstasy (inspiration) flowed in, reassembled the metaphysical jigsaw into the greatest poetry to which the sodden organism could be attuned, then broke the reverie. With all the help of inspiration we can do only a little better than our best.

The mating of like minds is often expressed by the meeting of bodies and I would like to include both under the heading of mutual attraction—but with full physical union on the one hand or long standing friendship on the other a whole new set of obligations arise. I refer only to the phenomenon of "getting off" with someone, to the magical moment when we are neither hurt nor bored, when the letters in a name spin its anagram, when a handshake proclaims the return of Ulysses and a look can awaken the hyacinth of unborn springs. Sometimes these two profound and unpunished sensations are blended, especially when we are studying the past lives of old artists and writers for then knowledge and love coincide and the dead whom we have exhumed are reincarnated by the imagination.

Here one is greatly helped by such things as association copies and if an attachment to these be sentimental, there is no greater sentimentalist than I, for I believe that communication with dead writers becomes particularly intense when one is reading their marginal annotations, their notebooks or letters. Good criticism is a form of spiritualism but the medium must possess the facts, not a lock of hair. The living denigrate the dead; they must or else they would be dominated by them but the handwriting of a dead man still retains something of his bygone arrogance. The Past, of course, is the natural subject of literature, though many writers ignore this or, to put it another way, it is what Time does to Action that is our particular province. Homer, Dante, Shakespeare, Milton, Flaubert, Proust, they all climbed under the tent. At five, ten, twenty, fifty, one hundred, or one thousand years ago, according to each writer, a point of maximum intensity was reached on which imagination could focus and so marinate people and events to perfection.

Do I believe in Art? If life be ecstasy there is nothing to say but "Alleluia," if that ecstasy be lost then what can Art do to relive it? And here we discover the weakness of any such word as belief. In the last analysis, at the moment when the bullet sears the flesh, when the plane plummets or the anaesthetic counts me out, can I really claim to believe in anything but panic and self-pity? No. Then how can I believe in Art? Or Liberty?

"Give me liberty or give me death"—does it mean any more than "give me Leamington or give me Bath?" In the ultimate crisis, to those without religious faith, surely all belief seems equally absurd? In moments of acute sea sickness or in that extraordinary onset of semi-consciousness known as being "taken ill" there is simply nothing or nobody but seems ridiculous and sinister, indifferent or hostile. I still suffer from occasional attacks of claustrophobia in lifts or crowded theatres and before the invisible hand starts throttling me—"fugitive from some just doom"—I receive an alarming impression of having walked into an enemy ambush. In those seconds on the edge of panic all my values collapse and crumble into common absurdity. One might argue that these are moments of irrational fear and that one might feel differently at the long-expected onset of death when resignation replaces anxiety. "On some fond breast the parting soul relies," and I hope that it is true, but I still think there should be one word for believing in art as I believe in it, in the sense in which we say, "I believe in colonic irrigation," and another for the faith of patriots and martyrs.

"Would you die for your country?"

"I have so many countries."

"Would you die for Queen and country?"

"Not if I could help it. I regard it as my duty to cling to consciousness until the last possible moment."

"Duty to yourself?"

"Duty to my consciousness."

"As an artist?"

"Certainly."

"As an artist, forgive me, you don't write much?"

"And I compose, paint, sculpt even less, but I am an artist all the same."

"What then is Art?"

"Art is the conscious apprehension of the unconscious ecstasy of all created things."

It is one process to perceive this ecstasy, another to be able to communicate it. Once perceived in terms of human consciousness, we set this ecstasy against man's knowledge of his fate and engender an attitude either of acceptance or rebellion, realist or romantic. I believe in the supreme importance, virtue, and necessity of this process for the history of Art is the chronicle of such human achievements as have approached nearest to perfection, of the elixir of humanity. This, I think, explains the homogeneity of genius; constantly, when we read of the childhood and adolescence of men of genius we are struck by how alike they are, by their effortless technical mastery of their medium at an early age, their precocious feats of memory, of understanding of adult states, above all, by the immense richness of imagery in a writer like Keats, of melody in a composer like Mozart which reveal their immediate insight into this blissful universal harmony.

I do not believe in original sin but as a mythological statement of the human condition it seems painfully true. The fall, and the likelihood of going on falling, explains far more to me than the idea of progress and perfectibility; we have a bias to ruin, an itch for self-destruction; our moments of ecstasy are sometimes intolerable and must be blotted out. The heart rusts, the soul silts up. I cannot accept this back-sliding as a theological fact, but I feel it may be biologically or physically correct, that in bodies the process of aging may instigate cruelty, lethargy, betrayal quite automatically; and I have remarked that any physical rejuvenation in myself—a slimming cure, a skiing holiday, a walking tour, even high altitudes in an aeroplane, induces a corresponding readaptation of belief, an impulse to universal love which endures till former conditions, over-eating, over-talking, over-competing, flu and fatigue, reassert themselves and the concept of love as the key and purpose to everything, the condition of the upper atmosphere, is once more enfeebled by the terrestrial envelope and the struggle for existence.

Even the lightness and brightness of all the materials connected with aeroplanes seem to point to a more light-hearted and light-headed way of life. The smiling air hostess is the archaic Greek Κορη in the Temple courtyard, the reassuring captain is the young bearded Zeus. In the air books seem inappropriate, the ectoplasm of the earthbound.

I have always been fascinated by the study of climate and in particular by its relationship to art. On the whole, art is a sun substitute—perpetual sunshine casts out art. Where are the art centers of the world? New York, Boston, Chicago, London, Paris, Brussels, Amsterdam, Munich, and Berlin, all with long winters. There is hardly any great painting south of Rome or Madrid, and an interesting map could be made of the concentration of genius, of the southern limit of antique shops, of easel painting (at what point does it become too hot to have pictures on the walls?), of good bookshops even. I noticed in the Tropics that European poetry only became significant just before it was going to rain and that incidentally it was no longer possible, owing to humidity or white ants, to enjoy fine bindings or first editions. Air-conditioning may increase the yield from warm places even as central heating has pushed the creative limit northward but the fact remains that if I were to say "I believe in Art," I would really mean, "I believe that in certain physical states (not extremes of pain, fear, lust, or ecstasy) the literature, painting, music, architecture, sculpture produced between latitudes 40 and 60 in the last two thousand years under seasonal conditions can justify existence to me while I also live between latitudes 40 and 60, and am subject to a similar awareness of the seasons."

I have noticed that Indians and Africans who spend some time in Europe very quickly assimilate European art which is not a racial but a geographical product; they take to it like umbrellas. All art, then, is relative, but the artist is eternal and if I could only be sure I were one it would not matter what else I believed. But only one part is an artist; another wishes to be remembered as lover, friend, sage or scholar, or simply an endurer, one who stayed to the end.

What Yeats wrote of Wilde, that "because of all that half-civilized blood in his veins he could not endure the sedentary toil of creative art" is true of most of us. Flaubert's day or indeed any other day spent between library and desk will often be felt a day wasted even as the sensation of movement, the most pointless journey will always seem valid by its combination of thought and action, of mobility with the indulgence of curiosity. An archaeologist's life seems to me among the most admirable. I believe that it is still possible for him to make discoveries of such significance that they may serve to put humanity back on the right path, discoveries about primitive Christianity or the nature of Egyptian and Greek religion, the lost books of Sappho and the Greek dramatists, Petronius, Tacitus, Livy, the *catalogue raisonné* of the Alexandrian library (I regard the burning of the Alexandrian library as an inconsolable private grief) or of buried works of art which will come to light in our time because we are so desperately in need of them.

Another profession I particularly admire is the Doctor's, above all the specialist in mental diseases who works on the frontier between psychology and the physiology of the brain and I also envy diplomats and Special Correspondents, for they are nomads without guilt. The capitalist, I mean the true capitalist, who lives by and through the manipulation of his capital, is also a free man after my own heart and when he combines great undertakings with a passion for the arts I feel he is to be ranked only a little lower than the artist himself, with Maecenas or the Medici, the princely builders, like the Popes and *Fermiers Généraux*. And yet what a miserable man is the artist with his vanity and envy, servility and egotism— and how much more miserable the capitalist who so seldom does anything for the living and competes for the prestige of the Past with rival collectors. If I were asked to name some characteristics typical of the mid-twentieth century, I would put first the uncritical worship of money, the spread of nationalism, the tyranny of the orgasm, the homosexual protest, and the apotheosis of snobbery. Money, sex, and social climbing motivate society.

Never have the rich lived so inconspicuously for themselves or done so little for other people—or been so rich for that matter, for I do not count the various altruistic tax-evasion schemes, the trusts, foundations, and municipal galleries which are now the rage, a form of giving away money that the state has already ear-marked, which permits the minimum human contact and plants on other shoulders the onus of discrimination. The ideal rich man of today is ideally mean, saving every sixpence for his posthumous trust rather than personally rewarding a poet or a painter, and purchasing only an occasional farm or a piece of Cromwellian silver or an impressionist like Sisley who is dead yet not altogether in the museums. Often he is homosexual and a snob about everything as well (though seldom a nationalist), and invariably an amateur painter or writer who is jealous of his colleagues, though eager to pick their brains. He paints best in winter, at Nassau, when all the other painters are in bed with flu, and writes most in summer, in his beach house. He no longer is privately printed but obtains very good terms. For money has emerged twin victor from the twentieth century wars— money for the Haves and Nationalism for the Have-nots. Never has wealth held so many attractions or provided such a sanction for the good life since the whole texture of living is altered for those who possess it. Money need no longer clog the mind and coarsen the sensibility. It provides an extra dimension. The rich can travel light, at last, airborne from one aesthetic experience to another; they dodge the winter, the wear and tear of sedentary toil, of families and fidelity, they are as remote from us as the cuckoo during the seven months when he is away. Only people engrossed in their work or who are perpetually in love can ignore this mobility.

So an alternative way of putting the question would be to say, is there anything you yourself believe in more than money, sex, or social climbing? Or nationalism? Any belief which enables you to contemplate without envy or inferiority the masters of life in this most luxurious of possible worlds? Here again I turn to my well worn trumps (1) the artist (and I would add the saint and the mystic if I knew more about them), (2) the lover, and (3) the joker, Hippocleides. Them and only them the capitalist cannot buy, the nationalist inflame or the snob deflate. They remain what the ancient Egyptians called "true of voice."

But there must be something else! Looking out of my garden window at the tall poplars and the Down beyond, listening to the confident squawk of an autumnal pheasant, the *fin-de-saison* stridency of the lawn mower, I am linked by my consciousness to the world of natural living of which for more than fifty years I have formed a part. Has this half-century of self-speculation given me nothing to affirm, nothing to render my leaving of the world of more consequence than the mowing of the grass, the shooting of a pheasant, the felling of a tree? *"Un homme au rêve habitué"* he died while still uncertain of the divinity of Jesus or the identity of Shakespeare, a sceptic of whom we can proudly write: *"Mort sur le champ d'ennui!"*

"We must live this life," answer Hippocleides and Voltaire, "as if every minute were precious except the last—a bad quarter of an hour about which we can do nothing." *"Supportons la vie qui n'est pas grand'chose et méprisons la mort qui n'est rien de tout."*

"Every third thought shall be my grave," counters Prospero, "you have perhaps ten, perhaps twenty years to prepare. Let every activity be subject to that end! Make a good death!"

"Consider a child," says Hippocleides. "What does everyone require of a baby? That it should eat well, sleep well, and laugh. Who wants to tell it of sorrow or fear, of death and disease, of sin and suffering? Children are our guests in the world and we must entertain them as well as we can and spare them the inconvenience of our mortal condition as we would a visitor from another planet. And what we would for them is surely right for us?"

I have left out one phenomenon besides the search for truth and the obsession with the form and shaping of a work of art—the devotion which is distilled, after years, from all the possessive kinds of love; which may have originated in boredom, unhappiness, habit, or lust, from an accident of fusion that creates something profound and selfless ("the giving which plays us least false") like the love of a parent for a child which yet keeps something of the child about it—a positive permanent illusion, a projection of lost early loves on to one person. In the field of discovery and the world of love miracles still happen. The presence of one of these long-suffering accomplices in our last act of existence may help to ease us out of it, or, when all those whom we have truly loved are dead, they may suffice to tip the scales for death, until dying becomes a renewal of communication with them. The rest is mineral emptiness.

III
SATIRES &
PARODIES

Felicity

As there seems a little space left over, I am utilizing it to thank those correspondents who have submitted unfinished manuscripts to me for advice and help. I am afraid they cannot be returned; for instance, I have lost all of Kip Streatham's novel, except the page beginning, "It felt pretty good to be out there under the moon with the gin running round in me like an electric hare and my arm as far as it would go round Myrtle." He will have to write another.

Hedda Bedales, who is "five feet ten and a half in her hikers," she tells me, has sent in a tale of primitive passion on a Hertfordshire farm somewhere up near the North Circular. Thirza, the heroine, refuses to take her bicycle out in the rain, and narrowly escapes a larruping. The second two hundred pages show a falling off.

But it is with real joy that I print some of the manuscript of Miss Aglae ("three syllables please, but it's not my real name anyhow") Oakenshaw's unpublished novel, "Absent from Felicity"—publishers, those lean subfusc creatures with rolled umbrellas and little blue engagement books, must keep a look-out for Aglae (-⌣⌣):

Felicity was dressing for dinner. A cosy gas fire burned in the grate toward which she held out her bare foot while she held out (in her hand I mean) a slinky open-mesh gold stocking. She loved to crinkle her toes in the firelight. Her foot didn't seem to belong to her, it was a little pink animal or something. She loved her bedroom, which had been her nursery, with its dado of beasts and its view out on the Hampstead garden.

There was a knock at the door. "Come in." It was Dads! "Hello, old chap," he said. "How's tricks?" She looked up lovingly at the curly head, tanned face, and open smile of her father. Dads was wonderful, only he worked so terribly hard. He was a blurb writer, and April was coming on so that he was absolutely indispensable. "Not been overdoing it, skipper?" she asked anxiously. "Only the Golding omnibus," he smiled back, but she thought he looked worried all the same. "Don't fret about me—I'm strong as a Steen." He laughed. It was one of their favorite jokes. "May there be no Cronin' at the Bar," she capped. "Hurry up now, old boy," he cried. "Don't keep your mother waiting." For Felicity's mother, Mrs. Arquebus, was a very special person. She pulled on her stocking and took a last look at the room. A bowl of hyacinths, her white bed with the green eiderdown, and very few pictures. A small oils by Barribal called *Green Chartreuse* hung over the mantelpiece, with its plaster gargoyles from the little shop near Notre Dame, and there were one or two etchings with masts and a choice Steggles of Rosebery Avenue that she had got, in an austere mood, out of the Picture Library when she took the Edward Wolfe back. And her books! She loved the little cabinet with its glass doors. There was just room for her favorite authors, Phyllis Bentley, Phyllis Bottome, Helen Waddell, Helen Simpson, G. B. Storm, Beverley, and Theodora Benson—and poetry, too, Humbert Wolfe of course, and some of the new writers who left one rather breathless, and whose books had lovely cold names like *Open the Sky* and *Armed October*. The door opened again. This time it was Mums. "Hurry up, daughter o' mine, there's a good fellow!" she cried. "Fellow" was Felicity's favorite nickname. She had brown curly hair, rather special brown eyes, and a nose with the weeniest tilt to it, "just room for a deck quoit," as Dads put it, and a very pretty figure. She loved green, smoked lots of cigarettes, adored dancing, but knew there were other things beside it, and was altogether a heathery honeyish brackeny kind of Hampstead Piskie, alternately the joy and tribulation of her family, servants, nanny, teachers, friends, and taxi drivers, in fact of everyone whose delight and misfortune it was to know her. Phew! She was just grown up. As Dads had said the other day, "Fellow used to be a drawing by Shepperson. Now she's a Gouache by Lewis Baumer." She repeated it to herself on her way down to the hall and cocktails. Tonight it was a party. There were two other successful blurb writers and their wives, Mr. Goulash the publisher, and two very nice young men for Felicity. A "poet" and a "thinker." "Mr. Beastly may drop in afterward," said Mums, who looked almost regal. "I'm thinking," said the thinker, "he has the root of the matter in him." "I've always found him charming myself," said Mr. Goulash; "the only realist in Flask Walk," said a blurb writer. "Is his new book *John Hanbury, Ironmaster*, or *John Hanbury, Ironmonger?*" whispered the other —"in writing the blurb that's going to be rather important; one used to be able to go by the picture on the wrapper, but with these beastly yellow-jacks one never can tell." They had out the silver fish knives and napkin rings "with two k's!" as Dads put it. That meant one of their grand parties.

Outside in the spring night the laburnums were hanging their golden bodkins over the wall, and the laurustinus loomed evilly out of the shadow. "Scrumptious, Sacred, and Profane!" cried one of the blurbies. "The moment I saw it I said, 'This is NOT a detective story.'" "I don't know what you mean by that word," said Miss Gibbon, who was a stickler for etymology. "And I don't know which word you mean either," riposted the blurbie. "And does Miss Felicity," he laughingly added, "inherit the family talent for 'appreciation'?" "Don't talk cocker," laughed Fellow—and she smiled secretly to herself at the idea of *Her* writing blurbs. For she was going to do something creative. A biography of her father, perhaps, with all the family jokes in it. Not that she wanted—she looked across at him, handsome, healthy, shaggy, smiling—still, you never knew, these athletes cracked up sooner than you expected, and blurb writing carried with it, she had heard, a high mortality. First the dedication—*to the memory of the dearest of Dads*—then the preface, "*I have not hesitated to set down the other side of the picture. Gilbert Arquebus was, in many ways, a very tiresome man. . . .*" Good heavens, what was she thinking! She smiled brightly at him, and reassuringly he smiled back. "Absent thee from Felicity," he reflected, "awhile." Yes. But why not for ever? More money all round. Conceited little bore. Expensive, too. Trying that grin on me now. All right! This evening she should have her first glass of port. More money all round! And then, maybe, he could get at that actress, the one who was playing the governess, a big fat bouncing creature who looked as if she had a temper. He began to hum "Singing in the Rain" to himself. Macking in my whack, I'm whacking in my mac, 'cos I'm glad to be back. . . . "Elia," he cried suddenly. "My adorable Elia! Who reads him now?" "Oh, Dads!" and Mums beamed loyally down the table. Special Person indeed! he thought. If they knew what a drag a writer's wife can be. The woman who shares your early struggles is very different from the one you would choose to share your later success. And why the hell should she? Port for her too. "I saw the first caterpillar today," Mums went on, "it was a looper." "You might really be in the depths of the country," said Mr. Goulash. The poet was telling a story, "'And what do *you* do?' I asked her. 'Paint.' 'And what do you paint?' 'Fans.' 'What fun—like Conder, I suppose; do you get a lot of fan mail?' 'Not fans, you idiot, vans. I don't paint silly fans, I paint useful vans.' She's a girl from the Tottenham cell." Tiresome young cub, thought Dads—and that dreary thinker, with his Scotch face hanging over the savoury. A glass of port all round. "A very special bin," he said, when the time came. "Not a has-bin, I hope," said Mr. Goulash. Dads scowled. "I want you all to drink a health," he said. "It's my birthday, don't forget!" The blurbies were still whispering. "Who wrote the last Charles Morgan?" said one—"I don't know who did the front; as a matter of fact, I did the back." "I did the front," said Dads, "if you still want to know." They didn't, for the cyanide was doing its work. "You were quite right not to like the laurustinus, Felicity," laughed Dads—"but my biography will have to wait." The way they fell they reminded him of a skittle alley, only quieter; each seemed to knock against the next one, there would be a wobble, and over they'd go. Last went the thinker, and Dads drummed impatiently on the mahogany with his cigar cutter while he was "passing." Soon all, with varying grace, had made the fatal exit, and it was a very lonely man indeed who, five minutes later, was speeding down Haverstock Hill on his way to the stage door.

Felicity Entertains

Good morning, my diary. I wonder if you remember me. It's been a neglected little diary all the summer! Well, this is Felicity. "Fellow" to you! And she's going to take you out once a week and fill you up with interesting things. Happy now?

This is the Try-out Season. A Try-out is when someone you meet abroad who seems awfully sweet is asked to the house for the first time and the family don the winter war-paint. It's not much good looking nice in lederhosen now, and the wretched youth has to prove he's got guts. I decided to start with the most eligible. Wilfrid Wendover. He's terrifically important in the Wine and Food Society. I've explained all about it to the family, and told them they must ask H. K. Boot to meet him, and have everything just so.

Dads tries his hen-pecked line. "And so my offspring considers our modest social accomplishments may pall on Mr. Wendover? The formidable H. K. Boot has to be called in to provide an intellectual equal? And what of the unfortunate host whose duty it is to feed Mr. Wendover in the manner to which he is accustomed and minister simultaneously to the more ethereal—I hope—necessities of old H. K.?"

"Rubbish, Dads, you know you adore H. K.!"

"Of course—but I prefer to worship from afar."

"Nonsense—we all know you were lovers."

"How can you talk like that in front of Mums!"

"Oh, don't mind me," said Mums; "if I was to be jealous of H. K. I'd have no peace."

"She's a dam' sight too long in the tooth for you anyhow,

isn't she, Dads?" said Baby, who'd been out on the Heath "Observing."

"See anything, Baby?" said Dads.

"Well, I'm pretty sure I spotted a schizophrenic fur cap. The real thing, congenital idiot I should think, absolute bin-fodder! But we're not observing special cases at present. Simply what everybody in England does at 3.57 for the 'Twixt Lunch and Tea' report."

"Talking of lunch and tea," I said (being one whom Psycho-analysis, Mass Observation, and the conversation of one's younger sister affect like a bad smell), "what are you going to give the English Brillat-Savarin for dinner?"

"I think we can leave that safely to Mums," he sliced back.

"Well, don't forget Miss Boot is the authoress of *With Gourd and Gherkin* and *A Weeny Tour in France*," said Baby.

"I don't suppose gherkins are in season," mused Mums.

Uncle Pat tried a bit of escapist stuff with the *Evening Standard*, but Dads was too quick for him.

"Ah—anything in the paper? Let's have a look at it. I wonder if you can give us any idea of a menu that will satisfy the exacting Mr. Wendover—and our old friend H. K.?"

"Roast mutton and caper sauce," suggested Mums, "and cheese straws, with a fish pie or something for a start and some soup, I suppose."

"Come, come—we must do better than that for Mr. Wine and Foodover." (Family laughter.) "Turtle soup, turbot, guinea fowl, salad and spatchcock," amended Dads. "Your real gourmet likes a simple dinner—something that won't re-move the emphasis from its proper place. The wine—he'll want something with a nose to it! I think that part of the com-missariat had better be left to me!" The cellar is in the cup-board under the stairs and Dads is the only person who's allowed there. "You, Felicity, after your expensive lucubra-tions at the Finishing School, will justify the experiment by putting the menu into French. And what about Baby?"

"I will observe."

"Well, it keeps her quiet," said Mums—but Uncle Pat had

got away with the *Evening Standard*, and Dads went after him. Uncle Pat is N.P.G., which doesn't mean what you think, but stands for Non-Paying Guest or Nobly Permanent, as Dads calls him.

The Fatal Night. Mums crunches a bit of paper with our names set out in order. Dads is busy between the cellar and the fireplace. He looks wonderful in his dinner jacket. Fawcett is lighting the candles, the perfect parlormaid. Uncle Pat's shirt-front crackles when he moves, and there's a black mark where he's tried to get the stud to do up again. Baby looks inoffensive, and Mums is absolutely regal in her brocade. I'm jittery myself. I can't help wondering if Will Wendover's going to seem different after that time on the raft. Still, I've got my green on! I finger my French menu:

Soupe à la Tortue

Suprême de Turbot
Pochaise

Poule de la Côte d'Ivoire
[Oiseau Dahomey]

Salade Arquebus

Spatchcock [I know when I'm beaten!]

Café—chocs.

The bell rings. Gosh, I'm frightened! Dads takes a step forward. "Now remember, Family. Be Bright! Mr. Wendover may put us all into one of his *Memorable Meals*, and we'll all like that. So F. H. B. (Family Hold Back) and we want a nice genial evening—NO POLITICS."

Fawcett opens the door. Dads beams. But in walks my brother Chris!

"Good God, what are you doing here? Why aren't you at Cambridge?"

"Thanks for the reception, Father. Well, if you must know, I've been sent down."

"Oh, Chris, how *could* you?"

"Sorry, Mums."

"Nothing dishonest, I hope?"

"No, Dads. For canvassing for the C.P. and making Communist speeches."

"You little rat!"

"Yes. I suppose you would say that. Who's coming to supper?"

"*Dinner*, Chris."

"If forty-five million comrades call it supper, I don't see why I should call it dinner."

"Oh, Chris!" cried Mums. "But here they are. Mr. Wendover, the Wine and Food expert, and Miss Boot. There's no time for you to change, you'll have to sit between Fellow and Babs."

"Right you are, Mums."

Will isn't as tall as I thought, and he didn't wear glasses on the raft. He's quite old really—over forty, and stoops a bit. Miss Boot is in a purple velvet suit with a purple ribbon to her eyeglass to match. She's done her hair in a short gray fringe.

"Sherry or cocktail?" says Dads, after the introductions.

"Manhattan," says the Boot.

"Sherry," says Wilfrid, giving her a dirty look.

"I wonder what you'll think of this?" says Dads, but not giving him any clue.

"Dinner is served, madam," whispers Fawcett, and the game is on.

"Ah," cries Dad. "What about a 'soup's on' of fish! Bring your sherry in with you—and we'll discuss it there."

With the usual knocking of knees we get our feet under the mahogany.

Wendy sloshes his sherry about, brings it up to his nose, sips it, throws his head back as if he's going to gargle—and pours it into the soup. We all do the same. Dads tries the turtle soup, catches Mums' eyes, and turns on the full current. One expects a fizzle of smoke to come from the top of her head. She's certainly in the Hot Seat. "Too Expensive," she lip-reads back. I get the idea, reach forward to the menu, grab my eyebrow pencil and alter it to *Soupe à la Tortue Fausse*. That's the first hurdle. There's still a terrific silence when Baby puts on her "observer's" voice and leans across: "Tell me, Mr. Wendover—do you do anything besides eat?"

Mums stops the rot. "Excuse my terrible daughter—she's been so impressed by hearing of Miss Boot's activities—*With Gourd and Gherkin* and *A Weeny Tour in France*."

"What—*the* Miss Boot? But I can't talk to you—you're a frightful heretic!" cries Wendy. "Do you realize, Mrs. Arquebus, that Miss Boot believes in decanting wine without standing the bottle up for forty-eight hours? And then she leaves the stopper in! Why, she's a regular Trotskyite—a Hotsy Trotskyite certainly"—and he bowed. "But definitely beyond the Party line."

"Oh, don't be a cabbage," guffawed old Boot. "One can't always agree with André and A. J. A. The trouble with the Committee is that they consider any criticism to be treason. But I think you're quite wrong. After all, Saintsbury himself said—"

"Anyone can quote Saintsbury and twist his meaning around," hissed Wilfrid; "and besides, we do not oppose criticism, we welcome it—only we make the very natural reservation that it must be informed—in fact, that it must come from a member of the Committee. If we permitted any prejudiced littérateur to air his or her view we should never get anything done. It's not a question of being loyal to Saintsbury. It's a question of 'Are you loyal to Simon? to Symons? to Wyndham?' If you insist on pretentious literary independence, Miss Boot, you will be instituting a parallel center and be considered an enemy of the feeding classes. I warn you and I repeat—" he thundered.

"But do tell us how *you* decant wine, Mr. Wendover," implored Mums, and Fawcett whisked away the turbot, which had got quite cold by now.

"Certainly, Mrs. Arquebus. Thirty-six hours before serving I stand the bottle upright. Twelve hours before serving I place it in the decanting machine after the cork has been electrically drawn, then I leave the decanter standing in the room in which it is to be used—thank you, some guinea hen—and I remove the stopper one minute for every year the vintage is old. The older the wine the longer it requires to come to life—or, as we say, 'to breathe.'"

"Then your wine will certainly catch cold," roared La Boot. "Take out its little stopper—yes, some guinea hen, please—I never heard of such a thing—and Barry Neame—"

"Well now, here's a test," said Dads. "Here's a wine from my own modest *caves*—oh, nothing remarkable—just a well-fendered little wine—one that's honest and obliging enough to engage in a symplegma or amorous wrestling match with this charming bird we're debating—I won't tell you what it cost or where it came from, but I'm going to ask our two experts here to guess. By the way, how do you like our feathered friend?"

"It's most interesting," answered Wendy. "A veritable Phoenix."

"The phoenix and the turtle." Miss Boot giggled—and suddenly they both began to quote.

> The claw, the jowl of the flying fowl,
> Are with the glorious anguish gilt.

"Yes, that's it," they laughed, and I heard Wendover whisper: "The only difficulty is who's got the claw?"

"Glorious anguish," answered Bootsy, "that's the sauce all right."

Dads doesn't like his guests to get on too well together. It makes him feel empty. "Now—what about the wine judging?" he said. "I'll offer a prize—whoever guesses it can have anything he likes in the room—you can see I don't think it's going to be very easy."

The wine was brought in in two decanters which Fawcett handled somewhat gingerly. They were rather clouded and you couldn't tell much about the stuff from its color. There was one stopper in, and one out, to satisfy both the experts, and a delicious winey smell steamed from the open one.

"Let me help you first, H. K.," said Dads, and then "God damn it! I've burned my fingers." The two tasters exchanged glances. "Mind you—it will take a lot of guessing," said Dads, and Wendy answered:

"I've never been wrong before. I think I know all the vintage clarets—though my period is pre-phylloxera."

"And I've never made a mistake," roared the Boot, "over a burgundy."

Dads filled both their glasses and they began to slosh the stuff about as before. When it was going round and round in the glasses they had to put them down and pick them up again with their napkins. As far as one could see, it was a kind of Virginia creeper color. Then they sloshed it round again. Slosh—slosh—once more—now up with it—sniff—gargle—glug—glug-glug—and down. Wendy did it once and frowned. Miss Boot had to do it all over again. The suspense was colossal. Uncle Pat looked less fuddled. Mums was fascinated, Babs was observing like Malinowski himself, and even Chris stopped running his fingers through his hair and making bread pellets.

Boot spoke first. "It's extraordinary. Quite unique. I've only tasted something like it once. And that was in France— on my 'Weeny Tour.' In that delicious debatable region between Bédarieux and Agde that some call Languedoc—and some call Roussillon—we had walked eleven kilometres after drinking three bottles of Frontignan—my friend and I—and had spent a pleasant day in arguing over the virtues of the unicorn, and its deadly enemies—the basilisk and amphisbaena—"

"Herkherm." Dads cleared his throat.

"Well, it's like a wine we had at a wayside inn," she finished, "so old, the cobwebs even were returned to dust, and the blushing cork dissolved around the penetrating screw. In fact, to come to the point—a Château Neuf du Pape—château bottled by his Holiness at Avignon!"

"Very warm," said Dads. "Now you, Wendover."

Wendy was still removing bits of stuff from his glass, but he looked up and said: "As far as I can judge, I should say Al-

gerian, one-and-six a bottle. Sidi Bel Abbés to be exact—
1937. Ah, I can see I'm right, and now, since I may choose
anything in the room, I'll have a whiskey-and-soda."

"Cook couldn't find no spatchcock, mum, she's turning out
some cheese straws," whispered Fawcett, and Chris jumped
up and said he must be off to his meeting.

"Good heavens, it's nine o'clock!" cried Miss Boot; "I think
we can drop you."

I heard Wendy talking to her as they went out: "*Oxford Poetry* 1910—but I edited it; and you wrote that thing about the
amphisbaena?"

"It's sweet of you to remember it after all these years."

"Not at all. It *formed* me."

Dads went into his study and slammed the door, and the
rest of us started on the chocs. What's so maddening is that the
Memorable Meals don't come out till Christmas. It's a quarterly.

Told in Gath

(With apologies to Mr. A*d*us H*xl*y)

"Vulgarity is the garlic in the salad of charm."—ST. BUMPUS.

It was to be a long weekend, thought Giles Pentateuch apprehensively, as the menial staggered up the turret stairs with his
luggage—staggered all the more consciously for the knowledge that he was under observation, just as, back in Lexham
Gardens, his own tyrannical Amy would snort and groan outside the door to show how steep the backstairs were, before
entering with his simple vegetarian breakfast of stinkwort and
boiled pond weed. A long weekend; but a weekend at Groyne!
And he realized, with his instinct for merciless analysis that
amounted almost to torture, that in spite, yes, above all, in
spite of the apprehension, because of it even, he would enjoy
all the more saying afterward, to his friend Luke Snarthes perhaps, or to little Reggie Ringworm, "Yes, I was at Groyne last
weekend," or "Yes, I was there when the whole thing started,
down at Groyne."

The menial had paused and was regarding him. To tip or
not to tip? How many times had he not been paralyzed by that
problem? To tip was to give in, yes, selfishly to give in to his
hatred of human contacts, to contribute half a crown as hush-
money, to obtain "protection," protection from other people,
so that for a little he could go on with the luxury of being Giles
Pentateuch, "scatologist and eschatologist," as he dubbed
himself. Whereas not to tip . . .

For a moment he hesitated. What would Luke Snarthes

have done? Stayed at home, with that splayed ascetic face of his, or consulted his guru, Chandra Nandra? No—no tip! The menial slunk away. He looked round the room. It was comfortable, he had to admit; a few small Longhis round the walls, a Lupanar by Guido Guidi, and over the bed an outsize Stuprum Sabinarum, by Rubens—civilized people, his hosts, evidently.

He glanced at the books on the little table—the *Odes of Horace*, Rome 23 B.C., apparently a first edition, the *Elegancies of Meursius* (Rochester's copy), *The Piccadilly Ambulator*, *The Sufferings of Saint Rose of Lima*, *Nostradamus* (the Lérins Press), *Swedenborg*, *The Old Man's Gita*. "And cultivated," he murmured, "too." The bathroom, with its sun lamp and Plombières apparatus, was such as might be found in any sensible therapeutic home. He went down to tea considerably refreshed by his lavage.

The butler announced that Lady Rhomboid was "serving" on the small west lawn, and he made his way over the secular turf with genuine pleasure. For Minnie Rhomboid was a remarkable woman.

"How splendid of you to come," she croaked, for she had lost her voice in the old suffragette days. "You know my daughter, Ursula Groyne."

"Only too well," laughed Giles, for they had been what his set at Balliol used to call "lovers."

"And Mrs. Amp, of course?"

"Of course!"

"And Mary Pippin?"

"Decidedly," he grimaced.

"And the men," she went on. "Giles Pentateuch—this is Luke Snarthes and Reggie Ringworm and Mr. Encolpius and Roland Narthex. Pentateuch writes—let me see?—like a boot, isn't it?" (Her voice was a husky roar.) "Yes, a boot with a mission! Oh, but I forgot"—and she laughed delightedly—"you're all writers!"

"Encantado, I'm sure!" responded Giles. "But we've all met before. I see you have the whole Almanach de Golgotha in fact," he added.

Mary Pippin, whose arm had been eaten away by termites in Tehuantepec, was pouring out with her free hand. "Orange Pekoe or *Chandu*, Giles?" she burbled in her delicious little voice. "Like a carricr pigeon's," he thought.

"*Chandu*, please." And she filled him a pipe of the consoling poppy, so that in a short while he was smoking away like all the others.

"Yes, yes," continued Mr. Encolpius, in his oily voice which rose and fell beneath the gently moving tip of his nose, "Man axalotl here below but I ask very little. Some fragments of Pamphylides, a Choctaw blood-mask, the prose of Scaliger the Elder, a painting by Fuseli, an occasional visit to the all-in wrestling, or to my meretrix; a cook who can produce a passable 'poulet à la Khmer,' a Pong vase. Simple tastes, you will agree, and it is my simple habit to indulge them!"

Giles regarded him with fascination. That nose, it was, yes, it was definitely a proboscis. . . .

"But how can you, how can you?" It was Ursula Groyne. "How *can* you when there are two million unemployed, when Russia has reintroduced anti-abortionary legislation, when Iceland has banned *Time and Tide*, when the Sedition Bill hangs over us all like a rubber truncheon?"

Mary Pippin cooed delightedly; this was intellectual life with a vengeance—definitely haybrow—only it was so difficult to know who was right. Giles, at that moment, found her infinitely desirable.

"Yes, and worse than that." It was Luke Snarthes, whose strained voice emerged from his tortured face like a cobra from the snake-charmer's basket. "Oh, decidedly, appallingly worse. The natives of Ceylon take the slender Loris and hold it over the fire till its eyes pop, to release the magic juices. Indicible things are done to geese that you may eat your runions with a sauce of *foie gras*. Caviare is ripped from the living sturgeon, karakul fur torn from the baby lamb inside its mother. The creaking plates of the live dismembered lobster scream to you from the *Homard Newburg*, the oyster winces under the lemon. How would *you* like, Mr. Encolpius, to be torn from your bed, embarrelled, prised open with a knife, seasoned with a few drips of vitriol, shall we say, and sprayed with a tabasco as strong as mustard gas to give you flavor; then to be swallowed alive and handed over to a giant's digestive juices?"

"I shouldn't like it at all!" said Mr. Encolpius, "just as I shouldn't, for that matter, like living at the bottom of the sea and changing my sex every three years. Not that it might not"—and he twitched his nose at Mary Pippin—"have its compensations."

"S-s-s-s-s-s-s-s-s-s-s-s-s-s-s-s-s-s-s-s-s-s-s-s-s-suppose," said Reggie Ringworm, who stammered, etc., "vat ve thilly oythter is weally weady and villing to be ab-s-s-s-s-orbed, I mean ab-th-th-th-th-th-thorbed, by our fwend, vat vat is in f-f-f-fact exactly ve end for which it has been cweated. Vat th-then?"

"What are we to think then," snarled Snarthes savagely, "of the Person or Purpose who created creatures for such an end? Awful!" And he took out his notebook and wrote rapidly, "The end justifies the means! But the end *is* the means! And how rarely, how confoundedly rarely, can we even say the end justifies the end! Like Oxenstierna, like Ximenes, like Waldorf, we must be men of means"—he closed the book with a snap—"men of golden means."

"I know what you mean," cried Mary Pippin from her dovecot. "That if Cleopatra's nose had been half an inch longer Menelaus would never have run away with her!"

Luke's face softened, and he spread out his splayed fingers almost tenderly. "And I don't mind wagering, if we can believe Diodorus Siculus, that, the nose unaltered, she bore a remarkable likeness, Mary, to you!"

"Ah, but can we believe old Siculus?" The other nose quested speculative. "Any more than we can believe old Paterculus, old Appian, Arrian, Ossian, and Orrian? Now a Bolivar Corona or a nicely chambered glass of sparkling Douro— even a pretty tea-gown by Madame Groult, I opine"—and he bowed to Mary—"these convince me. They have a way with one. Oh, yes, a way, decidedly! And just because they have that way it is necessary for me to combine them, how often, how distressingly often, with my lamentable visits to the Ring at Blackfriars, or to my meretrix in Holland Park. Why is it that we needs must see the highest though we loathe it? That happy in my mud—my hedonistic, radioactive, but neverthe-less quite genuine nostalgic *boue*, I should be reminded of the stars, of you, Miss Pippin, and of Cleopatra?" And he snuffled serio-comically, "Why can't you let Hell alone?"

A gong rang discreetly. The butler removed the pipes and Mrs. Amp and Roland Narthex, who were still in a state of kif, while the others went away to dress. Giles, who found something stimulating in Mr. Encolpius' nose, took out his notebook and wrote:

"Platitudes are eternally fresh, and even the most paradoxical are true; even when we say the days draw in we are literally right—for science has now come largely to the rescue of folk-lore; after the summer and still more after the equinoctial solstice the hours do definitely get shorter. It is this shortness of our northern day that has occasioned the luxuriance of our literature. Retractile weather—erectile poetry. No one has idealized, in our cold climate, more typically than Shakespeare and Dryden the subtropical conditioning. But we can consider Antony and Cleopatra to have been very different from their counterparts in the Elizabethan imagination, for on the Mediterranean they understand summer better and, with summer, sex.

"What were they really like, those prototypes of Aryan passion, of brachycephalic amour? Were Cleopatra's breasts such as 'bore through men's eyes' and tormented those early sensualists, Milton, Dante, Coventry Patmore, and St. John of the Cross? We shall never know.

"Professor Pavlov has shown that when salivation has been artificially induced in dogs by the ringing of a dinner bell, if you fire simultaneously into them a few rounds of small shot they exhibit an almost comical bewilderment. Human beings have developed very little. Like dogs we are not capable of absorbing conflicting stimuli; we cannot continue to love Cleopatra after communism and the electro-magnetic field have played Old Harry with our romantic mythology. That characteristic modern thinker, Drage Everyman, remarks, 'De-

stroy the illusion of love and you destroy love itself,' and that
is exactly what the machine age, through attempting to foster
it through cinemas and gin palaces, deodorants and depilato-
ries, has succeeded in doing. Glory, glory halitosis! No wonder we are happier in the present! If we think of the 'Eastern
Star,' in fact, it is as advertising something. And when we
would reconstruct those breasts of hers, again we are faced
with the diversity of modern knowledge. What were they
like? To a poet twin roes, delectable mountains; to a philan-
derer like Malthus festering cancers; to a pneumatogogue simply a compound of lacticity and heterogeneous pyrites; to a
biologist a sump and a pump. Oh, sweet are the uses, or rather
the abuses, of splanchnology! No, for details of the pathological appeal of these forgotten beauties we must consult the
poets. The ancients were aware of a good thing when they saw
it, and Horace knew, for instance, with almost scatological
percipience, exactly what was what.

"There are altitudes, as well as climates, of the mind. Many
prefer the water meadows, but some of us, like Kant and Bee-
thoven, are at home on the heights. There we thermostatically
control the rarefied atmosphere and breathe, perforce, the appropriate mental air."

In another room Luke Snarthes was doing his exercises.
Seated in the lotus position, he exhaled deeply till his stomach
came against his backbone with a smart crack. After a little he
relaxed and breathed carefully up one nostril and down the
other and then reversed the process. He took a nail out of the
calf of his leg, and after he had reinserted it, it was time to put
the studs into his evening shirt. "I was there," he murmured,
"when it started, down at Groyne."

When he had dressed he unlocked his despatch case and
took out a sealed tube. It was marked, "Anthrax—non-
filterable virus, only to be opened by a qualified literary scientist." "Jolly little beggars," he thought, and the hard lines on
his face softened. "I'll take them down to amuse Miss Pippin.
She looked the kind of person who'd *understand*."

"Snuff, peotl buds, hashish, or Indian hemp, sir?" said the

butler. Dinner was drawing to an end. It had been an interesting meal. For Giles and Luke (on the "regime"), grass soup and groundsel omelette, washed down with a bottle of "pulque"; for Mrs. Amp, whose huge wen, like Saint-Evremond's, made her look more than ever like some heavily wattled turkey, a chicken gumbo; for the rest Risi-bisi Mabel Dodge, bêche de mer, bear steak, and Capri pie.

"There's some *bhang* on the mantelpiece," said Minnie Rhomboid, "in poor Rhomboid's college tobacco jar."

"Delicious." It was Mr. Encolpius. "Common are to either sex artifex and opifex," he continued. "But, golly, how rare to find them contained in the same person—qualis opifex, Lady Rhomboid! I congratulate you—and this *barask*—perfection!" And he poured himself some more, while the snout wiggled delightedly.

"And you can drink that when Hungary is deliberately making a propaganda war for the recovery and re-enslavement of a hundred-thousand at last sophisticated Slovakians!" It was Ursula Groyne.

Poor Ursula, thought Giles, she carries her separate hell about with her like a snail its carapace! Not all the lost causes, all the lame dogs in the world could console her for the loss of her three husbands, and now she was condemned to the hades of promiscuity—every three or four years a new lover. Poor Ursula!

"And if you knew how the stuff was made!" The phrase was wrung from Luke Snarthes on his tortured calvary. "The apricots are trodden by the naked feet of bromidrosis-ridden Kutzo-Vlachs who have for centuries lived in conditions far below the poverty line! The very glass blowers who spun that Venetian balloon for you are condemned to the agonies of alembic poisoning."

"Doubtless," answered Mr. Encolpius urbanely, "that is why it tastes so good. It all boils down to a question of proteins. You, my dear Ursula, are allergic to human misery; the sufferings of Slovaks and Slovenes affect you as pollen the hay fever victim, or me (no offence, Minnie) a cat in the room. To ethics, mere questions of good and evil, I am happily immune, like my cara doncella here—am I right, Mary? Let Austin have his swink to him reserved, especially when it is a swink of the Rhomboid order. Go to the slug, thou ant-herd! If you could make up to kings (you remember what Aristippus said to Diogenes, Snarthes), you would not have to live on grass!"

"B-b-b-b-b-b-b-b-b-b-b-b-b-b-b-b-b-but all flesh is gwath, so ve pwoblem is only sh-shelved." It was Reggie Ringworm!

"Sit down, everybody, it's time for the séance," commanded Lady Rhomboid. "We have persuaded Madame Yoni."

In darkness they took their seats, Mr. Encolpius and Giles on each side of Mary Pippin, while Snarthes elevated himself to a position of trans-Khyber ecstasy suspended between the table and the laquearia. The *bhang*-sodden bodies of Mrs. Amp and Roland Narthex they left where they were.

The darkness was abysmal, pre-lapsarian. Time flowed stanchlessly, remorselessly, from a wound inenarrable, as with catenary purpose. Madame Yoni moved restlessly, like Bethesda.

In her private dovecot Mary Pippin abandoned herself to the eery. What a thrill, to be here at Groyne, and for a séance! There had been nothing like it since she had joined the Anglican Church, to the consternation of her governess, Miss Heard, because of the deep mystical significance (as of some splendid sinner repenting on the ashes of lust) of the words, "for Ember Days." All the same, she was not quite sure if she liked Mr. Encolpius. But what was this?—another thrill, but positive, physical. With mothlike caresses something was running up and down her arm—1, 2, 3, 4, 5,—spirit fingers, perhaps: the tremulous titivation continued, the moths were relentless, inexorable, 86, 87, 88. Then on her other side, along her cheek, she felt a new set of moth antennae playing. From the chandelier above came the faintest ghostly anticipatory tinkle—someone was on the move as well, up there! 98, 99 . . . Suddenly Madame Yoni screamed—there was a crash, as of three heads bumping together, and the lights went up to reveal Pentateuch and Mr. Encolpius momentarily stunned by the Ixionic impact of the fallen Snarthes. His power had failed him.

"W-w-w-w-w-w-w—" stammered Reggie Ringworm, but he was interrupted by a shout from Luke. "My God—the anthrax!" He took from his pocket the fragments of the broken tube. "At the rate of multiplication of these bacilli"—he made a rapid calculation—"we shall all be by morning, Lady Rhomboid, dead souls." His splayed face had at last found its justification.

"Death!" said Mr. Encolpius, "the distinguished visitor! One bids good-bye, one hopes gracefully, to one's hostess, and then, why then I think one degusts the Cannabis Indica. Well, cheerio, kif-kif!" And he picked up the Brasenose jar.

Imperturbable, schizophrene, the portraits of Groynes and Rhomboids by Laurencin and the excise man Rousseau looked down from the walls. So Miss Heard had been right, thought Mary. The wicked *do* perish. Than this there could have been no other conceivable termination to a weekend of pleasure!

> They say of old in Babylon
> That Harlequin and Pantalon
> Seized that old topiary, Truth,
> And held him by Time's Azimuth. . . .

Why had the nursery jingle recurred to her?

Luke removed a nail or two disconsolately. They would be of little use now. He tried to reassure Minnie Rhomboid. "After all, what is anthrax? What, for that matter, are yaws, beri-beri, dengue or the Bagdad Boil, but fascinating biochemical changes in the cellular constitution of our bodies, a re-casting of their components to play their new cadaverous roles? Believe me, Lady Rhomboid," he concluded, "there are more things in heaven and earth than are dreamed of in the British Pharmacopoeia!"

Giles took out his notebook. "La Muerte, Der Tod, Thanatos," he wrote.

"Your C-c-c-Collins perhaps?" stammered Reggie.

Giles began again: "It was at Groyne, during one of Minnie Rhomboid's most succulent weekends, that it all happened,

happened because it had to happen, because it was in the very nature of Luke Snarthes and Mary Pippin that exactly such things should happen, just as it was character not destiny, character that *was* destiny, that caused Napoleon . . ." He paused and looked up. The menial was regarding him reproachfully.

Where Engels
Fears to Tread

From Oscar to Stalin. A Progress. By Christian de Clavering. (The Clay Press, 12s. 6d.)

Reviewed by CYRIL CONNOLLY

At last the authentic voice of a generation! "You are all a lost generation," remarked Gertrude Stein of us postwar age groups, and now, thanks to Mr. Christian de Clavering, we know who lost us. Let me try and tell you all about this book while I am still full of it. First thing you know you have opened it, and there is the dedication:

"TO THE BALD YOUNG PEOPLE"

Then comes a page of fashionable quotations all in German. The middle part by Kafka, the fringes by Rilke and Hölderlin. The rest by Marx. Impeccable! And the introduction.

"Why am I doing this, my dears? Because I happen to be the one person who can do it. My dears, I'm on your side! I've come to get you out of the wretched tangle of individualism that you've made for yourselves and show you just how you can be of some use in the world. Stop worrying whether he loves you or not; stop wondering how you will ever make any money. Never mind whether the trousers of your new suit turn up at the bottom; leave off trying to annoy Pa. We're on to something rather big. The Workers' Revolution for the Classless Society through the Dictatorship of the Proletariat! Yes! It's a bit of a mouthful, isn't it! We're used to words of one syllable, words like Freud, Death, War, Peace, Love, Sex, Glands, and, above all, to Damn, Damn, Damn! Well, all that's going to be changed. Morning's at seven, and you've got a new matron.

"I'm told Mr. Isherwood is writing a book about the twenties. Mr. Isherwood is a Cambridge man, and we who made the twenties do not wish them looked at through the wrong end of a cocoa tin. Through either end. My precious twenties! He shan't have them! Avaunt. Avanti!"

(And so the autobiography starts. I will quote a few of the dazzling vignettes. For the reasons with which the author concludes, I have refrained from comment.)

Home. Background. Mother.

"Mother, who is that horrible old obesity with the black chin? I believe he's following us."

"Hush, that's Daddy."

And so dawned my second birthday.

Home.

"Mother, where is home this time. Heliopolis? Hammamet? Ragusa? Yalta?"

"Guess again."

"I know. Prinkipo."

"Warm."

"Monte Carlo."

"Very warm."

"Has it got a clever coastline? I know! Cannes!"

And home for the next two months it was.

"Mother—what does Father do?"

"He has his business, boy o' mine."

"And what is that?"

"He's a sort of accountant."

"On 'Change?"

"On the Turf!"

"Poor Mother, poor darling Mother—but we needn't see him, need we?"

"Of course not, precious, but I thought you were old enough to know."

I pulled the hood down and for a moment it was very stuffy inside the pram. . . .

Children's Party.

"What is your father, Christian?"

"He's interested in racing—my mother is the Honorable. What is *your* father, Edelweiss?"

"A mediatized prince. What sort of racing?"

"Oh, never mind now—let's ask Mother to play some *Rimsky*."

But I realized I couldn't stay on in Montreux Territet.

My mother an angel. My father a bookie!

"And don't forget, my boy, a tenner for every little nob you bring home with a handle to his name."

Eton. Henry's holy shade. An impression, above all, of arches, my dears, each with its handsome couple, and study fireplaces always full of stubs of Balkan Sobranie. And the naughtiest elms! While the battle of Waterloo was being fought all round me, I just sat still and watched my eyelashes grow. There were books, of course. Pater, Alma Pater, with his worried paragraphs. His prose reminded me of stale privet—and Petronius, who made me long to know more Latin. (I only learned two words, *curculio* and *vespertilio*, a bat and a weevil, but they got me everywhere, afterward, on Mount Athos.) And Compton Mackenzie as he then was, and Huxley, before he had acquired his Pope and Bradley manner, and Verlaine of course; Rimbaud, Mallarmé, Baudelaire.

"What is that book, de Clavering?"

"*Les Chansons de Bilitis*, sir."

"And what is this lesson?"

"You have the advantage, sir."

"What do you mean, boy?"

"Ah, sir, fair's fair. I told you what my book was. You must tell me what's your lesson."

"Elementary geometry."

"But it sounds fascinating! Then this delicious piece of celluloid nonsense is—I know, sir, don't tell me—a set-square?"

"I have been teaching it for twenty years, and never met with such impertinence."

"Twenty years, and still at Elementary! Oh, sir, what a confession." And it was a very purple face one glimpsed behind the blackboard. Ah, those Eton masters! I wish I could remember any of their names, for I was really sorry for them. What tragedies went on under their mortar-boards! Some of them were quite young, and one often got the impression that they were trying, inarticulately, to communicate; would have liked, in fact, to share in the rich creative life that already was centering round me. They used to teeter round my Baksts, and once I caught my housemaster sniffing at a very special bottle made up for me by Max of Delhez, and gingerly rubbing some on his poor old pate. Worldlings, yet deprived of all worldly grace, of our rich sex-life how pathetically inquisitive! They are all there still, I suppose, and I often wonder, when I motor through Switzerland in summer, if one will not find a bunch of them spawning round some mouldy *arête*, in their Norfolk jackets, like eels in the Sargasso Sea.

The boys of course took up most of my time. I soon found that it was easy to get on with them by giving them presents, and making them laugh. A dozen of claret here, a humidor of Coronas there, a well-timed repartee, and persecution was made impossible. It was easy to find the butts and make rather more skillful fun of them than anybody else. In fact, I give this advice to those of my readers who are still at school. In every group there are boys whom it is the fashion to tease and bully; if you quickly spot them and join in, it will never occur to anyone to tease and bully you. Foxes do not hunt stoats. But always defer to the original teasers, and hand your prey over to them for the *coup de grâce*. And boys like expensive presents, though they are genuinely embarrassed by them. All the same, they were a provincial lot. I never felt very safe unless I had several of them round me, in colored caps and gaudy blazers, puffing away at my cigarettes and looking for dirty jokes in the *Vie Parisienne*. By cultivating all the Captains of Games in this way I found my afternoons were left free. I would watch them troop away with their shinpads to some mysterious district on the way to Slough, then saunter up to Windsor with a book—on the bridge I would wave to any who seemed to be pushing a particularly big boat underneath it. Happy river of Eton-Windsor! I have always been very vague about its name, but I often pictured it winding away past Reading Gaol and into the great world somewhere—the world of the Ballet and the Sitwells, of Cocteau and the Café Royal.

"Hello, Faun, what a way to spend your *Après-midi.*"

It was Harold, my most uneasy disciple.

"I was just thinking that summer made a noise like the rubbing together of biscuits."

"Yes, it is hot," he replied. "If it goes on like this I shall have to buy some FLANNELS."

"And be mistaken for Peter Fleming?"

"Oh, you're cruel. But seriously, what *shall* we do?"

"Well, there's Tull's, and I haven't eaten a lobster patty since this morning—or one might buy a gramophone record—or a very cool Braque of half a dozen ash-blonde oysters—then there's that place one goes to London from."

"You mean the G.W.R.?"

"Thank you—and by now the school library will probably have heard of William Morris—or one might try the arches and see what one could pick up."

"Or the Castle."

"I'm bored with bearskins—but, my dear, that man—he's touched his cap—so familiar."

"You mean the headmaster?"

It seemed an evil omen.

Then there was the Corps. I quickly joined the signal section. You didn't have to carry rifles. It was there that I first met intellectuals, dowdy fellows mostly, who went in for Medici prints and had never heard of Picasso. I realized for the first time what a gap separated cultured and cosmopolitan art lovers like myself, people who cared equally for music, painting, and literature, from those whose one idea was to pass examinations; literature is a very different thing to a poet and to someone who has to make a living out of it. "What do you think of Apollinaire?" I asked one of them. "Good God, we won't get a question on that—he's well outside the period." "On the contrary, he's very much of it. His book on Sade is vital." "I thought you meant Sidonius Apollinaris." I could make no contact with them. But signaling was delightful. One

sat for hours beside a field telephone while little figures receded into the distance with the wire. "Can you hear me?"
"No." "Can you hear me now?" "No." "Well, try this."
"This" was the morse code machine, and nimbler fingers than
mine would fill the air with a drowsy song. Iddy iddy umpty
umpty iddy umpty iddy . . . However, all things come to an
end, and there were tiresome scenes—long waits in red-brick
classrooms looking at huge sheets of paper—"write only on
one side of the paper." But which side? and the precious minutes were wasted. Suddenly a lot of people I had always been
willing to avoid seemed to have no object in life but to want to
meet one. They would cluster round some old cannon outside
New Schools, gowns fluttering and tassels wagging. One afternoon, when the place was looking more Raphael Tuck than
ever, I went upstairs, and unforgivable things were said. It
seemed one was suspected of all the alluvial vices, in fact one
was not getting the best out of the curriculum. For the last
time I crossed the bridge over the mysterious river, past Tom
Browne's, where rather a good pair of "sponge bags" were
being created for me for Ascot, past Hills and Saunders, who
had turned out some passable groups of my tea-parties.
"These people are my friends," I would implore the photographer, "I want them to look fresh and good-looking and aristocratic and rich." "But, sir." "Remember, they are not the
Shooting Eight, or Mr. Crace's Old Boys, and I don't want to
sit in the middle with folded arms and a football. I shall stand
rather over to the side and at the back, and the only way you
will know I am the host is by this enormous cocktail shaker."

"Oh, my boy, my boy, 'ere am I sweating away on the Turf to
edicate you, and just when I 'ope you'll bring the nobs in you
go and get sacked. Sacked from Eton!"
   "Not sacked, Pater,—supered."
   But my father could never appreciate an academic distinction.

Before one can understand Oxford one must have lived in Capri, and it was there that I spent the next few months, cram-

ming. Mother had taken a quiet villa with a view of the funicular. At seventeen it was rather odd to figure fairly recognizably in five novels in three languages. But Monty and Norman were insatiable. "No one would think it absurd if you sat to five painters," they remonstrated, and I retorted that I had a jolly good mind to—but I was too busy at that time, sitting for Fersen.* It was my first introduction to *les paradis artificiels* (not counting Tidworth), and with all a boy's healthy craving for novelty I flung myself down on the Count's couches and sampled poppy after poppy through his amusing collection of Chinese pipes. When the time came for my Oxford vivâ, I was older than the rocks and my eyelids were definitely a little weary. I could not decide. Magdalen and *Sinister Street*, Merton and Max, Balliol and Gumbril? or the House—Peers and Peckwater? Max had praised my eyelashes. Harold said Balliol was perfect for case histories like mine, but I realized I should find it madly ungay. That Buttery! Finally it was the House I chose, two vast eighteenth century rooms which I did up in pewter and cinnamon. Harold supplied wax fruit, and antimacassars for the Chinese Chippendale chairs, I added incense, brass trays and Buddhas, and Robert a carpet from the Victoria and Albert (the Yacht, not the Museum).

My father had become reconciled to me. "'Appiest days of your life, my boy, and don't forget, a pony for every youngster you bring 'ome with a 'andle to his name. Good for the business." I was worried about my father. "Mother," I said, "don't you think Daddy is looking definitely *blafard?*" "Is he?" she replied. "You're sitting on the Continental Bradshaw."

Most of my Eton friends had also come up to the House, and, as my father had taken a flat in Bicester, "ponies" and "monkeys" came rolling in. I spent them on clothes and parties, on entertaining and on looking entertaining. Parties! "Are you going to de Clavering's tonight?" and woe betide the wretch who had to say no. Nothing much happened at the time, but he soon felt he was living on an icefloe, drifting farther and farther from land, and every moment watching it

* The Marsac of *Vestal Fires*.

melt away. De Clavering's tonight! The candles burn in their sconces. The incense glows. Yquem and Avocado pears—a simple meal—but lots and lots of both, with whiskey for the hearties and champagne for the dons. "Have a brick of caviare, Alvanley? More birds' nest, Gleneagles? There's nothing coming, I'm afraid, only Avocado pear and hot-pot." "Hot-pot!" "Christian, you're magnificent!" "Caviare and hot-pot—Prendy will be blue with envy!" And then dancing, while canons go home across the quad, and David stomps at the piano. I took care at these parties to have a word and piece of advice for everyone.

There was an alert young man in a corner, looking rather shy. "I know—don't tell me," I said to him, "it's your first party." "Yes." I pinched his cheek. "Si jeunesse savait!" I laughed. It was Evelyn Waugh.

Another merry little fellow asked me if I could suggest a hobby. "Architecture," I gave in a flash. "Thank you." It was John Betjeman.

"And for me?"

"Afghanistan."

It was Robert Byron.

"And me?"

"Byron," I laughed back—it was Peter Quennell.

And Alvanley, Gleneagles, Prince Harmatviz, Graf Slivovitz, the Ballygalley of Ballygalley, Sarsaparilla, the Duc de Dingy, the Conde de Coca y Cola—for them, my peers, I kept my serious warnings.

"These bedroom slippers, Dingy? I flew them over from my *bottier*."

"You ought to look a little more like a public school prefect, Alvanley. The front cover of *The Captain*, it's rather more your *genre*. There! Wash out the 'honey and flowers,' and try a fringe effect. I want to see a pillar of the second eleven."

"Good jazz, Gleneagles, is meant to be played just a little bit too slow."

"Graf Slivovitz, this isn't the *Herrenclub* in Carpathian Ruthenia, you must take off your hat. Yes—that green growth with the feudal feathers."

"Sarsaparilla, only the King rouges his knees when he wears a kilt, and then only at a Court ball."

"Harmatviz, I can smell that Harris a mile away. What on earth is that terrifying harpoon in the lapel?"

"That, de Clavering, is a *Fogas* fly."*

"More Yquem, Ballygalley?"

"What's that?"

"That—if you mean the thing under your elbow—is how I look to Brancusi; the other is a kind of wine. Stand him up, will you, Ava?"

"Before the war we heard very little of the Sarsaparillas— he would not dare wear that tartan in Madrid."

"Before the war I hadn't heard of you, Coca y Cola, either; Count, this is a democratic country."

"I am democrats, we are all democrats. *Vive le roi.*"

"Thank you, Dingy, you must have been reading *Some People*. Now I want all the Guinnesses and Astors to go into the next room and get a charade ready. Alvanley, Gleneagles, Harmatviz, and Slivovitz—you will drive quickly over with me for a few minutes to Bicester to say good-night to father."

"No I don't think."—"My price is ten guineas."—"Jolly well not unless we go halves."—"Where is my hat and gotha?"—and madcap youth was served.

My crowning moment. The Summerville Grind. Peers and their mothers and sisters in mackintoshes and shooting-sticks. My mount. A huge animal whose teeth need cleaning. For the first time in my life I wear a bowler hat. And my racing colors. White silk shirt with a broad blue stripe—but zigzag! Alvanley and Gleneagles on each side of me—off! I was petrified, my dears; the first fence was enormous and my animal seemed hours getting over it. There was time for me to get down, and I rolled over. On it thundered, its great ugly stirrups banging together. A man leaned over me. "Not hurt, are you?" he said. And then, *plus fort que lui*, "Where *did* you get that shirt?" It was on a sigh that I answered, as I lost consciousness, "Sire, at Charvet's." It was the Prince.

---

* An amusing fish from the Balaton.

And there was talk—all kinds—the banter of my friends.

"Ah, de Clavering, if you were only of the nobility. I would ask you to stay at Dingy. What a pity you are not a real goodfellow."

"Apfelstrüdel! He is coming to Schloss Slivovitz with Pryce-Jones, is not that good enough for you?"

"Slivovitz—how picturesque it must be. But at Dingy we have to consider the *convenances*, my aunt Doudeauville, my Uncle Sagan. . . ."

"She 'appens to be *my* aunt Doudeauville too.* Her mother was of the German branch."

"I can find no Harmatviz on Madame Sacher's tablecloth."

"Rosa Lewis says the Claverings are an old Scotch family."

"Sarsaparilla would know that."

"Before the war we heard very little of the Sarsaparillas, now it appears . . ."

"Ah, bonjour, Coca y Cola, how is the Alvis?"

"Very well, would you like to look under the bonnet?"

"Haw, haw, haw, what a suggestion."

"But seriously, de Clavering—you are rich, you are intelligent, why have you no titles? Have you spoken to the King?"

"He may have no title, but I would trust him with my waistcoats."

"And I shake him by the hand—and say—'Well, what the hell, who cares?'"

"Bravo, Harmatviz, it's a democratic country. *Vive le roi!*"

Then there was brilliant conversation at Balliol, where the food makes long journeys to the dowdy sitting-rooms, under tins.

"We were discussing, de Clavering, whether it was more correct to say Theophylactus Simocattes or Simocatta—"

"You should consider yourself very lucky, Sparrow, to be able to say either."

"And what the collective noun is for a group of pelicans; there is a gaggle of geese, of course, and a pride of lions."

* By the marriage of Graf Hubertus Mary von and zu Slivotiz-Slivovitz with Katarina Auburn-Cord.

"A piety of pelicans, I suggest."

"Thank you—how delightfully Thomas Browne. I shall repeat that."

"I don't know which I dislike most, people who repeat my epigrams or people who copy my ties—and, by the way, I hope you don't mind. I've brought Raymond Radiguet."

"Where's he up?"

"He's not up. He lives in Paris."

"Paris! If I get an All Sogger I am determined to go there. It's right on the way to the British School."

"I know a very nice little hotel near the *Bibliothèque Mazarine*."

"I can't see why they don't build an arcade from Brick Top's* to the Ritz." Nobody laughs. As usual, one can find no contact with them.

My twenty-firster. Fifty people in fancy dress. The orchestra from the *Grand Ecart*. A large silver waste paper basket. "To Christian de Clavering, the Great Commoner—Alvanley, Alba, Ava, Abercorn, Andrassy, Aberconway, Argyll, Auersperg"—you can imagine the signatures. As the college barge, which I had taken for the occasion, glided up the Cher, life's goblet seemed full to brimming. But Nemesis pursued me. The dons descended. I suppose they hadn't had enough invitations. It appears that those afternoons which I spent under some hot towels in Germers were full of goings-on, lectures, tutorials, Heaven knows what. Divinity seemed a prominent element in the City of Lost Causes. I went down. Oxford, like Eton, had never really "given."

London at last.† The twenties. Parties. Parties. Parties. And behind them all an aching feeling.—Was it worth it? What is it all for? Futility. . . .

"Christian—you must dine with me tonight!"

"Gawain—I can't—I've engaged myself to the *'Derries*."

"Are you the manager?"

---

* Always my favorite nightbox.
† A London then where everybody knew everybody and we all squeezed into one telephone book!

"Yes, sir."

"My name is de Clavering. I should like to say I have never eaten such a disgusting meal. *Même à la Cour.* But haven't I seen you before?"

"Oui, monsieur, je vous connais depuis l'Eldorado."

"Es usted el cuadro flamenco?"
  "Sí."
  "Sí."
  "Sí."
  "Sí."

"Beverley, my dear, such a gaffe! I've just gone up to the old Dowager of Buck-and-Chan and mistaken her for the old Dowager of Ham-and-Bran!"
  "*Christian!*"

"She's got what the Americans call 'that.'"
  "What?"
  "What the Americans call 'that.'"
  "What's that?"
  "'That'—that's what she's got."
  "But what the Americans call what? I don't even know that."
  "Oh, my dear Duchess!"
For it was sometimes my privilege to give instruction to a very great lady.

"M. Picasso—Mr. Hemingway. M. Hemingway—Señor Belmonte. Mr. Nicolson—Mr. Firbank—and now shall we begin without Miss Stein? I'm starving."

"I can't decide whether to stay with Lorenzo in Taos or Crowley in Cefalu—where *does* one go in August?"

"Dear Evelyn, *of course*, put me into it!"

"Voulez-vous téléphoner à Mr. Proust de venir me trouver dans les bains de la rue de Lappe?"

"Herr Reinhardt ist zuschloss?"

"You know Diaghilev, of course, Dingy?"

"I've found the title for you, Breton—*Surréalisme*."

"And for this rather brusque poem, Osbert, I shall need the 'meg.'"*

Parties. Futility. You can read of most of them in old gossip columns. I still remember my tropical party, when a punkah was heard for the first time in Egerton Crescent. Palms and bananas decorated the rooms. The central heating (it was in July) provided the atmosphere. Some stewards from the P. & O. worked away at the punkahs, or at distributing *reistafel* and planters' punch. The guests wore shorts, sarongs, stingah shifters, or nothing at all.

"But this is *me*," I remember saying, holding up a slim volume. "Why haven't I been told about this before, Dadie? Who is this T. S. Eliot?"

"He works in a bank, I believe."

"Works in a bank—and writes *The Waste Land!* But he should be here, at my Tropical Party! Go and fetch him."

But there is a new disturbance, and Bolitho, our butler, is at my elbow.

"Some young people, sir."

"Their names?"

"The *Blackbirds*."

"Ask them to come up. We shall want some more room. Patrick, help me spread Elizabeth somewhere else. Ronald, come out from under that sofa, you're hunching the springs.†

---

* A megaphone, and such small ability as I may have acquired with it, now constitute my "platform manner."
† Firbank's shyness was proverbial.

Fallen out of the window, you say, with Brenda? Never mind, for the moment. I want to be alone. I want to read this book."

And then the blow fell. A summons, next day, to the Royal Automobile Club. "I'm ruined, my boy. I'm ruined. 'Aven't got a penny left. Those pals of yours, Alvanley and Gleneagles. They've skinned me. You'll 'ave to earn your own living from now on. Oh, your poor mother!" "It's poor me, you old banana. I've no intention of earning my own living, thank you."—"Ow, wot a boy, wot a boy." And I flung out. Tears. Consultations.

"I can always sell my Gris." "But what will you do then?"

"Oh, write—paint—don't fluster me."

"And we were to have gone to the Londonderry del Vals!"

"Poor mother."

One thing stood out with terrible clarity in those dark days. The old life was over. I could never associate any longer with those friends who had been used to look to me for advice, loans, old clothes, and entertainment. They would see to that. The Ritz, the Blue Lantern, must know me no more.

Exile. A few months in Paris—but Montparnasse, now, my dears, *Montparnasse;* a few offers for my memoirs; then Berlin, Munich—and finally, Greece. There, "in the worst inn's worst room," I existed, miserably, on fried goat and raki. To write or to paint—to work—but how? Write only on one side of the paper. But which side? It was the old dilemma. A wandering exile, the quays of the Piraeus knew me, the noisy bars of Terreno, the Dôme and the Deux Magots, Bohême and Silhouette, and that place in the Marokaner Gasse. I ate roseleaf jam with the good monks of Holy Luke, and fried locusts with the dervishes of Moulay Idris. And one crazy 4th of June, lobster salad with my housemaster! My slim figure lingered, winterbound, in dim cathedrals, and there were beaches where summer licked me with its great rough tongue. Ah, summer! There's a crypto-fascist for you! The spring I never cared for. It held nothing but a promise, and I, too, was promising. The autumns I adored; they smelt of cassia. But poverty was crippling. To whom life once had been a bed of roses—no, of *Strawberry-leaves*, there remained only the "Welcome" at Villefranche, the old Boeuf in the Boissy D'Anglas, the Pangion. It was not good enough. I came back to live with my mother.

It was then that I saw the light. One day I wandered into a little book-shop near Red Lion Square. It was full of slim volumes by unfamiliar names—who were Stephen, Wystan, Cecil, and Christopher? Madge? Bates? Dutt? These blunt monosyllables spoke a new kind of language to me. I looked at the books. Not at all bad, and some of these young poets, I realized, had even attended my university! One quatrain in particular haunted me.

> M is for Marx
> and Movement of Masses
> and Massing of Arses
> and Clashing of Classes.

It was new. It was vigorous. It was real. It was chic!

> Come on Percy, my pillion-proud, be
> camber-conscious
> Cleave to the crown of the road

and

> It was late last night when my lord came home
> enquiring for his lady O
> The servants cried on every side
> She's gone with the Left Book
> Study Circle O!

And everyone was called by their Christian names! So cosy! From that moment I've never looked back. It's been pylons all the way. Of course they didn't want me, at first. The meetings behind the Geisha Café—they suspected me of all sorts of things, I'm afraid—I said quite frankly: "I realize I shall never understand eclectic materialism but I'm terribly terribly Left!" And I showed them one or two things I'd written for the weekly reviews, all among the waffle receipts and the guest house advertisements.* And I called myself Cris Clay. Then—on a drizzling February morning—came my first Procession! It was for me a veritable *Via Crucis*, for we had to march up St. James's Street—past Locks, and Lobbs, and

---

* Soon to be published under the title of *I Told You So.*

Briggs, and Boodles. All my past was spread out before me. There weren't very many of us, and it was difficult to cheer and shout our slogans

> One, two, three, four
> Pacifism means War.

I raised my eyes to White's bow window.

Yes, there they were—Alvanley and Gleneagles, with their soiled city faces and little moustaches, their bowlers and rolled umbrellas—and, good heavens, there were Peter, and Robert, and Evelyn! I never felt more ridiculous. When suddenly something made me look round. "De Clavering, old horse!" "Well, I'm spifflicated." "You old *finocchio!*" "*Spinaten!*" It was too good to be true.

"But, Harmatviz—I see you don't know the first thing about the cut of a corduroy."

"Not a red shirt, Slivovitz—a red tie if you must."

"And you, Coca y Cola—you look like a scarecrow."

"These are good workmen's pants, de Clavering, real dungaree!"

We gave a boo to the bow window that made the *Tatlers* rattle in their holders.

"But how did you get here?"

"I was expelled for plotting against the Regent in favor of the traitor Otto."

"I was turned out for lack of enthusiasm for the present regime and communicating with the traitor Wilhelm."

"I wanted to annoy Sarsaparilla."

"Anyhow, we're all good anti-Fascists," cried Comrade Graf Slivovitz.

I wanted to say something more—that I had even been told by the Party that I should be more useful outside it, but I couldn't speak. Old friends had met, traveling a stony road, coming to the same hard conclusions, and together.

And that's about all. There are one or two things I've left out, the war, the slump, the general strike, and my conversion to Catholicism, because I'm so vague about dates. But I think this will remain—A Modern Pilgrimage. And now for the reviewers. I think they'd better be careful. They'd better be very careful indeed. A line is being drawn. I'm going to say it again, and very slowly. A line is being drawn. Quite quietly at present—just a few names jotted down in a notebook—one or two with a question mark after them. They have another chance. And the rest don't. Those lines mean something. Tatatat! Yes, my dears, bullets—real bullets, the kind of bullets they keep for reviewers who step across the party line. One day you're going to see something rather hostile. It will make you feel, perhaps, a little uneasy. It's heavy—and stubby— and rather pointed. Guess? Yes. A machine-gun. POINTED AT YOU. And behind it, with his hand on the trigger, Comrade—no, COMMISSAR—Cris Clay. Did you write such and such an article? Yes (No). It doesn't matter which. Tatatat. It's no good then bleating about how you voted in the last election, or where your sympathies have always been. We don't want your sympathy. We don't want you at all.

You subscribed to the *News-Chronicle*, did you? I am afraid you will be under no necessity to renew that subscription.

You wrote for the *New Statesman?* What did you write about? "Gramophone records."

"To sit on the fence is to be on the wrong side of it—line him up, Gollancz."

"Yes, Commissar."

"And you—what were you?"

"Turf-Accountant."

"Your face seems vaguely familiar—but that doesn't make it more pleasant—line him up, Stephen."

"It was no accident, Pryce-Jones, that you have lived near three royal palaces."

"But—"

But I am anticipating. There are two ways to review a book like mine, a right and a wrong. The wrong way is to find fault with it, for then you find fault with the book clubs behind it, in fact, with your advertisers. And if I seem too clever it's because you're too stupid. Think it over. The right way is to praise it, and to quote from it in such a way that you can all learn my lesson. I stand no nonsense. Remember, my dears, a line is being drawn. Tatatat. See you at the Mass Observatory.

> Something is going to go, baby,
> And it won't be your stamp-collection.
> Boom!

And that I think could particularly be meditated by the Fascist Connolly.

CRIS CLAY.

PARIS—BUDAPEST—PARTON ST.
1936-1937.

Bond Strikes Camp

Shadows of fog were tailing him through the windows of his
Chelsea flat; the blonde had left a broken rosette of lipstick on
the best Givan's pillowcase—he would have to consult last
night's book matches to find out where he had grabbed her. It
was one bitch of a morning. And, of course, it turned out to be
the day! For there was always one breakfast in the month
when a very simple operation, the boiling of an egg so that the
yolk should remain properly soft and the white precisely hard,
seemed to defeat his devoted housekeeper, May. As he decapi-
tated the fifth abort on its Wedgwood launching pad he was
tempted to crown her with the sixteen-inch pepper mill.
Three minutes and fifty-five seconds later by his stopwatch
and the sixth egg came up with all systems go. As he was
about to press the thin finger of wholemeal toast into the prepared cavity the telephone rang. It was probably the blonde:
"Don't tell me: it all comes back—you're the new hat check
from 'The Moment of Truth,'" he snarled into the receiver.
But the voice which cut in was that of his secretary, Miss
Ponsonby. "He wants you now, smart pants, so step on the
Pogo."

Swearing pedantically, Bond pulled away from his uneaten
egg and hurried from the flat to the wheel of his souped-up
Pierce Arrow, a Thirty-one open tourer with two three-piece
windscreens. A sulphurous black rain was falling and he
nearly took the seat off a Beatnik as he swerved into Milner. It
was that kind of a Christmas. Thirteen minutes later his lean
body streaked from the tonneau-cover like a conger from its

hole and he stood outside M.'s door with Lolita Ponsonby's great spaniel eyes gazing up at him in doglike devotion.

"Sorry about the crossed line," he told her. "I'll sock you a lunch if they don't need you at Crufts." Then the green lights showed and he entered.

"Sit down, 007." That was Grade C welcome indicating the gale warning. There had been several lately. But M. did not continue. He surveyed Bond with a cold, glassy stare, cleared his throat and suddenly lowered his eyes. His pipe rested unlit beside the tobacco in the familiar shell-cap. If such a thing had been possible, Bond would have sworn he was embarrassed. When at length he spoke, the voice was dry and impersonal. "There are many things I have asked you to do, Bond; they have not always been pleasant but they have been in the course of duty. Supposing I were to ask you to do something which I have no right to demand and which I can justify only by appealing to principles outside your service obligations. I refer to your patriotism. You are patriotic, Bond?"

"Don't know, sir, I never read the small print clauses."

"Forgive the question, I'll put it another way. Do you think the end justifies the means?"

"I can attach no significance of any kind to such expressions."

M. seemed to reflect. The mood of crisis deepened.

"Well, we must try again. If there were a particularly arduous task—a most distasteful task—and I called for a volunteer—who must have certain qualifications—and only one person had those qualifications—and I asked him to volunteer. What would you say?"

"I'd say stop beating about the bush, sir."

"I'm afraid we haven't even started."

"Sir?"

"Do you play chess, Bond?"

"My salary won't run to it."

"But you are familiar with the game?"

"Tolerably." As if aware that he was in the stronger position, Bond was edging toward insolence.

"It has, of course, been thoroughly modernized; all the adventure has been taken out of it; the opening gambits in which a piece used to be sacrificed for the sake of early development proved unsound and therefore abandoned. But it is so long since they have been tried that many players are unfamiliar with the pitfalls and it is sometimes possible to obtain an advantage by taking a risk. In our profession, if it be a profession, we keep a record of these forgotten traps. Ever heard of Mata Hari?"

"The beautiful spy?" Bond's voice held derision. The school prefect sulking before his housemaster.

"She was very successful. It was a long time ago." M. still sounded meek and deprecating.

"I seem to remember reading the other day that a concealed microphone had replaced the *femme fatale*."

"Precisely. So there is still a chance for the *femme fatale*."

"I have yet to meet her."

"You will. You are aware there is a Russian military mission visiting this country?"

Bond let that one go into the net.

"They have sent over among others an elderly general. He looks like a general, he may well have been a general, he is certainly a very high echelon in their K.G.B. Security is his speciality; rocketry, nerve gases, germ warfare—all the usual hobbies." M. paused. "And one rather unusual one."

Bond waited, like an old pike watching the bait come down.

"Yes. He likes to go to nightclubs, get drunk, throw his money about and bring people back to his hotel. All rather old-fashioned."

"And not very unusual."

"Ah." M. looked embarrassed again. "I'm just coming to that. We happen to know quite a bit about this chap, General Count Apraxin. His family were pretty well known under the old dispensation though his father was one of the first to join the party; we think he may be a bit of a throwback. Not politically, of course. He's tough as they come. I needn't tell you Section A make a study of the kind of greens the big shots go in for. Sometimes we know more about what these people are like between the sheets than they do themselves; it's a dirty business. Well, the General is mad about drag."

"Drag, sir?"

M. winced. "I'm sorry about this part, Bond. He's 'so'—'uno di quelli'—'one of those'—a sodomite."

Bond detected a glint of distaste in the cold blue eyes.

"In my young days," M. went on, "fellows like that shot themselves. Now their names are up for every club. Particularly in London. Do you know what sort of a reputation this city has abroad?" Bond waited. "Well, it stinks. These foreigners come here, drop notes of assignation into sentries' top boots, pin fivers on to guardsmen's bearskins. The Tins are livid."

"And General Apraxin?" Bond decided to cut short the Wolfenden.

"One of the worst. I told you he likes drag. That's—er—men dressed up as women."

"Well, you tell me he's found the right place. But I don't quite see where we come in."

M. cleared his throat. "There's just a possibility, mind, it's only a possibility, that even a top K.G.B. might be taken off guard—if he found the company congenial—perhaps so congenial that it appealed to some secret wish of his imagination—and if he talked at all (mind you, he is generally absolutely silent), well then anything he said might be of the greatest value—anything—it might be a lead on what he's really here for. You will be drawing a bow at a venture. You will be working in the dark."

"Me, sir?"

M. rapped out the words like a command. "007, I want you to do this thing. I want you to let our people rig you up as a moppet and send you to a special sort of club and I want you to allow yourself to be approached by General Apraxin and sit at his table and if he asks you back to his hotel I want you to accompany him and any suggestion he makes I request you to fall in with to the limit your conscience permits. And may your patriotism be your conscience, as it is mine."

It was a very odd speech for M. Bond studied his finger-nails. "And if the pace gets too hot?"

"Then you must pull out—but remember. T. E. Lawrence put up with the final indignity. I knew him well, but knowing even that, I never dared call him by his Christian name."

Bond reflected. It was clear that M. was deeply concerned. Besides, the General might never turn up. "I'll try anything once, sir."

"Good man." M. seemed to grow visibly younger.

"As long as I'm not expected to shake a powder into his drink and run away with his wallet."

"Oh, I don't think it will come to that. If you don't like the look of things, just plead a headache; he'll be terrified of any publicity. It was all Section A could do to slip him a card for this club."

"What's its name?"

M. pursed his lips. "The Kitchener. In Lower Belgrave Mews. Be there about eleven o'clock and just sit around. We've signed you in as 'Gerda.'"

"And my—disguise?"

"We're sending you off to a specialist in that kind of thing— he thinks you want it for some Christmas 'do.' Here's the address."

"One more question, sir. I have no wish to weary you with details of my private life but I can assure you I've never dressed up in 'drag' as you call it since I played Katisha in *The Mikado* at my prep school. I shan't look right, I shan't move right, I shan't talk right; I shall feel about as convincing arsing about as a nightclub hostess as Randolph Churchill."

M. gazed at him blankly and again Bond noticed his expression of weariness, even of repulsion. "Yes, 007, you will do all of those things and I am afraid that is precisely what will get him."

Bond turned angrily but M.'s face was already buried in his signals. This man who had sent so many to their deaths was still alive and now the dedicated bachelor who had never looked at a woman except to estimate her security risk was packing him off with the same cold indifference into a den of slimy creatures. He walked out of the room and was striding past Miss Ponsonby when she stopped him. "No time for that lunch, I'm afraid. You're wanted in Armory."

The Armory in the basement held many happy memories for Bond. It represented the first moments of a new adventure, the excitement of being back on a job. There were the revolvers and the Tommy guns, the Smith and Wessons, Colts, lugers, berettas, killer weapons of every class or nationality; blow-pipes, boomerangs, cyanide fountain pens, Commando daggers and the familiar heap of aqualungs, now more or less standard equipment. He heard the instructor's caressing voice. "Grind yer boot down his shin and crush his instep. Wrench off his testicles with yer free hand and with the fingers held stiffly in the V sign gouge out his eyes with the other."

He felt a wave of homesickness. "Ah, Bond, we've got some hardware for you. Check it over and sign the receipt," said the lieutenant of marines.

"Good God, what's this? It looks to me like a child's water pistol."

"You're so right—and here's the water." He was given a small screw-top ink bottle full of some transparent liquid. "Don't spill any on your bib and tucker."

"What'll it stop?"

"Anything on two legs if you aim at the eyes."

Bond consulted the address of his next "armorer." It was a studio off Kinnerton Street. The musical cough of the Pierce Arrow was hardly silent when the door was opened by a calm young man who looked him quickly up and down. Bond was wearing one of his many pheasant's-eye alpacas which exaggerated the new vertical line—single-breasted, narrow lapels, ton-up trousers with no turn-ups, peccary suède shoes. A short covert-coat in cavalry twill, a black sting-ray tail of a tie, an unexpected width of shoulder above the tapering waist and the casual arrogance of his comma of dark hair low over the forehead under his little green piglet of a hat completed the picture of mid-century masculinity. The young man seemed unimpressed. "Well, well, how butch can you get? You've left it rather late. But we'll see what we can do."

He turned Bond toward the lighted north window and studied him carefully, then he gave the comma a tweak. "I like the spit-curl, Gerda, we'll build up round that. Now go in there and strip."

When he came out in his pants, the barracuda scars dark against the tan, a plain girl was waiting in a nurse's uniform. "Lie down, Gerda, and leave it all to Miss Haslip," said the young man. She stepped forward and began, expertly, to shave his legs and armpits. "First a shave, then the depilatory—I'm afraid, what with the fittings, you'll be here most of the day." It was indeed one bitch of a morning. The only consolation was that the young man (his name was Colin Mount) allowed him to keep the hair on his chest. "After all, nobody wants you *all* sugar."

After the manicure, pedicure, and plucking of the eyebrows it was time to start rebuilding. Bond was given a jockstrap to contain his genitals; the fitting of an elaborate chestnut wig so as to allow the comma to escape under it was another slow process. And then the artificial eye lashes. Finally what looked like a box of tennis balls was produced from a drawer. "Ever seen these before?"

"Good God, what *are* they?"

"The very latest in falsies—foam rubber, with electronic self-erecting nipples—pink for blondes, brown for brunettes. The things they think of! Which will you be? It's an important decision."

"What the hell do I care?"

"On the whole I think you'd better be a brunette. It goes with the eyes. And with your height we want them rather large. Round or pear-shaped?"

"Round, for Christ's sake."

"Sure you're not making a mistake?"

The falsies were attached by a rubber strap, like a brassière, which—in black moiré—was then skilfully fitted over them. "How does that feel? There should be room for a guy to get his hand up under the bra and have a good riffle." Then came the slinky black lace panties and finally the black satin evening skirt with crimson silk blouse suspended low on the shoulder, a blue mink scarf over all and then the sheerest black stockings and black shoes with red stilettos. Bond surveyed himself in the long glass and experienced an unexpected thrill of excitement; there was no doubt he had a damned good figure.

"Well, you're no Coccinelle," said the young man, "but you'll certainly pass. Hip-square! Drag's a lot of fun you'll find. One meets quite a different class of person. Now go and practice walking till you drop. Then get some sleep, and after that, if you're good, we'll make up that pretty face and launch you at the local cinema."

After practicing in high heels for a couple of hours, Bond went back to his couch and lay down exhausted. He dreamed he was swimming under water on a stormy day, the waves breaking angrily above him while, harpoon in hand, he followed a great sea bass with spaniel eyes that seemed to turn and twist and invite him onward down an ever-narrowing, weed-matted gully.

When he awoke it was dark and he fell avidly on the Blue Mountain coffee and club sandwich Miss Haslip had brought him. "Now we'll start on the face—and here's your evening bag." Bond transferred his water pistol, ink bottle, Ronson lighter, gun-metal cigarette case and bill folder and emptied the contents of his wallet; a vintage chart from the Wine and Food Society, an "Advanced Motorists" certificate, another from the Subaqua Club, a temporary membership card of the Travelers, Paris, the Caccia, Rome, Puerto de Hierro, Madrid, Brook, Meadowbrook, Knickerbocker and Crazy Horse Saloon, Liguanea, Eagle, Somerset (Boston) and Boston (New Orleans), ending up with a reader's pass for the Black Museum. When he had done, Colin emptied the whole lot into a large envelope, which he told Bond to put in the glove compartment, and handed back the water pistol and key ring. "Try these instead," and Bond was given a powder puff, a couple of lipsticks, some Kleenex, a package of cigarettes (Senior Service) with a long cane holder, some costume jewelry and a charm bracelet and a membership card in the name of

Miss Gerda Blond for the Kitchener Social Club, Lower Belgrave Mews, S.W.

In a compartment of his evening bag he found a pocket mirror, tortoiseshell comb, enamel compact and a box of eye make-up with a tiny brush. "When you get mad at someone it's a great relief to take this out and spit on it. The harder you spit, the more of a lady you'll seem." Mount showed him how to apply the little brush, the mascara and black eye-shadow. "When you don't know how to answer, just look down for a little—lower those eyelashes, that'll fetch them—and make with the holder. And do be careful in the Loo. That's where nearly all the mistakes are made. Now we're off to the Pictures."

"What are we going to see?"

"*La Dolce Vita.*"

In the dark cinema Bond noticed a few interested glances in his direction. A man in the next seat put his hand on his knee. Bond knew the drill; a policewoman in Singapore had shown him. You take the hand tenderly in yours and extend his arm across your knee. Then you bring your other hand down hard and break the fellow's arm at the elbow. He had just got it all set up when the lights went on.

"I wanted you to see that picture, it gives you so many approaches," said Colin Mount. "You can try Ekberg—the big child of nature—or one of those sophisticated cats. Now off you go. Better take a taxi, that hearse of yours looks too draughty."

In Lower Belgrave Mews, Bond rang the bell, showed his card and was immediately admitted.

The Kitchener was discreetly decorated in the style of 1914 with a maze of red plush and some old war posters. The familiar, rather forbidding face with pouchy eyes and drooping moustache and the pointing finger, "Your King and country need you," recruited him wherever he looked. There were two upstair rooms, in one of which people were dancing. The other held a few divans and tables and a little bar. They had once formed a large double drawing-room. On the landing above, the bathrooms were labeled "Turks" and "Virgins."

Bond sat down at a table, ordered "Eggs Omdurman" washed down by a "Sirdar Special." He noticed several couples dancing sedately to the Cobbler's Song from *Chu Chin Chow* on a pickup. There were posters of Doris Keane in *Romance* and Violet Loraine in *The Bing Boys* and of Miss Teddy Gerrard. The subdued lighting from pink lampshades, the roomy banquette, the liver-flicking welcome of his "Eggs Omdurman" and the silken recoil of the "Sirdar Special" made him feel for the first time content with his preposterous mission. Had he not worn the kilt at Fettes? He was in it now, up to the sporran. All at once a woman's low voice interrupted his reverie. "Dance?" He lowered his eyes, as he had been told, and thought furiously. To refuse, in fact to tell her to get the hell out, was his first reaction—but that might arouse suspicion. He had better play along. "Thanks. I'd love to," he managed in a husky contralto and looked up past a mannish red waistcoat and tweed jacket into a pair of faintly mocking brown eyes. It was Lolita! Speechless with disaster, Bond wondered how long it would be before the story was all over the office. If only his disguise could last a couple of rounds. And then he remembered. Was he not 007 and licensed to kill with his water pistol? He tensed himself and let the sweat dry on his forehead. In a moment he was hobbling on to the dance floor, where it was much darker, to the strains of "Japanese Sandman." His secretary seemed transformed: capably she maneuvered him into an obscure corner where they rocked up and down as she began to hold him closer, sliding a leg between his and shifting her hand slowly and expertly down his spine. He began to wonder how the jockstrap would hold. Suddenly she drew back a little and looked him in the eyes. "What's your name?"

"Gerda"—he croaked—"Gerda Blond."

"It's your first visit to the Kitch, isn't it?—well, Gerda, I could fall for you in a big way. I bet you could give someone a good butt in the eye with those charleys." She ran a finger gently up a full, firm breast and gave a start when the nipple shot up trigger-happy as a Sensitive Plant. "Gerda, I want to ask you a question." Bond lowered his eyes. "Have you ever slept with a woman?"

"Well, no, not exactly."

"Well, you're going to tonight."

"But I don't even know your name."

"Just call me Robin."

"But I'm not sure that I can tonight."

"Well, I am. And let me tell you; once you've been to bed with me you won't want anyone else. I know what men are like—I work for one. No girl ever wants a man once she's made it with a dike. It's the difference between a bullfight and an egg-and-spoon race."

"But I can't imagine what you see in me."

"Well, you've got a pretty good figure and I like that in-between color, like a Braque still life, and I adore the wizard tits—and then you're not like the other mice, sort of virginal and stand-offish—and I'm crazy about the spit curl." She gave it a sharp tug.

"That's not a spit curl," pouted Bond. "That's my comma."

"Have it your way. And I like your husky voice and those droopy eyes and right now I'm imagining your little black triangle."

"Oh, belt up, Robin!"

"Come on, Gerda, we're going back to my place."

Miss Ponsonby began to lug him off the dance floor. Immediately, out of the corner of his eye, Bond caught sight of a stout figure in a dinner jacket at another table, a bald head and fishy stare and a pair of enormous moustaches, even as a thick forefinger shot up like an obscene grub and began to beckon to him. A deep voice rumbled: "Would the two little ladies care to accept a glass of champagne?"

"Certainly not," snapped Miss Ponsonby. "Father would turn in his vault."

"Thanks a lot. No objection," came Bond's husky contralto. His secretary wheeled round. "Why, you black bitch—you filthy little tart, I suppose you support a basketful of bastards at home all bleating their bloody heads off. Go along and I hope the old Tirpitz gives you a Lulu." She gave Bond a ringing slap across the eyes and burst into tears. As she left she turned to the new arrival. "You watch out with that bint. Mark my words. She'll do you in."

Bond held his smarting cheek. The foreign gentleman patted his arm and pulled him on to the banquette. "What a headstrong young lady—she gave me quite a turn. But here comes our champagne. I have ordered a magnum of Taittinger Blanc de blancs, '52—it never departs from a certain 'tenu'—independent yet perfectly deferential." He had a trace of guttural accent but what impressed Bond most were the magnificent whiskers. He had seen them only once before on a Russian, Marshal Budenny, Stalin's cavalry leader. They gave a raffish Eighth Army-turned-innkeeper look to the big-nosed military man and were perhaps symptomatic of the formidable General's atavism.

Bond collapsed on to the alcove divan and raised the paradisal prickle to his lips, remembering Monsieur Georges, the wine waiter at the Casino Royale who had called his attention to the brand in the first of his annual agonies.

"Perhaps I had better introduce myself," said the General. "I am a Yugoslav traveling salesman here to make certain business contacts and tonight is my evening of relaxation. All day I have been in conference and tomorrow I have to go down early in the morning to Salisbury Plain. Vladimir Mishitch. Just call me Vladimir; the accent is on the second syllable."

Bond noticed he had not inquired his own name and finally volunteered with downcast eye, "My name is Gerda. I like traveling too but I'm afraid I haven't anything to sell."

"One never knows. *'La plus belle fille du monde, ne peut donner que ce qu'elle a.'*" The General stuck his hand into Bond's blouse and ran his fingers through the hair on his chest. "That's a nice rug you've got there, Gerda." Bond lowered his eyes again. "And that—that is pretty too. How do you call it?"

"That's my comma."

"I see. I'm afraid I make more use of the colon. Ha! ha!" Bond did not know whether to seem amused or bored, and said nothing. "Tell me, Gerda—" the General's voice took on a warmer color. "Have you ever slept with a man?"

"Well no, not exactly."

"I thought not, Gerda—your little girl friend—the paprika-hühn—she would not allow it, hein?"

"Well, it's something we've all got to do sooner or later."

"And I suggest you do it right now—for when you've been to bed with a real man, a man of age and experience, you won't ever want anyone else. It's like the Salle Privée at the Sporting Club after a tea with your P.E.N."

He inserted a torpedo-shaped Larranaga such as seldom reaches these shores into an amber holder and poured out the ice cold champagne until Bond unaccountably found himself sitting on his lap in some disarray, while the General broke into stentorian song:

> How you gonna keep them
> Down on the farm
> After they've seen Paree!

Bond broke away.

"Aren't you going to have a dance with me?"

The General roared with laughter. "I have never learned to dance except our Yugoslav ones and those we dance only with comrades."

"I expect I could pick them up."

"Yes. Like I have picked up you. I will play one to you in my hotel and you will dance like an Ustashi."

"But they were all Fascists, weren't they?"

The General laughed again. "They danced very well at the end of a rope. Like Homer's handmaidens—with twittering feet."

Bond found the allusion faintly disturbing. "It's too hot, let's go."

The General paid the bill from a bundle of fivers and hurried down the stairs; it was only, Bond noticed, a little after midnight. "We will take a taxi, Gerda, it is less likely to be followed."

"But why should anyone want to follow you, Vladimir?"

"Business is business; don't worry your pretty little head."

The taxi turned off St. James's Street and stopped in a cul-de-sac. "But this is not a hotel."

"No, Gerda, furnished service flatlets. Mine is in the basement, so we go down these steps and don't have to face your night porters—so puritanical—and so expensive. Though anyone can see you're not an ordinary lady of the town." He covered a falsie in his large palm and cupped it hard. "Pip—pip."

"Leave me alone. I've got a headache."

"I have just the thing," said the General and paid off the taxi, almost flinging Bond in his tight skirt and high heels down the steps into the area. For the first time he felt a twinge of fear. To the taxi driver he was one of London's many thousand fly-by-nights off to earn their lolly—yet no one else in the great indifferent city knew his whereabouts nor what manner of man was preparing to have his way with him. At home in Chelsea his black shantung pyjamas would be laid out, the evening papers and the *Book Collector* spread on his night table, the digestive biscuits and Karlsbad plums, a bottle of San Pellegrino, a jigger of Strathisla. Lately he had taken to spinning himself to sleep with a roulette wheel or some Chopi xylophone music from the Transvaal asbestos mines. . . .

Vladimir opened a Yale and then a mortice lock and let them into a typical furnished basement flat, a beige sitting room with a somber bedroom beyond. The fog was beginning to probe again, like a second day's grilling by Interpol. "Here, swallow this for the headache—and have a glass of whiskey—Teachers, Cutty Sark, Old Grandad or do you prefer vodka or slivovitz?"

"Old Grandad—and what about you?"

"Oh, I'll help myself to some vodka." It was a tiny error but a revealing one. But perhaps the General argued that a Yugoslav drank slivovitz enough at home.

Bond put a cigarette in his mouth and just remembered in time to let the General light it. He took the yellow pill which he had been given, palmed it and pretended to swallow it with a grimace. "I hate all these pills and things. I don't believe they're any good at all."

The General raised his vodka. "To Friendship."

"To Friendship," chorused Gerda, lifting up her Old-Grandad-on-the-rocks. She was thinking fast. The purpose of the pill she hadn't swallowed must have been to make her sleepy but hardly to put her out. She had better play drowsy.

"Let's have another toast," said the General. "Who is your best friend?"

Bond remembered the gambit pawn. "Guy Burgess."

The General guffawed. "I'll tell him. He'll be delighted. He doesn't often get a message from such a pretty girl."

Bond lowered his eyes. "He was my lover."

"One can see that by the way you walk."

Bond felt a mounting wave of fury. He opened his bag, took out his mascara and spat viciously. The General looked on with approval. Bond produced another cigarette. "Here, catch." The General tossed over his lighter. Bond, with the eye brush in one hand and the pack in the other, brought his legs neatly together as it fell on his lap.

"Where were you at school, Gerda?"

"Westonbirt."

"And so they teach you to catch like a man—what is a woman's lap for? She widens it to catch, not brings her legs together. And when she drowns she floats upward not downward. Remember that. It may come in useful."

Bond felt trapped. "I'm so sleepy," he muttered. "I don't understand."

"Quick, in here." The General pushed him into the bedroom with its electric fire and dingy satin coverlet. "Undress and get into bed and then look under the pillow."

Bond took off his blouse and skirt while the General gallantly turned his back, but kept on his stockings, pants and "bra," then got out his water pistol and filled it, dropped the pill behind the bed and finally climbed in and felt under the pillow. The first thing he found was a tube of some oily-looking substance, the next was a shoe horn with a long cane handle, the last was a piece of paper with "No one is the worse for a good beating" printed in heavy capitals. "Ready," he called and lay quietly until the General in a blue quilted

vicuna kimono came simpering in. Bond made a kissy noise
and as the General climbed on to the bed and advanced his
hairy handlebars reached out with the water pistol and shot
him full in the eye.

The General wiped his face with a silk handkerchief. "Temper, temper," he giggled as the liquid ran down his chin.
"What a silly toy for a naughty little girl. Who do we think we
are, a black mamba?" He picked up the shoe horn and dealt
Bond a vicious cut across the falsies.

"Help, help, murder," screamed Bond and once again as the
General drew back his mind began to race furiously. Somewhere along the line he had been double-crossed. But when?
He lay back drowsily. "Vladimir—it was only my joke. I'm so
sorry. Now let me sleep."

"Soon you shall sleep—but we have all to earn our sleep.
Now shall I beat you first or will you beat me?"

"I will beat you, Vladimir, or I shall certainly drop off before my turn comes. Besides I've never beaten anyone before."

"Tell that to Guy Burgess." The General handed over the
long shoe horn and lay down on his stomach. You can kill a
man with a short stick, Bond remembered. Get his head forward. Hold the stick in both hands and jab one end up under
his Adam's apple. It had all seemed so easy in Armory. But
the General's broad shoulders were in the way. "How dare
you speak to me like that." Bond jumped up and ran for the
bathroom.

As he hoped, the General lumbered after him. "Come out,
you young fool, I can't sit around all night while you play
hard to get. I'll miss my train to Porton."

Porton! The anthrax boys! Bond's nipples stiffened at the
name. "I won't come out till I get my little present."

"Fifty pounds—if you'll go the limit."

"I want half now."

The ends of some five-pound notes protruded under the
bathroom door. Bond pulled hard but the General, he
guessed, must be standing on them on the other side. That
meant he was right by the door which opened inward. Bond
would have to fling it open, get Vladimir's head forward and

ram his throat in one continuous movement. He was in peak training, his opponent would assume him to be half asleep—it could be done. He counted down from five (the nearest he ever got to a prayer), threw open the door and discovered the smiling General with his hands deep in his kimono pockets and head thrown far back. There was a strong smell of cigar and Floris mouthwash. Still holding the shoe horn in one hand, Bond lunged forward with the other, got hold of both ends of the handlebars to bring his head down and gave a tremendous tug. There was a screech of rending cardboard and the General gave a yell of pain; a gummy red patch was spreading where the whiskers had been. Bond stared into the cold blue eyes and this time they fell before him.

"I'm sorry, James," said M. "It was the only way I could get you."

Bond drew himself up; his eyes flashed fire, his comma glistened, his breasts firmed, the nipples roused and urgent; his long rangy body flared out above his black silk panties, he looked like Judith carving Holofernes. In two seconds of icy concentration he saw everything that had to be done.

"It's been going on so long. I've been through too much. Don't think I haven't fought against it."

Bond cut him short. "I thought fellows like you shot themselves." M. hung his head. "Have you got a gun—sir—?" M. nodded. Bond looked at his watch. "It's a quarter past two. You may employ what means you prefer but if I find out you are still alive by nine o'clock I shall alert every newspaper here, Tass and United Press—Moscow, Washington, Interpol and Scotland Yard, *Izvestia* and the *Kingston Gleaner* with the whole story. If it had been anyone else, I might have urged you to leave the country but with modern methods of eliciting information you would be blown in a day."

"You're quite right, James. I've staked all and I've lost. I hope you'll believe me when I say it would have been for the first and last time."

"I believe you, sir."

"And now perhaps you'd better leave me, 007; I shall have one or two reports to make."

Bond flung on his blouse and skirt, worked into his stilettos and snatched up his bag and tippet.

"One last question, James. How did you guess?"

Bond thought of simply confessing that he hadn't guessed, even when the water pistol had proved a dud. Right down to the Taittinger M.'s arrangements had been perfect. But that might look bad on his file. Then it came back to him. "You spoke of Homer's handmaidens with 'twittering feet' when Ulysses hanged them. That was in Lawrence of Arabia's translation. Robert Graves objected to it. I remembered that you had said Lawrence was your friend. It might have occurred to you that Graves could be mine."

M.'s face brightened and the sickening love-light shone once more. "Good lad!"

It made Bond want to spit in his mascara. "Sir." It was the guardsman's simple dismissal. Without a backward glance he let himself out and stamped up the area steps into the fog. In a few hours the finest Secret Service in the world would be without a head: Miss Ponsonby and Miss Moneypenny would lack an employer. All over the world transmitters would go silent, quiet men grip their cyanide or burn their cyphers, double agents look around for a publisher.

And he would be home in his black pyjamas, snoring up an alibi in his big double bed. There could be only one successor, one person only immediately fitted to take up all the threads, one alone who could both administrate and execute, plan and command. M., as he said, had played and lost. Come egg-time 007 Bond (James) would no longer be a mere blunt weapon in the hands of government. "*M. est mort! Vive le B.!*"

And when all the razzamataz had subsided, he would put on his glad rags and mosey round to the old Kitch. . . .

"Taxi!" The cab drew up to him in the dim light of St. James's Street. "King's Road, corner of Milner," he rasped.

"Jump up in front, Lady, and I'll take you for nothing."

Bond jumped.